BUSINESS POLICY

BUSINESS POLICY

Edited by

J.C. VOHRA

SBS Publishers & Distributors Pvt. Ltd.

ISBN : 81-89741-22-5

Business Policy

First Published in India in 2006

Published by:
SBS PUBLISHERS & DISTRIBUTORS PVT. LTD.
2/9, Ground Floor, Ansari Road, Darya Ganj,
New Delhi - 110002, INDIA.
Tel: 0091-11-23289119 / 41563911
Email: mail@sbspublishers.com

Printed at Printline, New Delhi.

PREFACE

Policies are guidelines or general limits within which the members of an enterprise act. They are general statements or understandings which guide thinking and action. Policies exist at various levels of the enterprise—corporate, divisional and departmental. They are valuable because they allow lower levels of management to handle problems without going to top management for a decision each time.

The present book is designed to help the participants to develop an understanding of basic inputs required, making and implementing business policy decisions and also familaries them with the issue and practices involved.

This book has been divided into 14 chapters, which will provide complete knowledge of Business Policy—An Introduction; Implementation of Corporate Plans; Policy Planning in Business; Business System; Organization Functions; Production Policy; Personnel and Financial Policy; Corporate Structure; Process of Control; Industrial Growth and Policy; Role of Managers; Strategy and Structure; Foreign Collabration Policy; Foreign Trade Policy etc. to the students.

Hopefully this book will prove a dependable work to management students and teachers besides the researchers in the field.

Editor

Contents

1

Business Policy—An Introduction

POLICIES are the guiding principles that govern human action usually of routine and repetitive nature. They are general statements which guide thinking and action of the company's official attitudes towards the range of behaviour within which it will permit or desire its employees to act. According to Koontz, O'Donnell, "Policies are the general statements of understadings which guide or channel thinking and action in decision making. They limit the area within which decision is to be made and ensure that decisions will be consistent with and contribute to objectives." Thus, policies delimit the area within which decisions are to be made, and ensure that decisions will be consistent with the overall business objectives. A business policy is an established guiding cannon premised on an objective devised to govern the activities of a business enterprise and from which the basic precepts of contact are derived. A policy is a steering mechanism used by the top management to ensure that activity proceeds in the desired direction. While objectives provide the ends which is management should try to achieve, the policies provide the goals which everybody should keep in mind while achieving the ends.

ELEMENTS OF BUSINESS POLICY

(1) The Firm

The firm can be defined in a rather broad sense to mean a business entity (corporate or other form) or any other kind of entity (academic, military, government, religious). Within the firm it is useful to consider separately the resources, characteristics, capabilities, limitations, and organization, even though these overlap to some degree. Management can be viewed as within the firm and yet apart from it, in the sense that general managers are responsible not only for the firm but for all its relationships with other elements in the policy concpet. In this book, as in other literature, references to the company, the corporation, the firm, the enterprise, or the business are used somewhat interchangeable, and all refer to the business entity that is labled here as the firm.

Resources are defined here as those things under management's control that can be utilized to reach the firm's objectives. Resources in the classical economic sense are land, labour, and capital. Assets on the balance sheet are resources:

Money, on hand and due from others

Inventories of products and materials

Plant and equipment

Liability and equities on the balance sheet represent the ownership of the assets. the relationship and condition of these balance sheet items should be analyzed along with other factors as a parrt of policy or strategy evaluation.

Human resources, the people in the company, are an important resource not shown on balance sheets. Intangible resources are also valuable:

Patents, franchises, leases, and other contractual rights

Knowledge of the business and its environment

Goodwill and favourable relationships

Reputation of the firm and its leaders

Skills and capabilities of its people

Established sales routes

Dealer organisations

Sources of supply

Any other contractual or customary relationship important to the firm.

The organization of the firm (both structure and members) has a great deal to do with how the other resources are utilized. The choice of the firm's organisation form is a strategic kind of choice by management, because it will affect the way in which the firm achieves its objectives. But the existing oragnisation at any time of strategic analysis must be taken into consideration as a part of the firm that is supposed to follow some strategic path. Organisation structure and behaviour can usually be changed by strategic action. However, the organisation will influence the choice of objectives and strategies.

Experience and past performance can indicate capabilities and limitations of the firm. Performance, as shown in the financial statements and other available records, needs to be analyzed in detail along with the analysis of the current position of a firm. Experience and past performance, along with resources, should help to indicate what the firm is and the kind of business it is in.

The assessment of strengths and weaknesses is an important element of strategic planning, says. Howard Stevenson. Items for strategic evaluation include directions, strategies, overall policy commitments and past practices. This process enables managers to learn from their past successes and failures. To improve the process, Stevenson suggests that managers make measures and criteria (including goals) explicit, define attributes as well as strengths and weaknesses, and understand the difference in the use of strenths and weaknesses.

Experience can indicate something more than skill and knowledge: it should help identify what the firm does best-what has been called its "distinctive competence" (a term attributed to Philip Selznick). Distinctive competence is a crucial part of Andrews's definition of corporate strategy mentioned earlier, in which the focus of resources is the way in which to convert distinctive competence into market advantages.

In every business you must consider, “What does it take to win?” in the oil business you must drill. If you do not drill, you do not win. In construction you must bid to win. In every business you must be able to do something will in compete and succeed.

The precept that the best single indicator of probably for future behaviour is past behaviour may well just as true from a company as for an individual. Changes in behaviour can be made and often must be made, but the past force and direction of momentum can never be safely ignored.

(2) Time

Time, in the policy concept, has three components: *(a)* the pint in time when the analysis is made, *(b)* the point when the selected strategy is implemented, and *(c)* the time span, which is the period of implemnetation, performance toward objectives, and measurement of progress. In a sense, the illustration of the time span of a strategy may be partly artificial, because its visualization or establishment is not as final as the illustration would suggest. Changes take place, and new strategies and often employed before old ones are fulfilled. However, it is necessary to recognize the nature of the other elements of policy at a specific point in time (when formulating or reappraising any of the elements) and to designate the period of time (or continuity, if a permanent objective is involved) for the employement of the strategic alternative considered.

Changes in any of the elements of policy may interrupt the time span that was intended origanally, making necessary a new appraisal with possible changes in the time period, the strategies, or even the objectives. Even without specific changes in conditions, managers need to periodically ressess their objectives and strategies and to continually monitor the environment and the performance and progress of the firm.

“Strategic issue management” (SIM) is a term used by Ansoff for a system to watch for early but weak signals to avoid strategic surprise. He emphasizes the real time character of SIM. “It follows no fixed planning calender; rather, the surveillance is continuous.

Timing is critical also in the sense of both the time when managers discern impending or actual changes in the environment and the time when they decide to make changes in objectives or strategies of their firm. Premature changes or initiatives can be as unsuccessful as changes made too late. For example, industry as a whole has been much more receptive to innovations in energy conservation since 1974 than was the case even a decade earlier.

(3) Opportunity

New opportunities abound in the changing environment and can also be created within the firm. Opportunity has a positive connotation, and we can differentiate the term "opportunity" form terms with negative connotations. such as "problem," distrubance," or "threat." Yet it requires attention, effort, and resources to respond to or create opportunities, and those commitments of resources are seldom made without some risk of loss or failure. At the very least, the choice of one alternative bears a price of alternative forgone (which is the way economists define cost). The risk of loss or failure associated with each strategic alternative should thus be weighed against its expected gain and success. Managers expect higher gain from higher risks, but other factors also enter into the assessment of risk and decisions about an acceptable level of risk. Flexbility to change from one strategy to another, when conditions en route to an objective indicate the need to consider changes, can help to reduce or control risk. Timing has an important effect upon risk. Long-term commitments of large amounts of resources involve substantial risk because of the uncertainty of the future and would therefore be expected to have a higher payoff than strategic alternatives offering more flexibility in the timing and use of resources.

Strategic alternatives include all the kinds of major strategic choices that need to be made toward the attainment of objectives. They may be functional as well as comprehensive, external, or internal. As in the case of objectives, however, it is useful to limit the extent of what we call strategy to a relatively few (compared with all the possible detail general means of attaining objectives or avenues toward objectives. Some typical strategic alternatives are discussed in Chapter 8. The details of breaking down major strategies into programmes, projects, plans, or tasks are part of the implementation of strategy and the on going management of the firm.

(4) Environment

Environment literally means the surroundings, external objects, influences or circumstances under which someone or something exists. The environment of any organisation is "the aggregate of all conditions, events and influences that surround and affect it." Since the environment influences an organisation in many ways, its understanding is of crucial importance. The concept of environment can be understood by looking at some of its characterstics.

Characteristics of Environment

Business environment (or simply environment) exhibits many characterstics. Some of the important—and obvious—characteristics are briefly described here.

1. ***Environment has a Far-reaching Impact.*** The environment has a far-reaching impact on organisations. The growth and profitability of an organisation depends critically on the environment in which it exists. Any environment change has an impact on the organisation in several different ways.

2. ***Environment is Complex.*** The environment consists of a number of factors, events conditions and influences arising from different sources. All these do not exist in isolation but interect with each other to create entirely new ses of influences. It is difficult to comprehend at once what factors constitute a given environment. All in all, environment is a complex phenomenon relatively easier to understand in parts but but difficult to grasp in its totality.

3. ***Environment is Multi-faceted.*** What shape and character an environment assumes depends on that perception of the observer. A particular change in the different environment,

or a new development may be viewed by different observers. This is frequently seen when the same development is welcomed as an opportunity by one company while another company perceives it as a threat.

4. ***Environment is Dynamic.*** The environment is constantly changing in nature. Due to the many and varied influences operating, there is dynamism in the environment causing it to continuously change its shape and character.

   Since the environment is complex, dynamic multi-faceted and has a far reaching impact, dividing it into external and internal components enables us to understand it better.

Characteristics of Policy

A statement should have the following characteristics to be called a policy:

(1) ***Consistency.*** A policy should provide for consistency in operations of an organisation. The policy should not create conflicts in the organisation. It should ensure uniformity of operations at various levels in the organisation.

(2) ***Written Form.*** A policy should be in writing as far as possible. A policy takes concrete shape when it is be in writing. It will ensure uniformity of application at all times.

(3) ***Participation.*** A policy should be developed with the active participation of top management. Policy formulation calls for serious thinking and participation of all the top level executives.

(4) ***Clarity.*** A policy should be clear, definite and explicit. It should leave no scope for mis-interpretation.

(5) ***Expression of Intentions of Top Management.*** A policy should be an expression of intentions of top management. It should present the principle that will guide the organisational actions.

(6) ***Relationship to Objectives.*** The policy should be derived from the objectives. It should faciliate the achieving of organisational objectives.

(7) ***Broad Definition.*** A policy should be stated in broad terms. The purpose of policy statement is to serve as a guide to practice now and in future. So it should be stated in the broadest possible term.

Types of Policies

Policies may be classified into the following categories:

1. ***General and Specific Policies.*** As to the area of freedom policies may be classified as general and specific. General policies are stated in broad terms to give freedom to units of the organisation. On the other hand, specific policies are intensively defined to restrict freedom of action.

2. ***Orginiated, Appealed and Imposed Policies.*** On the basis of origin, policies may be classified as Originaled, appealed and imposed policies. *Orginated policies* are deliberately formulated by top managers on their own initiative in order to guide the actions of their subordinates. They are generally put in writing and embodied in a policy manual. *Appealed policies* are formulated on the appeal or request of subordinates. Subordinates make an appeal to deal with a particular case which is not covered by earlier policies. *Imposed policies* arise from the influence of outside forces like government, trade unions, trade associations, etc.

3. ***Written and Implied Policies.*** Written policies are explicit declaration in writing. Implied policies are those inferred from the behaviour or conduct or organisational members, particularly of top executives. Where no written policy exists on a particular topic or the expressed policy is not enforced, subordinates interpret the actions of their superiors and make decisions accordingly. For instance, if promotions are made on the basis of seniority, there is an implied promotional policy, even though nothing is expressed in writing. Written policies are always.

4. ***Organisational and Functional Policies.*** In terms of scope, policies may be classified as organisational policies and departmental policies. Organisational policies are the overall policies of an organisation and they are formulated by top management. Departmental or functional policies are meant for specific functions or departments of business *e.g.*, sales policy, production policy, financial policy, personnel policy etc. They are derived from organisational policies to guide the efforts of people in particular departments. Organisational or basic policies are used uniformly throughout the organisation whereas departmental policies are applied in particular departments.

Importance of Policies

Sound and clear-cut policies provide the following benefits:

1. Coordination. Sound policies facilitate unity of purpose by focussing attention on organisational objectives. They are helpful in securing uniformity of action throughout the organisation. Policies promote intelligent cooperation and initiative. They provide a guide for thinking in future planning and promote intelligent cooperation.

2. Quick Decisions. Policies ensure prompt action on the part of subordinates. They delimit the area within which a decision is to be made. Lower level executives can decide with confidence and need not consult their superiors again. Every policy sets forth the proper course of action to be followed in a given situation. It saves time and effort by pre-deciding recurring problems.

3. Effective Control. Policies provide the rational basis for evaluating performance. They help to ensure that actions are in accordance with the objectives and interests of the organsiation. They tend to prevent deviations from planned course of action. In the absence of clear-cut policies, management is prone to become lost in the maze of details to the extent that their overall efficiency is impared. Policies are derived from objectives but provide the frame work for procedure and programmes. They serve as ground rules for operating plans.

4. Better Decentralisation. By formulating policies top management can delegate authority for routine matters. Unless policy is clearly defined it is not possible to decentralise as excutive responsibilities and relationships are not clear. The executives to whom authority is delegated can act with effectiveness and coordination with the help policies. From the prescribed policies the necessary managerial practices and procedures can be derived. Policy avoids the need for repeated guidance and indicates expected behaviour. Policies foster an intelligent exercise. They facilitate delegation by providing "guidelines to the delegate in order to help him in determining what appropriate action to take and what action will be within the limits of the stated policies. In effect, a policy informs the delegatee what is trying to be attained by making known the general course of action to be followed."

The entire process of management is coordinated and organised by means of management policies. The fabric of management is held together by the wrap and woof of policies. They make for uniformity of action and consistency in work. A policy reflects the intention and courses of management. Policies reduce the range of individual decisions and encourages management by exception. They set broad patterns of behaviour.

Sound policies prevent deviations from planned courses of action, make for consistency of action, promote intelligent co-operation, foster initiative and serve as guides to thinking for future.

Limitations of Policies

(1) Policies do not cover all the problems. Sometimes unforseen situations arise which are not covered by the existing policies.

(2) Policies are not ever lasting.

(3) Policies are no substitute for human judgement. Policies only delimit the area within which decisions are to be made.

(4) Policies are repeatedly used plans and bring about rigidity in operations. They leave no room for initiative by the subordinates.

Procedure to Formule Business Policies

Policy formulation refers to the designing of policies. The formulation of policies is generally a function of all managers. However, the higher a manager is in the organisation the more important is his role in policy-making. However, policies can be effective only when they are acceptable to those who are to use them. Therefore, the various functional and departmental executives should be actively involved in the formulation of policies. Contrary to popular impression policy-making is not reserved at the top, though higher level managers play a more important role in policy-making. Policy formulation is in effect planning. Policy-making is a vital phase of planning and is based upon the underlying objectives of the organisation. Policy formulation is largely an art as it involves the use of judement and experience. However, scientific analysis is helpful in generating and evaluating alternative. Policy-making is a highly skilled function requiring finest qualities of managerial talent. It is pervasive and far reaching in its effects on the affairs of the organisation. The formulation and administration of policies is one of the critical tasks of management. Only by thinking and deciding in terms of policy can executives successfully direct and control large organisations. The process of policy formulation consists of the following steps:

1. ***Definition of Purpose.*** The first step in policy formulation is to define clearly the objectives and philosophy of the company. A policy is a means towards the achievement of certain goals. Therefore, the basic concept of the business should be defined. For instance, the notion of an automobile manufacturing plant may be to develop a 'massclass automobile. In addition to such a conceptional idea, purpose

needs to be defined in terms of relevant guidelines for measuring performance, and desired performance targets. If, for instance, a firm is interested in rapid sales growth, the relevant guideline may be total industry expansion and target may be to grow at the industry growth rate plus 5 per cent. The selection of specific targets and the appropriate base lines for measuring performance should be based upon an analysis of a firm's opportunities and risks, its available resources, and the performance of its various constients.

2. ***Preparation of Strategic Intelligence.*** The next step is to secure information—questions, insights, hypotheses, evidence relevant to policy. As a minimum, this intelligence should consist of *(i)* detailed description of what the company is and how it defines its sphere of operations, *(ii)* a prediction of future environmental opportunities and risks and their likely impact on the company's competitive position, and *(iii)* an identification of corporate strengths and weaknesses and resources required to cope with future opportunities and risks. This step thus consists of an analysis and understanding of internal and external environment of the firm.

3. ***Policy Analysis.*** After policy alternatives are indentified each of the alternative is examined in the light of its contributions to chosen objectives. Examination of alternative policies and evaluating the consequences of various alternatives and their effects on preferred values and norms are significant elements of the policy formulation process.

4. ***Policy Alternatives.*** Once objectives and a general philosophy of business have been defined, alternative operating policies need to be indentified and analysed. The policy maker should attempt a comprehensive overview of policy problem and alternative policies. This step is central

to the task of policy formulation. Thus a comprehensive list of policy alternatives needs to be generated, the probabilities of the consequences of each alternative need to be assessed, and their consequences need to be evaluated in terms of satisfying corporate objectives.

5. ***Time Sequencing.*** This step in formulation of policies involves the designation of timed sequence of conditional moves based upon price analysis of possible competitive responses and counter attack. The tentative policy may be tested to find out its impact on the organisation. The policy finally selected is then communicated to all those involved in its execution.

6. ***Policy Review.*** Policy formulation also involves a periodic re-examination of the assumptions underlying current policies and an evaluation of organisational performance to date. A periodical review of policies is necessary to keep the policies up-to-date and useful.

7. ***Strategic Choice.*** The selection of consistent operating policies which, in the judgement of top management, best fit available resources and best serve the organisation's purpose, provides the basic guidelines for executive action. The establishment of specific policy represents the most visible evidence of strategic commitment.

Objectives of Studying Business Policy

As we know business policy focusses on top and general management, a basic question arises: Why should be study it particularly when not all of them are expected to reach at the top or perform general management functions? Normally, they start their career in a functional area; only very few start in corporate planning division. From this point of view, this question becomes quite important. This question can be solved only by analysing the basic objectives of business policy course. Policy course emphasises following aspects.

(a) Development of analytical and decision making skills through cases and other reading material which are multi-functional and multi-departmental in nature. Following are basic objectives of policy.

(b) Integration of the knowledge and the methods learned in previous courses, *e.g.*, statistics, economics, production, marketing, finance accounting and personnel.

I. (i) It helps in learning, understanding, and appreciating the knowledge research in other areas by integrating these together.

(ii) Business policy course provides understanding of uniqueness and setting of operations in different industries.

(iii) The policy study emphasises the limitations of specialised knowledge in solving complex business problems. Since a specialist looks at the problem from his own speciality, he is likely to overlook the total interest of the organisation. The policy study may provide him an understanding of how his knowledge can be integrated with others so that suitable decisions are made.

(iv) The study of policy enables students to understand how various steps of strategic management process can be carried on; how the strategies can be formulated and implemented; and how the organisation can overcome its weaknesses and emphasise its strengths.

(v) It emphasis undestanding of interrelationships among sub-systems in the organisation and problems top managers face in avoiding suboptimisation of parts.

(vi) The basic objective is to gain knowledge and understand the central significance of policy and strategy to top management and its organisation. This means an understanding of how total enviornmental forces affect the functioning of the organisation. This is the basic core of systems approach in management also which is largely followed in management of large and complex organisations.

(vii) The basic objective of any discipline is to impart knowledge. Knowledge comes through the study of existing literature which provides base for further research. A considerable body of knowledge purporting to make general statements about policy course runs through several dimensions.

II. Top managers of the organisation have attitudes, values, and ways of thinking that are unique to them and which also have a distinctive impact on decision processes. Knowledge of policy inculcates these attitudes in the students. What a manager knows by way of policy course is quite helpful in developing the attitudes, values and aspirations which he brings to his tasks. There are several implications of developing attitudes appropriate for top management functions.

(i) Policy course also puts emphasis on innovation in management practices through creativity. Since the manager has to work in an environment of diversity and variability, he has to find out a way of lying in the world full of uncertainty. He develops such attidues through his learning by business policy.

(ii) A manager takes decisions on the basis of totality of factors involved in them because he takes a generalist's position. As compared to generalist, a specialist tends to look. As beyond his area of specialisation leaving many more things to be desired. A generalist, on the other hand, has a tendency to look at the problem from every corner. This attitude results in decision making on the basis of all relevant facts rather than on the basis of one discipline alone. This is likely to yield better result.

(iii) Business policy course tries to develop professional orientation among managers which is distinct from self-seeking contrives. The introduction of social responsibility and ethical consideration in policy formulation and implementation has put emphasis on looking organisational objectives in larger social perspective in larger social perspective. A generalist is, thus, required to focus more attention on his aspect as compared to specialists.

(iv) A generalist develops the attitudes of making decisions under the condition of partial ignorance which is the reality of business system in any country. Thus he works on satisfying decisions rather than optimising decisions. He puts emphasis on cost traders in terms of the timing of decisions, the nature of the solution, problem implementation and so on.

III. Perhaps the major contribution of the policy course lies in developing appropriate skills necessary for viewing the total organisation. Effective managers need different skills and the relative importance of these skills may very with the level in the organisation Katz has identified three kinds of skills necessary for managers. These are technical skills, human or administrative skills, and conceptual skills. Their relative importance varies with the level of management.

(i) Human or administrative skills are concerned with how it is done. There skills are the ability to work with people effectively thereby getting their full support for achieving organisational effectiveness.

(ii) Technical skills are concerned with what is done. These pertain to knowledge and proficiency in activities involving methods, processes, and procedures. These involve working with tools and specific techniques. Such skills are learned by accountants, engineers, typists, and time-study men. These skills are the distinguishing features of job performance at the operative level.

(iii) Conceptual skills or general management skills are concerned with why it is done. These skills refer to the ability to see the whole picture; to recognise signficant elements in a situation; and to understand the relationship among these elements. Such skills are necessary to deal with abstractions, to set models, and to set plans.

Thus technical skills deal with things, human skills deal with people, and conceptual skills deal with ideas. Since people in the organisation perform different kinds of job, they required different kinds of skill mix.

Business policy course tries to develop all these skills.

(a) The second type of skills which policy course tries to inclucate in the students relate to integration of various factors such as resources, times, goals, and so on, Integration of various subsystems of the organisations is also required. For this purpose, a manager has to treat an ogranisation as an organic entity comprising a system in itself, but related to the larger systems of its environment. In this process, a manager must pull the separate concepts he has studied in functional and basic discipline courses and to adapt them to a less structured set of problems.

(b) General management skills centre-upon relating the organisation with its environment and upon coordinating departmental specialities and their point of view, Knowledge of general management is needed not only by general or top managers but a sensitivity to these processes is helpful at various levels of organisation. The assential skills for strategy formulation and implementation which are concerned mostly with analytical and administrative processes make every manager more effective irrespective of his level in the organisation.

(c) Administrative skills can be developed by policy course by providing an opportunity to students to judge the actions in the light of various objectives set. The strategies selected can be judged as consistent or inconsistent according to criteria which may be developed. The students can use their knowledge of other fields with balanced view to find out whether their strategies are able to achieve objectives.

(d) A top manager requires analytical skills so as to size up quickly and accurately the situation presented in terms of identifying the core problems and issues involved, analysing the facts to identify opportunities and threats in the environment and identify the strengths and weaknesses of his organisation so that he integrates these with the environment. Though total management education tries to achieve this objective, the role business policy is crucial in this respect.

Business policy course, though focusses on top management point of view, is also important for other level managers and even functional managers in that it enables the participants to take total view of the organisation and the environment in which context they have to function. Business policy course may enable them to intepret the instructions they receive from above more broadly; perceive the significance of their own area's potential contribution as organisational priorities shift; and couch the recommendations or proposals they send upward in term that make sense to a general manager and are related to their conception of the organisational objectives. Such managers may not function as general managers but with a general management view point they can influence the strategic decisions.

COMPONENTS OF PLANNING

The scope of planning is very wide. An enterprise has several aims. Accordingly, it has to build up a hierarchy of plans. The various types of plans may be described as under:

1. Objectives are the goals or purposes towards which business operations are directed. They are the end points of planning as planning is done to achieve objectives. They are established to guide the efforts of an organisation and each of its constituents. Setting of objectives is the first step in planning. Objectives should be expressed clearly and precisely. Management cannot be effective without carefully defined objectives. Goals are broad statements while objectives are specific and in measureable terms objectives embody the broad goals towards which the group activity is directed. They are the building blocks to planning "Objectives are the goals, aims or purposes that organisations wish to achieve over verying periods of time." Objectives are often expressed in terms of standards, targets, quotas, dead lines, etc. Objectives are the key to sound and the basis of effective management.

An enterprise has multiple objectives: Long-term and short-term, organisational and departmental, internal and external, main and subsidiary, general or specific, economic and social etc. Different objectives should be properly integrated into a network or hierarchy. According to Drucker, "to manage a business is to balance a variety of needs and goals.....Objectives are needed in every are a where performance and results directly and vitally affect the survival and prosperity of the business. These areas are: market standing; innovation; productivity; physical and financial resources; profitability; manager performance and development; worker performance and attitude; public responsibility."

Objectives are very important as they provide a sense of purpose, serve as standards of performance, help in fixing responsibility, add to coordination, enable greater delegation of authority and serve as guides to action Objectives set up the framework for planning and, therefore, a meaningful formulation of enterprise objectives is a necessary first step in the planning process. They indicate the destination of an enterprise.

2. Policies are general statements of understandings created for the attainment of ojectives. They serve as broad guides to thinking and action on the part of members of an organisation. They indicate the manner in which particular situations should be handled by the organisational members. A policy can be defined as the guidelines or mode of action underlying certain operations. It is general guide to action. It does not tell a person exactly what to do, but it does point out the direction to go. In other words, "a policy is a verbal, written or implied statement outlining the guiding course adopted and followed by a manager. That is to say, a policy establishes the overall guides or boundaries which provide the general direction in which managerial action takes place. The guides provided by policies help to keep the activities moving along the routes intended by managers." A policy defines the area within which a decision is to be made. It expresses the intentions of the management and is a multi-purpose plant that continuously guides action. It is a standing answer to recurring problems; a continuing decision that applies to repetitive situations. They set up broad limits for decision making so that subordinates need not seek approval for every individual action. This saves time and effort. They help in ensuring that action conforms to objectives and there is harmony of effort. As a plan action, a policy relates efforts to objectives and helps in securing uniformity of action. A policy gives meaning to objectives, makes for stability and instills confidence in the employees. It helps delegation of authority and coordination. A good policy statement porivdes supervisors with guidelines for dealing in a consistent manner with issues which arise from time to time. Without policies each situation might to be rethought before action could be taken. Policies define limits within which executive discretion may be used. The application of policies requires initiative, and judgement. It also provides a yardistick for evaluation of alternative courses of action. "Policies tend to predecide issues, avoid repeated analysis and consideration of general courses of action and give a unified structure to other types of plans, thus permitting managers to delegate authority while maintaining control."

Policies may be general or specific, functional or departmental, voluntry or imposed, written or implied, originated or appealed. They should always be clear, precise, flexible, consistent and integrated. They should be based on acts, resources and environments of the particular enterprise. They should be stated in broad terms to facilitate the organisation. They should be stated in broad terms to faciliate recurring use. Different policies should support one another and must reflect the internal and external environment of the organisation. To be effective, policies should be developed with the active coorperation of all concerned. All policies should be in writing and must be communicated to those who will use them so that they may be fully understood. The managerial policies should be revised from time to time to keep them up-to-date and effective. They should be precise yet flexible. They should be understood by all members of the organisation.

Policies are linked are linked to objectives yet differ from them. Objectives describe what is being sought after, policies describe how the objectives are to be accomplished. Both are equally important to effective action. A policy should be differentiated from practice which is the usual mode of handling a given problem. A practice stresses expediency and things as they are while a policy stresses direction and things as they should be.

Distinction between Policies and Procedures

Policies are specific guidelines and constrains for managerial thinking and action. They are planned expressions of the organisation's official attitude towards certain issues. But procedures, on the other hand, are systematic ways of handling regular events. They involve chronological sequence of actions required to the particular tasks. They are operational guides to action and routinise the way certain recurring jobs are to be done. The other points of difference between policies and procedures are as follows:

(a) Policies are guides to decision-making while procedures are guides to action.

(b) Policies have some room for managerial thinking and discretion while procedures are generally detailed and rigid.

(c) Policies are generally framed by the top management and procedures are laid down at somewhat low-level in the light of policies.

(d) Policies form part of strategies of the organisation while procedures are operational as tactical tools.

The difference between policies and procedures can be further explained by means of an example. An industrial concern may adopt a policy of centralised recruitment and selection through the labour department. The labour department may then chalk out the procedure of recruitment and selection. This procedure may consist of several steps like inviting applications, preliminary interview aptitude and other tests, final interview, medical examination and issue of appointment letter.

3. Procedures. A procedure or routine is a chronological sequence of steps to be undertaken to enforce a policy and to attain an objective. It is a standard or uniform manner of doing repetitive work. It is more specific than policy and is a definite guide to action. It specifies the way in which particular work is to be performed so as to ensure that whoever performance it will do it the same way. A procedure emphasizes details while a policy concentrated on general approaches. For example, a company may have the policy of promoting employees on the basis of merit. In order to implement it, the procedure may consist of definition of merit, records of performance, tests and interview to identify the most meritorious. Similarly, there may be procedures for purchasing raw materials, selecting personnel, redressing grievances. In fact, a standard procedure is necessary for every repetitive activity. A procedure is different from a method which outlines the specific manner in which a particular step in the procedure is to be performed. For example, to measure merit employees may be compared in terms of punctuality, discipline, output and accidents. This is a method of merit rating. A procedure is also different from a schedule which specifies the time limit for each step in the procedure. Scheduling is the process of establishing a time sequence for the work to be done. It is essential to ensure continuity of operations to evaluate performance and to create order and regularity in executing policies and programmes. A policy delineates an area of operation, a procedure lays down the path through that area. A policy is guide to decision-making while a procedure is an operational guide to action. A procedure is a means of implementing policy.

4. Rules. A rule is a rigid and definite plan that specifies what is to be done or not to be done in a given situation, without deviation. It allows to flexibility in dcision-making. Rules help in maintaining and enchancing efficiency. It is a specific guide to action and permits no discretion or judgement. No deviation is expected from the stated course of action. A rule does not lay down a sequance of steps. It may or may not be a part of of procedure. The rule "no smoking in the factory" is not a parrt of any procedure. On the other hand, the rule that "all orders must be acknowledged within 48 hours of their receipt" is a part of procedure. A rule reflects what a manager expects of his subordinates. A rule generally carries with it the penalty for violation.

5. Programmes. The planning process culminates with programmes and budgets. Programming helps to develop the most economical way of doing things in a uniform manner. A programme is a concrete scheme of action to accomplish a given task. It specifies the steps to be taken resources to be used, time limits for each step and the persons who are to carry it out. A programme is a sequence of activities designed to implement policies and accomplish objectives. A programme is thus a mixture of objectives, policies, procedures, rules etc. A major programme, *e.g.*, development of a new product may be supported by several derivative programmes concerning factory building, machinery, raw materials, technical personnel, etc.

6. Budgets are estimates or projections of expected results expressed in numerical terms. A budget is a financial plan. It establishes restrictions within goals are to be reached and serves as an yardstick of measuring performance. It may relate to income and expenses or production or sales. Budgeting is an element of planning but budgets serve as a means of coordination and control also. They express different plans into a common language (money) and serve as standards of evaluating performance. To be effective, a budget should be flexible and should provide for unforseen events.

7. Strategies. A strategy is a particular type of plan designed to intepret and adjust other plans. A strategy represents conscious decision to initiate certain actions directed towards specific purposes. It seeks to meet specific situations or crisis, *e.g.*, price reduction by competitors, strike by employees, etc. Plans and policies have to be changed according to changes in underlying conditions. Strategies help in adjusting and executing them. Competitive strategies are based on projected activities of competitors. Strategies are different from tactics which is a course of action designed to execute a strategy. A tactic designates policy in operation with respect to method and procedure.

Strategies are designed in response to phenomena occurring within and outside the firm. Strategies are formed in various functional areas *e.g.* product strategies, market strategies, financial strategies, etc. Strategy should be differentiated from policy. Policy is the general guideline while strategy is the course of action. Stretegy many exist without a policy. For instance, a supervisor may have a policy of enforcing discipline but his strategy may be to wait until enforcement is demanded by workers. The waiting strategy is not likely to be embodied in the policy. Policy and strategy may, at the time, be coextensive. For example, a business policy may be to distribute through retailers. The strategy is the same but it implies that action to implement policy will be taken at the right time.

8. Projects. A project is a distinct cluster of functions and facilities for a definite purpose. It is a part of a general programme which can be designed and excuted as a distinct plan in itself. It is a time bound plan consistent of details, the time schedule, exact method of performing each step, provision for place and resources and special method designed for unique conditions. It is marked separate from normal operations because of its special significance. In a programme of developing a new product, for example, publicity may be a project Project help simplify coordiantion and control by identifying an integrated work package within a hetrogeneous mass of activities and resources.

Sometimes policy is confused with the term strategy. A policy is a guide to thinking and action on the part of executives. On the other hand, a strategy lays down the direction in which human and physical resources will be deloped and applied in order to maximise the chances of achieving a selected objective in the face of difficulties.

Plans are sometimes classified as single-use plans and multiuse plans. A *single-use plan* is designed to meet a specific situation or purpose. It is used up one for the particular task and has to be framed new for a different task. A *multi-use* plan or repeated use plan is designed to be used over and over again in recurring situations. It is a standing guide to thinking and action. Objectives, policies, rules procedures are 'multi-use plans while programmes, budgets, strategies, schedules, and projects are considered as single use plans.

Strategy and Tactics

It is beneficial to make distinction between strategy and tactics so that managers can concentrate themselves on strategic functions rather than engaging in tactical functions. Organisational decisions range across a spectrum, having a broad master strategy at one end and minute tactics at the other. The major difference between strategy and tactics is that strategy determines what major plans are to be undertaken and allocates resources to them, while tactics, in contrast, is means by which previously determined plans are excuted. Beyond this, major difference, there may be some other differences which can be understood better by analysing military use of strategy and tactics.

Strategy is system of carrying through on originally considered plan under a constantly shifting set of circumstances. Strategy furnishes tactics with the opportunity to strike and with the prospect of success. It does this through its conduct of the armies and their concentration on the field of battle. On the other hand, however, strategy concept accepts the results or every single engagement and builds them. Strategy retires when a tactics victory is in the making in order later to exploit the newly created situation. A basic objective of strategy accordingly is to 'break the will of the army, deprive him of the means to fight, occupy his territory, destroy or obtain control of his resources or otherwise made him submit.' The objective of tactics is success in a given action which is only one part in a group of related military action. A further distinction between strategy and tactics as used in Military Science is made on the basis of delegation of decision making authority. Strategy decisions are not delegated too low in the organisation. Normally the authority is not required for the most effective decisions.

Such a distinction between strategyand tactics is quite sharp. however, business is different than war in its true perspective not only in terms of its objectives vis-a-vis its competitors but also in terms of process of achievement of objectives. In business, there is seldom a win-lose situation as is the case with the way. Therefore, the distinction should be made between strategy and tactics in business terms. Such distinctions can be made as follow.

1. Strategy has a long-term perspective; specially the successful strategies are followed for quite long period. In occasional cases, it may have short-term duration. Thus depending on the nature and requirement, its time horizon is flexible, however, emphasis is put on long-term. On the other hand, time horizon of tactics is short-run and definite. The duration is uniform, for budget prepartion.

2. Strategies are most important factors of organisation because they decide the future course of action for the organisation as a whole. On the other hand, tactics are of less importance because they are concerned with specific part of the organisation. This difference, though seems to be simple, becomes important form managerial action point of view.

3. The formulation of strategy is affected considerably by the personal values of the person involved in the process. For example, the goals of an organisation is affected considerably by the personal values of the persons concerned. This aspect will be taken for further discussion in this later. On the other hand, tactics is normally free from such values because this is be taken within the context of strategic decisions.

4. Generally separate group of managerial personnel are involved in strategy and tactics fourmulation and their implementation. As discussed earlier, strategic decisions are never delegated below a certain level in the managerial hierarchy. The basic principles in this context is not to delegate below the levels than those possess the perspective required for must effective strategic decisions. Tactical decisions can be taken by personnel at lower levels because these involve minute implementation of strategic decisions.

5. Element of uncertainty is higher in the case of strategy formulation and its implementation. In fact, strategic decisions are taken under the conditions of partial ignorance. Tactical decisions are more certain as these are taken within the framework set by the strategy. Thus evaluation of tactics is easier as compared to evaluation of a strategy.

6. The formulation of strategy is both continuous and irregular. The process is continuous but the timing of decision is irregular as it depends on the appearance of opportunities, new ideas, crises, management initiative, and other non-routine stimuli. Tactics is determined on a periodic basis by various organisation. A fixed time table may be followed for this purpose.

7. As discussed earlier, strategy is developed at the higher level of management either at the headquarter or at divisional offices and relates. Tactics is employed at and relates to lower levels of management.

8. Total possible range of alternatives from which a manager can choose his strategic action is greater than tactics. A manager requires more information for arriving at strategic decision to its environment, this requires information about the various aspectss of environment. Naturally the collection of such information will be different. Tactical information is generated within the organisation particularly from accounting procedures and statistical sources.

❒

2

Implementation of Corporate Plans

MOST corporate planning exercises result in the identification of future growth objectives as well as future expansion, dispersion and diversification activities. By a series of studies and brainstorming sessions-based on analyses of strengths and weaknesses, identification of opportunities and threats—business organisations identify the areas of future growth, dispersion and diversification. Some of the analyses and discussion which go into the formulation of the final corporate plan is often very sophisticated involving such complex exercises as environmental scanning, competitive strategy analysis, technology forecasting, etc. But surprisingly, many such corporate plans finally do not get implemented! Part of the problem of non-implementation could be the top management's attitude towards corporate planning, particularly if the objective is to keep up with corporate rather than to use it as a vital tool for managing the destiny of the organisation and using the corporate plan as a commonly shared blueprint for future growth and development. We need not pursue these themes further for the simple reason that if the basic objective in conducting a corporate planning exercise lacks management commitment towards its implementation and is intended to be "decorative" in purpose, the implementation is bound to be of a low order. However, most corporate plans do not get implemented because at the time of the formulation of the corporate plan, several assumptions are implicity made, *e.g.*

(a) Growth-even of the order of doubling or trebling the organisation's activities in five years can be managed by getting additional people, accommodation, equipment, etc.

(b) The people within the organisation would eontinue to be motivated and committed towards the attainment of the long run objectives formulated by the corporate plan. A secondary assumption in this regard is that the personnel who are likely to be inducted during the plan period would subscribe to the current values and styles of the organisation.

(c) Even if new factories or sales offices are to be located at new places, managing such multiple location operations would not present any substantive problem.

(d) The current level of organisational effectiveness could always be sustained and improved to respond to the problems of future growth, diversification and multi-location, multi-product, multi-technology operations.

It can be safely said that all these assumptions are usually invalid since they do not take into account problems of organisational dynamics involved in managing growth, multiplicity of locations, technologies and products and most importantly, sustaining or improving organisational effectiveness. It is for these reasons that many carefully analysed and documented corporate plans do not get substantially implemented.

Need for Organisational Development

The process of corporate planning—particularly formulation of action plans for implementing the corporate strategies and achieving the long term organisational objectives-must encompass the following:

(a) The organisational requirements particularly in the areas of management structure and systems-inherent in implementing the corporate plan; and

(b) The assessment of current level of organisational effectiveness and the requirements of improving such organitional effectiveness by either the required interventions or action which will influence processes leading to greater organisational effectiveness.

These requirements fall in the area of Organisational Development (or OD as it is often called) necessary for implementing the corporate plan. While many people perceive OD to be essentially a behavioural exercise, in reality several other aspects of management development are inherent parts of such OD exercise. Whtle there is no consensus amongst the practitioners as to what constitutes OD, it could be visualised as an organisational process initiated by management to cope up with the demands of continued organisational efficiency and effectiveness.

Warren Bennis identifies the problems which should be addressed while undertaking organisational development as follows:

(i) problems of destiny-growth, identity and revitalisation;

(ii) problems of organisational effectiveness.

(iii) problems of human satisfaction and development; and

There are many modes of organisational development and several instruments or interventions available for achieving such development.

Responding to the Problems of Growth, Identity and Revitalisation

In regard to problems of growth, identity and revitalisation, the basic instrument often used is a series of internal discussious which raise these issues amongst managers at all levels and the interaction between managers leads to a consensus in regard to these three requirements of the future. Ideally the best instent is the corporate planning process itself since all the participating managers are required during the process of corporte planning to examine the organisational strengths and we nesses, the opportunities and threats and then formulate the corporate mission and objectives for achieving the desired growth, identity and revitalisation of growth and diversity.

The exact terminology might be different but often grow for purposes of corporate planning is expressed in terms expansion, related and unrelated diversification and choice new locations, products and technologies for attaining sue growth. The definition of the corporate mission in the corport plan is really the perindic redefinition of its identity, which then gets reflected in distinctive organisational as well as function strategies. The requirements of revitalisation are often reflects in the corporate plan in terms of action plans for improvement human capabilities, replacement of technologies by newer ones, systemic and structural changes for coping up with the requirments of growth and diversity.

It has always been apparent to perceptive managers that the participation of its high performing managers in the corporation planning process is in itself an act of organisational development. During the process of corporate planning, the participing managers, particularly younger managers, are required shed off their functional or operational reference points, forced to look at the uncertain future (particularly the likely environment and competition) and asked to develop organisational strategies and objectives from the viewpoint of the organisation as a whole (rather than mere growth or improvement of their respective functions or operations). It is for this reason that many of us contend that the greatest benefit of corporate planning is in the not output-in terms of quantitative growth targets specific strategies, etc. (which in any case do not always get implemented)—but in the process leading to management development and "mind stretching" of the participating managers. It has often been noticed that managers who have been closely involved in their organisation's corporate planning process, become thereafter more confident, less managerially insecure and far more pro-active and positive in their managerial style and action. In the best sense of the term, this represents organisational development.

However, we must accept that not all managers can participate in the corporate planning process for several reasons. The first and the primary reason is the number would be too large for a process which is as creative as corporate planning. The involvement of too many managers seethes with many difficulties—the problems of maintaining the confidentiality of some of the sensitive parts of the corporate planning exercise, developing a consensus (and the real risk of a creative exercise; like corporate planning degenerating into an exercise of developing "democratic" consensus), the ability of managers to contribute to the process and so forth. It is for this reason that those managers who do not participate in the corporate planning exercise should be provided with an opportunity of understanding and accepting the considerations which have led to the formulation of corporate objectives and making contributions towards the implementation of the corporate plan. Such participation will contribute towards their accepting the corporate aspirations of future growth and development inherent in the corporate objectives. Many a times this is sought to be done by making presentations of the corporate plan to such managers after it has been finalised. A major problem is that such a presentation cannot simulate the process of introspection and analysis which forms the most critical and productive parts of the corporate planning exercise. It is for this reason that the requirements of the modes and mechanisms for developing such understanding, acceptance and contribution to implementation requires to be identified as a part of the organisational development process.

Responding to the Problems of Human Satisfaction and Development

In the area of human satisfaction and development, OD has to be primarily viewed in the light of enhancing the quality of the behavioural climate within the organisation. For this purpose, OD interventions are usually thought in terms of personal, inter-personal and group process interventions.

Such interventions are usually preceded by a diagnosis of the current state of the behavioural climate addressed to such issues as:

(a) Are the key people in the organisation involved and committed?

(b) What is the level of congruence between organisational objectives and personal objectives?

(c) How effective are the inter-personal and group processes in terms of accomplishment of common tasks?

(d) What is the feeling of mutuality and collaboration amongst peers as well as superior-subordinates? What is the nature and quality of relationship of trust and confidence between them?

(e) What are the perceptions relating to accountability, responsibility, authority and control in relation to the various managerial roles?

(f) How participative are the planning and decision making processes (where such participation is perceived to be desirable and necessary)?

(g) What is the degree and type of value conflicts?

(h) How well do people work in teams and share achievement jointly with others?

(i) Are the values of people pro-active or reactive in nature? Are they positive or negative in terms of introducing change?

(j) How well does the organisation reward achievement and punish continued failures?

(k) What is the quality of achievement orientation amongst people and pride in belonging to the organisation?

Two basic behavioural science technique or a combination of both are used in such interventions. They are:

(a) Some form of sensitivity training laboratory; and

(b) Transactional analysis.

Of course, OD work in this area addresses many other issues but usually the OD processes are built around the concept of change agents. For this purpose, a few people in the organisation, who are identified as opinion leaders and high achievers, are chosen to act as the catalyst group. Usually they are required to analyse, explore or understand the various issues outlined above, often working with an internal or external OD adviser or trainer and formulate their responses for enhancing the quality of the organisational climate. Thereafter, the change agents are used as instruments for introducing the desired change by a process of interacting with others in the organisation. Such intraction could be in terms of day-to-day inter-personal relationship or by group process. Periodically the change agents meet and review the progress and identify areas which require shifts in terms of formulating new approaches to organisatjonal development. It is not unusual for OD work to spread over two or three years before substantive changes in the organisation's behavioural climate are visible.

Sensitivity training laboratories usually consist of T-Groups (often with diverse membership). Though T-Groups are often thought of as unstructured, agendaless group sessions of members and a professional trainer (who might be an insider or outsider) who acts as a catalyst and facilitator-several variations of the T-Group model have been evolved in the past.

Some of the variations from the traditional model are:

(a) In many cases, the trainer also participates in the discussion primarily for raising new issues, clarifying positions, highlighting implications of statements and assumptions, underlining implications in terms of role relationships (rather than pronouncing on what is desirable); and

(b) In contrast to the earlier method where all the data were generated in the T-Group meeting itself, many T-Groups now provide prior material for discussion, for example, role descriptions real life cases involving behavioural problems, position papers for responding to problems organisational climate, etc. Some trainers in use innovative methods like role reversals (often as a role analysis technique) to inculcate greater understanding of one's own role in the context of the role-set in within which the concerned manager has to function.

While sensitivity training based interventions are essentially aimed to improving group processes or dynamics, Transactional Analysis (or TA as it is often called) is aimed towards enhancing quality of inter-personal relationship. The transactional analyses theory postulates that personalities are made up of three ago states:

The parent,

The adult, and

The child.

Analysis of the transactions and communications between people is a major aspect of TA. The basic assumption is that enhancement in the quality of transactions and communications would make the concerned managers more effective in their organisational roles and personal lives.

Responding to the Problems of Organisational Effectiveness

In regard, to the third and possibly the most important dimension of OD aimed at responding to problems of organisational effectiveness, a great deal of understanding and insights have been developed in the last two to three years. Much of the understanding and insight has come about due to the pioneering work done by McKinsey and Co. Inc., the world renowned management consultants, in identifying the elements which determine organisational effectiveness. Even more important is their finding that the balance and harmony between these elements-relative to the context of the organisation's product, market, technology and people-determine the level of organisational effectiveness.

The McKinsey 7-S Model: Definitions and Illustrations

The 7 elements which comprise this model are:

(a) Strategy;

(b) Structure;

(c) Systems;

(d) Superordinate Goals;

(e) Staff;

(f) Style; and

(g) Skills.

The first three elements are often called the three "hard" Ss because they are susceptible to changes by managerial direction. In contrast, the remaining four elements are called the four "soft" Ss because while their impact and influence in terms of organisational effectiveness is real, changes can be effected over a long period of time by influencing managerial attitudes in relation to these four elements rather than by direction from top management.

Each of these elements together with a few illustrations drawn from the Indian context are discussed in the subsequent paragraphs.

Strategy

Strategy is the distinctive future product-market technology choice an organisation makes and the manner and mode of implementing such choices in the competitive marketplace.

An example where a well-articulated and clearly defined business strategy has significantly contributed to growth and continuing profitability is that of Reliance Textile Industries, which markets its products under the brand name VIMAL. The distinctive elements of their successful business strategy have been the appropriate choice of the market segments and the ability to align their own internal managerial and operational capabilities to suit the specific requirements of the target market segments. Also, they have been remarkably effective in relating their strategies to the overall environmental conditions and, the timing of their entry into the different segments. Arising out of this, they have chosen to cater to the "high-priced, high-quality" segment and have acquired the latest technology and the best processes for yarn spinning and weaving. They have marketed their products in a non-traditional way by staying away from traditional markets and by providing the required back-up support to marketing in terms of advances growth, credit-deposit ratio, cost effectiveness, etc., are well defined and there is considerable clarity relating to responsibility, accountability and autonomy of operations at each operating level.

(a) Dealer relationship;

(b) Advertising and sales promotion;

(c) Design strengths; and

(d) Distribution channels.

Structure

Structure is the way the total organisational task is organised in terms of authority and accountability upto the lowest managerial responsibility centres.

An example of an organisation which has been able to manage growth very effectively primarily due to the structure that has been evolved in the State Bank of India. They have evolved a structure which has enabled them to effectively control the operations of over six thousand branches catering to the different segments in banking operations. The structure essentially consists of a group of branches placed under a Regional Manager who is the *de facto* chief executive of the region headed by him. The Regional Managers and the Managers heading the large branches report to the respective Chief Regional Managers, who in turn report to the Local Head Office. Twelve such Local Head Offices have been constituted. At different levels, the tasks in relation to deposit growth, advances growth, credit-deposit ratio, cost effectiveness, etc., are well defined and there is considerable clarity relating to responsibility, accountability and autonomy of operations at each operating level.

Simultaneously, the State Bank has differentiated its business in terms of commercial and institutional banking, personal banking, agricultural banking, small industries banking and international banking. The structure interweaves the roles for planning, co-ordinating and monitering such functional tasks in the operating structure. As a result, the evolved structure has become a managerial instrument on the one hand for planning and monitoring overall financial performance and on the other hand for formulating strategies, objectives and, plans in relation to each distinctive part of the business.

Systems

Systems are the procedures by which an organisation's managers plan, decide, control and allocate resources.

Systems would include budgeting systems, performance reporting systems, management information systems, performance appraisal systems, capital projects analysis and monitoring systems, etc. What is important in relation to systems is not the existence of the systems or the degree of design sophistication of the systems, but whether they are accepted by the top management of the organisation as instruments for management of operations, and whether it is perceived at the lower echelons of management that the top management uses these systems for managing the operations. Moreover, the management processes beginning from the lower levels should be based on such systems and their use should be "metabolic" (rather than out of the need for conforming to the ground rules of systems administration).

A good example would be the parta system used by the Birla Group of Companies. The system is not sophisticated but it is the centrepiece of management of operations right down to the lowest management levels. The parta is essentially the pre-determined budget of the net cashflow from operations, before tax and dividend, which has been agreed upon between the Chairman and the President of the unit. The level of the understanding of this system is different at different levels. While the President of the unit (or division) is concerned with the total parta, at the lower levels the focus is more on managerial factors at the relevant level like cost of raw materials, sales volume, pricing, capacity utilisation, manufacturing efficiency, etc., which affect the parta rather than on the total parta.

Superordinate Goals

Superordinate goals are higher order objectives beyond profit, return on investment and similar measures. For example, leadership in management of high technology business, or providing the highest quality of customer service are examples of such superordinate goals.

An example is Associated Bearing Company Limited, a member of the SKF Group, which has chosen market leadership through product quality as its superordinate goal. The focus of their operations is on being the most outstanding producer of the range of products manufactured by them.

Style

Style is what the top management of a company does (and the way it does it) rather than what it says or what is projected in the Chairman's report or in the press conferences.

The style of the top management of Modi Rubber Industries Limited is the way it uses the dynamics of the marketplace as the pivotal reference point for corporate strategies and policies, and for decision-making. For example, it has adapted foreign technology to suit the buyer needs in the Indian conditions, obtained a high market share by way of offering distinctive product features, provided excellent customer service, and used imaginative distribution and marketing policies. It has acquired commanding market share through acquisition of competing companies and focussed on servicing the truck operators who have been identified as the key determinants of business success in the type market. In other words, their style of operation is totally dictated by the marketplace.

Staff

Staff relates to human resources and related dimensions such as morale, attitude, motivation and behaviour. Larsen and Toubro Limited is an example where the proactive and achievement orientation of the managers, which has been built right down to the lower levels, has contributed significantly to the organisation's overall effectiveness.

Skills

Skills are those dominating attributes or capabilities which demonstrate what the organisation does best.

An example could be the marketing skills of Hindustan Lever Limited or Brooke Bond India Limited in reaching out to their consumers even at very distant locations by way of excellent distribution logistics to ensure that the product is available to the consumer at a convenient supply-point. Another example, would be Larsen and Toubro's ability to meet delivery schedules of plants ordered by meticulous production planning, materials planning, coordination with clients and continuous monitoring of the progress on such orders.

Our earlier understanding was that organisational interventions could only be centered around the three hard Ss, *viz.*, Strategy, Structure and Systems, by mandating and specifying explicit changes required by the managers down the line. The McKinsey 7-S model challenges this belief. While the interactive nature between these clements have long been recognised, the McKinsey model has emphasised the four soft Ss as key elements of organisational effectiveness and alerted us to the fact that even though they are not susceptible to change by direcHon from top management, without organisational responses towards these four elements, the desired effectiveness cannot be achieved. The model has also provided us with the new understanding that in relation to these elements (notwithstanding their somewhat abstract definitions) they are the real determinants of organisational development and further that they can be influenced rather than changed.

At a more specific level, organisational development by formulation of strategy is achieved by the corporate planning itself. However, it needs to be understood that strategy needs to be spelled out not only in organisational terms, but translated also in functional terms in respect of such functions as:

(a) Marketing;

(b) Production;

(c) Procurement;

(d) Finance;

(e) Personnel;

(f) Employee relations, etc.

The other aspect relating to strategy formulation which is increasingly evident in corporate planning is the translation of strategies into action plans which identifies specific strategic events in the achievement of strategy in terms of:

(a) The managerial responsibility for planning, organising and implementing the event;

(b) The deadlines for accomplishment;

(c) The resources required;

(d) The requirements of co-ordination; and

(e) The arrangements for progress review and follow-up.

Perhaps the most interesting recent development in the strategic area has been the understanding that strategic planning may be a bottleneck to continued creativity and organisadonal effectiveness since it is a onetime exercise (with five years gap). It is increasingly contended that a detailed formal and structured corporate planning exercise—while extremly helpful in terms of identifying the future at that point of time—also has the disadvantage of freezing the thinking of the managers and the cutput assuming the proportions of a religious text by which all managerial responses and activities are to be guided. Moreover, the time gap between two corporate plans often becomes a strategic plan holiday! It is contended that while a structured strategic planning exercise is extremely valuable, two other factors must be taken into account:

(a) Notwithstanding the rigour, the depth and the richness of the environmental scanning, analyses of strengths weaknesses, opportunities and threats, they are no more than reasoned assumptions.

The reality is likely to be substantially different in several matters due to uncontrollable factors; and

(b) Strategy formulation is a creative process and too much structuring, analysis and reason inhibits the process of creativity. It is contended that creative thinking about strategy is often a product of the ability to view a set of past and current happenings and to relate them in a meaningful way to the organisation's future.

In this understanding, it has been increasingly argued that strategic thinking is even more critical to organisational effectiveness than strategic planning. Viewed in this context, managers must develop such strategic thinking capability and display it by strategic management rather than merely implementing the strategic plan. Organisational Development in this area is increasingly focusing on incalculating such strategic thinking capabilities and developing the skills of strategic management. In many ways, such skills are sought to be built by interaction with external environment-rubbing shoulders with people who have knowledge of and insights about the marketplace, the society and the technological horizon, by introducing a process of continuous environmental scanning and bouncing off ideas relating to strategic management action with knowledgeable senior managers, industrialists, policy makers and professionals. Many of us believe that the ability to select this group carefully, to maintain a pro-active orientation in such continued interaction to identify the right issues, and to listen, discern and act upon the insights generated are of the essence in strategic management.

In regard to structure, most corporate planning exercises indicate that the current structure would be inadequate to deal with the desired future plans of growth, dispersion and diversification formulated by the corporate plan. It is often found that accountability for results is hazy, responsibilities are not clearly defined, and authority and command over resources are not commensurate with the expected performance. It also becomes clear that such problems in the current structure will be compounded many times over due to three factors:

(a) The increase in the level of activity;

(b) The introduction of multi-location operation; and

(c) The proliferation of products and technologies arising out of diversification.

In regard to the first dimension, the common fallacy rests on the assumption that managing a company which is double the size of current operations merely requires double the number of people. This arithmetical understanding fails to take into account the qualitative changes that accompany increases in size beyond a point and the complexities introduced in communication, planning, resources allocation, decision-making, monitoring, taking remedial action and most importantly, shared understanding of organisational objectives and strategy.

In regard to the second dimension *viz.*, introduction of multi-location operations, it is often assumed away that so long one can have agreed budgets of performance targets and get periodic performance reports, such multi-location operations can be managed effectively and efficiently. Many organisations have found to their grief that the corporate graveyard is marked with organisations which make such assumptions.

In regard to the third and the last dimension, *i.e.*, introduction of multiple products and technologies, the problems relating to newer roles, changes in emphaiss between the different driving functions *i.e.*, marketing, production, personnel, finance, etc., require different product-market activities to be structured differently. Such structures have to be designed to fit unique context of the product-market-technology requirements, if the required degree of organisational effectiveness is to be achieved.

When the requirement of an OD intervention by way of structural reorganisation is identified, the debate often turns around the issue of the best agency for doing it *i.e.* whether it should be done in-houses or whether outside professionals should be called in. Many a time it is not taken into account that the relative capabilities of these two sets of people are quite different but complementary in the context of the requirements of effective structural reorganisation. It is getting increasingly recognised that in such exercises perhaps the most fruitful combination is professional experts working jointly with an in-house team. It is important in such joint exercises to define the following:

(a) The nature of the structural problems which currently exist and which are envisaged with expansion, diversification and dispersion;

(b) The broad approach to resolution of the problems identified (*e.g.*, constitution of semi-autonomous product or regional profit centres, establishment of corporate offices with distinctive functions, redefinition of managerial roles relating to technology, marketing, planning and development etc.);

(c) The role of the in-house team;

(d) The expected output in terms of organisational specification, role description, implementation, etc.;

(e) The process and requirements of deriving information required for analysis of the structural problems by data collection and interviews with various levels of managers:

(f) The time requirement for completing the exercise; and

(g) The role of the various agencies involved in the exercise in implementation.

The recommended collaborative approach in restructuring exercises has many advantages. It results in complementary requirements of objectivity being supported by organisational knowledge and insights, conceptual skills and experience of similar exercises being enriched by what is feasible and possible in the organisation's unique context, etc. But the most important benefit is in terms of implementation. If the In-House Team-usually composed of a very senior manager with an overall organisational perspective and three others, usually highly capable young managers with understanding of production marketing and personnel is also given the responsibility for implementation, given their involvement in the development of the new structure, they are able to carry it out most efectively and efficiently. There are many requirements of effective structural reorganisation, but the primary one is the outside expert's acceptance within the organisation and his ability to carry the management team by a process of continuous interaction. He should be able to convince the managers by his analysis and organisational logic that notwithstanding the changes suggested, they are not only useful and desirable, but necessary in terms of the organisational development required for coping up with the planned expansion, dispersion and diversification.

Corporate plans often identify requirements of systems design (or steamlining) as part of organisational development required to implement the corporate plan. Such systems development in most cases is identified in relation to introduction of the budgeting system and the related management reporting system. Such systems changes make it possible in the expanded and diversified organisation to set performance targets to allocate resources to relate actual performance to such targets and most importantly to review performance on a mutual and collaborative basis with a view to identifying the remedial action required to be taken to attain the original goals.

The other most often identified requirement for systems development relates to the performance appraisal system. Many a times, it is found that the current performance apprajsal system does not identify the high achievers, the reward and punishment system does not make managers' performance objectives congruent with organisational objectives and that it provides very little help in terms of identifying the needs for training and development as well as job rotation for enhancing managerial skills. Systems changes are often introduced to remedy these problems. increasingly, two other tools are being used in recent years with great effectiveness in achieving the desired organisation development:

(a) Job rotations amongst high achievers to develop general management skills. In the process, it leads to development of the required organisational perspective and understanding of the mutuality of various functions.

(b) Action research programmes whereby outstanding managers are taken out of their current jobs and given a time bound project to study, analyse and formulate responses to major problems experienced in another set-up in the company (and to implement it within a time schedule, usually of one to two years). The required organisational help for providing suggestions, guidance and advice is provided for in snch a scheme but it is left to the manager undergoing the action research programme to seek such help rather than such help being provided automatically.

In regard to the four soft Ss. *i.e.* Superordinate Goals. Staff, Style, and Skills, the OD effort can never be a structured exercise leading to mandated changes. These elements can only be influenced over a period of time rather than changed by direction of the top management. The first requirement for organisational development in these areas is the diagnosis of current inadequacies in each of these elements. It is, thereafter, necessary to formulate corporate responses to such problems. Usually they take the following forms:

(a) Symbolism. By their actions top managers in their own work situation must signal that they have introduced the desired changes regarding these elements. This symbolism is particularly important in regard to the top management group's action because it is then likely that it will percolate down the managerial level. An illustrative situation could be that participative management is desired, but not seen to be practised by tho top management which is perceived to be cloistered. Clearly a determination has to be made and such determination acted upon with purpose and volition that top management also wishes to share some of their planning, decision-making, controlling activities with lower level managers.

(b) Demonstration. By reflecting in the planning, organising, decision-making, policy formulation the various desired changes in relation to these elements in day-to-day operational terms. The most important requirement in this regard is the perception down the line that the organisational desire to introduce improvements in the four elements is evident in the top management's actions rather than their directions and specifications in these regard. For instance, if marketing is to be the driving force or skill for enhancing. organisational effectiveness, it must be seen that considerable effort and resource allocation is directed towards what end by way of formulating the appropriate marketing policy, making the necessary resource allocations, translating them into organisational practices, enforcing such practices, etc.

(c) ***Specification.*** By setting down in terms of written policies, principles, manuals, guidelines, etc. the desired objectives in relation to these four elements. While this is useful, unless it is backed up by action in relation to the three earlier requirements, it is unlikely that mere specification will contribute towards the required Organisational Development.

(d) ***Recognition.*** By constantly recognising and rewarding posative contributions in regard to these elements, the organisation can signal to the people in the organisation that it values such contribution for improving organisational effectiveness. Such recognition and reward must percolate to the lowest level because here again the need is for the credibility of the organisation's genuine desire to improve organisational effectiveness in relation to these elements.

It need to be mentioned that if changes in Strategy, Structure and Systems are imaginatively fashioned and implemented with the required purpose, sincerity and understanding, they make significant (and visible) contributions towards the improved effectiveness of the four soft Ss, *i.e.* Superordinate Goals, Staff, Style and Skills.

❐

3

Policy Planning in Business

LONG-RANGE planning has been high on the hit parade at management meetings and conferences in recent months, and as a technique it promises to be the next addition to the formula for "progressive" management. Moreover, the fact that consultants are much interested in it is a reliable harbinger that, ready or not, top executives are going to be hearing a lot about why they should embrace it. In fact the interest is so great-particularly as compared with accomplishment to date that there is real danger of the whole thing rapidly becoming a fad.

But just because a fad sometimes turns into a fiasco when introduced in a company, it does not follow that management can ignore the long-range planning task. Fad or not, here is something management must look at seriously-cautiously, perhaps, but nonetheless purposefully—that is, unless the company wants to undergo deliberate or unconscious liquidation.

Unfortunately, as pointed out recently, it is difficult to find plans to study and learn from. In the few companies where real projects of this kind have been undertaken there is reluctance to disclose the conclusions drawn by the planners, for fear that this might reveal to competitors the company's most closely guarded secrets on strategy and tactics. However, there is less hesitation to discuss how the planners went about getting the answers, and any executives who are considering the establishment of long-range planning in their firms can learn a great deal from a study of the ways in which other companies have approached the problem.

For this reason, and also because I think the administrative problem of introducing the planning activity and nursing it through the early stages is critical, I will concentrate on various organizational devices, on the approaches used to develop plans, and on some words of advice gathered from talking to executives who made a few mistakes along the way.

Trends and Countertrends

Long-range planning is that activity in a company which sets long-term goals for the firm and then proceeds to formulate specific plans for attaining these goals. There seems to be some indication that five years is the appropriate time span. A shorter period hews too closely to operating problems and discourages the consideration of planning problems, whereas a longer period becomes too nebulous as a basis for developing "supporting" plans, *i.e.*, detailed statements of what must be done in order to meet the long-term goals.

Up to now, not many companies other than the giants have done very much about such long-range planning on any formal basis. Typically, managements in small and medium-size companies are too busy trying to make a profit for the current months to find time to think about what the company will be doing five years from now. Yet these same managements are making frequent decisions with long-term implications-decisions which, in many cases, are even more critical for them than for their bigger competitors, simply because they cannot as easily afford a costly error on a new product or a new plant.

Of course, no successful company is able to get along without some kind of forward planning. In the past, however, this has usually taken the form of one or two top executives setting the general direction of growth. It may have been no more explicit than a strong urge to expand sales. Even where companies have joined the rush to diversification, the purpose has often been expressed in terms of adding volume rather than in terms of making effective use of company resources or reinforcing particular weak spots. Only in isolated instances has a wide group of company executives been involved in laying out detailed plans for the growth of the enterprise which they manage.

What accounts, then, for the sudden flurry of attention to planning? In particular, why is so much interest being given to the committee type of organization for planning?

Certainly a part of the explanation lies in the fact that the financial analysts in search of growth companies have reacted favourably to those situations where management has attempted to forecast the specific shape and scope of potential growth arid then taken positive action in anticipation of future demands. With this stimulus, a strong "follow-the-leader" influence has developed. More aud more top managements, trying to get something started, have looked around at what others have done. And they have seized on the organizational devices used by the very big companies which, because of their size and complexity, have almost inevitably had to set up some kind of formal group effort.

Support and Opposition

However, the habits and traditions of the past are not easily overcome. Down the line, the feeling still persists that planning is the main function of the chairman and the president and vice presidents and lower echelons should concentrate on running the company. So it is not enough for top management itself to awaken to the need for more formal planning. Someone very near die top must also take the initiative in pushing long-range planning of tbe company-wide kind; otherwise tbe chances are remote that it will ever be started.

Even in an organization conditioned to welcoming new developments and improvements in techniques, the long-range. planning function will probably not be self-generating. The trouble is that in most companies the rules of the game are such that the managers concentrate on short-term objectives. Budgets, performance ratings, and bonuses almost always are focused on the near term; accomplishments toward long-term objectives, by contrast, are more difficult to measure, and in most instances no attempt at measurement is even made. It is not surprising, I therefore, that after years of conditioning under these circumstances managers are less than enthusiastic about the "obvious" advantages of long-range planning. For example:

The president of a company with five divisions, each of which was headed by a general manager who had complete responsibility for sales and production, was disappointed because his general managers were not taking a "long-term view." But as one of the general managers commented to an outsider; "I'm too damn busy with day-to-day problems to even think beyond the current year's operations. We have to submit budgets, and this takes us 12 months ahead, but that's as far as we go. I'm judged on profit performance year by year."

Another kind of resistance stems from the fact that, in order to be effective, long-range planning must be comprehensive and in the process "look under all corners of the rug." Often the initial reaction is to regard the development of a master planl as a meddlesome, unnecessary intrusion. Many vice presidents and highly placed executives look upon it as a direct reflection on the caliber of the management in their respective departments; and, no matter how careful the precautions, the planners will find it difficult to avoid such an interpretation.

Indeed, I would venture the hypothesis that the most serious obstacle to fong-range planning is not so much the drain on management time, the actual problems of doing good planning, or the danger of revealing company strategy, as it is the subtle, but occasionally open, opposition of some executives which appears in the early stages of the development.

Hence top-management support is obsolutely essential. I am aware that if you add up all the speakers and writers who stipulate top-management support in the area of their particular interests, each and every activity in the company appears to need such baking and that is a physical impossibility. But the argument in the case of long-range planning is overriding, if only because the activity has always been thought of as so distinctly top-level.

Company Approach

Once the board of directors or the chief executive has committed the company to undertake long-range planning, the most critical decision to be made is how to approach the organizational problem—particularly the question of who is to be responsible for carrying the work through.

To get down to specifics, let me describe how one company approached this part of the long-range planning task, and then evaluate its efforts in comparison with those of several other companies.

Operating Managers

The president of Company A appointed a senior vice president with a background in sales as chairman of a planning committee. With the advice of the president, the chairman selected for the committee six managers from among the immediate subordinates of the vice presidents: one each from product development, purchasing, staff engineering, research, production, and personnel. The chairman of the committee asked a junior executive from the market research department to serve as secretary of the committee, with the understanding that the task would require only about one-third of his time.

The chairman preferred not to assemble a special staff for the planning committee, and he suggested that the members of the committee draw upon existing staff personnel in their various department for the studies required by the committee. An outside consultant was retained to meet with the committee, with the explicit understanding that he would act only as an adviser. Here is how the group functioned:

Sales Forecasts. The president had changed the planning committee with formulating a plan which would achieve a doubling of the company's sales within five years, without specifying how this goal was to be met. The committee decided to begin its work with an examination of the growth potential of the company's existing products. Considering such factors as population trends, a rising standard of living, and a high level of personal income, the planners estimated the total market for each of the products for the next five years.

They now attempted to estimate what share of the total market company A could expect to get with each of its products. At this stage, the committee reckoned with expected improvements which the research group predicted for existing products, as well as with the best guess on the efforts of competitors in the various markets. The forecast assumed that expenditures for advertising, sales promotion, and sales salaries would rise proportionately with sales.

After surveying the domestic markets, the committee turned to the foreign markets and estimated the possible five-year growth in various countries over the world.

The total potential growth in existing products fell short of the total sales goal set by the president. To fill this gap the committee turned to new products. A detailed appraisal of the sales potential year by year was made for each of the four most promising new products then in various stages of development by the research department. Incidentlly, the committee was the first to see that since one of the products had a large potential market yet was still in the early stage of research for large-scale production, there was both need and opportunity for making a closer study of possible acquisition of an existing company as an alternative to new plant.

At this point, the sales forecasts for existing products and new products were presented to the top executives. In their judgement, the estimates served as a reasonable basis for proceeding with more detailed studies of sales, production, manpower, and finances.

Sub-committees for Special Studies. With this general outline for company growth established, the members of the committee were able to break up into sub-committees to make more comprehensive studies in each area. For instance, the assumption previously made, that the dollars spent for advertising, sales promotion and sales salaries would have to be increased proportionately as sales increased had to be examined by a sub-committee of marketing specialists. The committee felt that as sales volume increased perhaps a smaller percentage of the sales dollar would be needed for these purposes. On the other hand, as competitors intensified their efforts and as company A sought an increasingly larger share of the total market, there was some reason to believe that a bigger share of the sales dollar would be needed to generate the expected volume of sales.

Before each sub-committee began any extensive studies, it was asked to prepare a description of how it proposed to collect the data needed for its final report. This proposed approach was presented to the entire committee for discussion, and many time-saving and money-saving suggestions were offered. For instance, the need for one expensive study was eliminated by the consolidation of two completed studies made by separate departments but not previously circulated outside the departments.

Concurrent with the sales study, a group of production representatives worked out a year-by-year schedule for existing production facilities. As shortages of facilities became apparent, they planned the type and location of new facilities needed over the five-year period. They also investigated the company's sources of raw materials and forecasted the pattern of price movements which might be expected. Finally, this group estimated the year-by-year capital requirements for the new facilities and predicted the manufacturing, freight, and warehousing costs for each product. A specialist on linear programming was called in to assist with this phase of the study.

A personnel group was also active. By keeping in touch with the deliberations in the sales and production sub-committees, it was able to draw plans for organizational changes, training needs, and recruitment requirements which would fulfill the expectations of the sales and production sub-committees.

Future Steps. The first five-year plan is not yet finished. The final stage is to compute the total capital requirements for new facilities and for working capital purposes. By projecting the budgeting procedure five years ahead, pro-forma profit and loss statements can be prepared for each of the years. Crude calculations of return on investment made at many stages to test the feasibility of certain individual projects will then be refined in the light of data available on all phases of the master plan.

Two years of the five-year planning period will have transpired before the committee is able to present a detailed master plan which the chairman believes is reliable as a basis for management action. The next task of the committee will be to project the plan for an additional two years. Each year thereafter the committee will review the four years of plans remaining and add a fifth year, so that a five-year plan will always be avilable for management guidance. The methods developed and the evidence gathered daring the preparation of the first five fear plan will greatly simplify future projections, and the committee will concentrate on refining the projections and making detailed studies of proposals which have long-term implications for the company.

Solid Accomplishments

During the months of staff work and meeting, the committee members constantly found it difficult to avoid being sidetracked on studies of urgent operating problems; but under the subtle prodding of the chairman, who tolerated occasional detours, the group has made steady progress in assembling a mass of data, interpreting it, and drawing conclusions in terms of specific plans for future expansion. The president is enthusiastic about the committee's work; he sees a blueprint emerging that can serve as a general framework within which management can make specific decisions on sales, production facilities, new products, manpower needs, and capital requirements.

In addition, the planning committee has have been a valuable training ground for developing future top executives. The members of the committee, who were already key operating managers, have been introduced to the difficult task of planning before being moved into positions where they have a major responsibility for thinking ahead. And having prepared and understood the plans, the members of the committee are ready to make the moves which will put those plans into effect when the "go-ahead" is given. In several instances, departmental projects have been initiated as a result of committee discussions without waitng for completion and approval of the over-all plans. The company enjoys the further advantage of having a real "team" of managers at the second level who have learned to work together.

Finally, the committee chairman has been able to sharpen his evaluation of each committee member's ability to put aside operating pressures and to devote a portion of his energies to the broader tasks of management. By combining executives who are especially imaginative and "creative" with men who tend to be more analytical and "scientific," and by mixing a great range of company experience, the chairman has been able to achieve a happy blend of bold, expansionist-oriented thinking and rigorously logical planning based on factual data.

Difficulties Experienced

Despite some solid accomplishments during its tenure, the planning committee's work has not always gone smothly. The members of the committee, as well as the vice presidents they report to, are extremely busy with operating problems; and while they recognize the value of the committee's, both they and their bosses put top priority on immediate problems. In a way, this situation has been advantageous in that it has forced the committee member to delegate much of the spadework to subordinates, but without any question the committee's progress has been slowed by the continual pre-occupation with immediate problems.

Also, the vice presidents of the company are not charged directly with responsibility for planning, and this probably accounts for a certain amount of indifference towards the aims of the committee.

Another difficulty growing out of such an approach, which centres the planning function below the vice presidential level, is that at certain stages the committee members may not be fully informed about proposals under consideration by the president and vice presidents. Although most committee members have welcomed the opportunity to deal with broad; company policies and problems, nevertheless they have experienced real frustration when, after weeks of study and discussion, a planning proposal has been rendered obsolete by top management's announcement of a move which the members of the committee did not know was under consideration.

Up to now, no workable line of communication has been set up for keeping the planning committee posted on the disposition of its proposals. As one committee member put it, following a two-hour presentation to the executive staff (composed of the president, executive vice president, and vice presidents): "There goes another four month's work down the well. We'll probably never hear from it again." Top policy decisions are made by the executive staff; and since the committee members do not participate in these deliberations, they cannot appreciate the part that their studies may have played in the final decisions.

Another problem has been the sharing of information. As the sub-committees got set to work on various aspects of the master plan, some tended to hold off beginning their jobs until they had received the conclusions of other groups. Of course, it was to be expected that operating men would be inclined to plan within the specifications set by others; yet, to make the most effective progress, each group needed to be working with the others so that ideas could flow back and forth. For instance:

During the production sub-committee's study of the possibilities of expanding plant facilities, such factors as comparative costs, ease of distribution to markets, and availability of raw materials were considered. The group assumed that the management organization could adjust to whatever proposal it devised, and only after it had settled on a plan was a personnel sub-committee invited to prepare supporting programmes for a management staff and a work force.

If, from the start, a personnel sub-committee had been studying the ideal expansion plan, considered from the standpoint of organization and personnel, it might have added an additional dimension to the production group's deliberations and thus have helped it to come up with a more practical proposal. As it was, the personnel sub-committee simply "planned" within the limits set down by the other sub-committee.

Alternative Approaches

Top executives who anticipate or have experienced that shortcomings of Company A's approach may want to consider different systems. A company that began with a planning committee similar to Company A's, but was discouraged by the difficulty of combining planning and operating responsibilities in the same persons, abandoned this approach in favour of a group whose members were assigned full-time to the planning activity. As before, the members of the committe were selected from the various departmeuts of the company, but under the new arrangement they were completely relieved of operating responsibilities.

There is a noteworthy advantage in such an approach in that a more detailed master plan could be deveioped sooner. But most chief executives would be horrified at the prospect of having a group of operating managers at least, if they were good man taken away from their jobs completely for a very long period of time. Almost immediately these operating managers would be tagged as staff men and, as a result, lose their preferred positions for influencing the line managers. This raises the question of what kinds of variations from Company A's approach are possible and practical.

Top-Level Vice Presidents

Company B, which, like Company A, had a centralized management consisting of functional departments reporting to vice presidents, decided in favour of the following kind of committee organization:

The president of Company B gave his highest-ranking assistant additional duties as vice president for planning and administration.

This vice president became chairman of a 15-man planning committee composed of all the other vice presidents. A sub-committee was appointed for each project which the planning committee decided to investigate. (Note how much less comprehensive the aims of this group were than the aims of Company A's planning committee). A vice president was always selected as chairman of the sub-committee, which might include other vice presidents as well as company officials who were not members of the planning committee.

An assistant vice president for planning was appointed. He became an ex-officio member of each sub-committee and coordinated their activities. The chairman of the sub-committee was responsible for the writing of the report to the planning committee, although he was free to call upon anyone to assist him in collecting and organizing data.

The planning committee did not attempt to formulate an over-all five-year plan, but studied a variety of individual projects, some of which were initiated by the president, some by members of the planning committee, and others by executives at various levels in the company. All of the projects had long-term implications.

Originally, a sub-committee was dissolved when its recommendations on a project had been accepted by the planning committee; but over a period of time, as the proposals began to fall into a definite pattern, the chairman of the planning committee decided to appoint standing sub-committees. For instance, the sub-committee on facilities came to be in continual operation and reviewed all projects which concerned the company's physical plant and equipment.

As the organization evolved, the top planning committee became a review committee, while the real spadework of collecting and interpreting facts and judgements went on in the sub-committees. The chairman convened the 15-man planning committee only to consider a report by one of its sub-committees. This happened on an average of four times per year.

The prompt and serious attention given to recommendations emanating from the planning activity created an extremely favourable atmosphere. There was never a delay in setting a meeting once the sub-committee was ready to report, and members gave top priority to attendance at these meetings. The president and board of directors responded similarly in taking up recommendations submitted to them. Because of this favourable top-management attitude, the subcommittees encountered little resistance in persuading various members of the company to undertake staff work, some of which was quite extensive.

At the same time, Company B's planning was not, obviously, as ambitious as Company A's. There was no master plan systematically accounting for the activities of all major company functions for a prescribed period of future years. It might be said, therefore, that in the short term Company B sacrificed the potentials of Company A's over-all planning for a thorough study of projects stemming from immediate problems. I do not mean to imply, however, that this is a case of "either-or", that there is no middle ground between the approaches of Companies A and B. Indeed, as we shall see, other alternatives have already been proved practical at least in the case of divisionalized companies.

Divisional Heads

Ordinarily, a company which is decentralized into divisions, each with a general manager responsible for sales, production, manpower, and profits presents a simpler long-range planning problem than that of either Company A or B. Within a division, the general manager and his staff are trained to work together on overall divisional problems. Thus in effect each division becomes a separate planning center concentrating on a single product or line of related products. Such a setup can be advantageous in long-range planning as the following example illustrates:

The president of Company C asked each of his eight division managers to prepare a five-year plan for his division. Each plan was to be presented at an all-day meeting at the home office attended by the president and all the vice presidents. The home office meetings were primarily intended to keep the top staff informed. The president and vice presidents were free to comment on the plans, but any modifications had to be made by the general manager of the division.

Members of the home office staff were available to assist the general manager in preparing his plan, but for the most part the division personnel did the work. For instance, all the plant managers in a division were active in drawing up production plans. The division controller also played an important role in assembling quantitative data.

The caliber of the initial presentations varied greatly. Moreover, they were so disparate as to organization content, and criteria that comparisons among divisions were difficult. But by co-ordinating subsequent reports through a member of the home office staff who was assigned the task, greater uniformity was attained.

At first there was resistance to Company C's planning attempt. Some managers argued that their divisions were doing very well profitwise and that they should not be dictated to on the question of whether or not to prepare a long-term plan. But since the first round of presentations, when several skeptics became convinced by what they saw come out of the other divisions, the opposition has dwindled, and almost without exception the managers have accepted the planning job with a high level of enthusiasm. They have discovered that a well documented plan provides the best evidence they can muster to persuade the home office to allocate additional funds to their divisions.

At the same time, the presentation of long-range plans has put top executives at headquarters in a better position to judge the performance of the divisiox managers. In a few instances the early presentations disclosed a lack of staff work even for day-to-day operations, much less for the more difficult task of forward planning. Those divisions with the most refined cost systems, budgets, and market research were able to produce more comprehensive plans from the outset. The emphasis on long-term planning in the meeting high-lighted the efforts of those managers who were planning for long-term return on investment concomitantly with good profits from current operations.

It is interesting to note, in passing, that while top management effectively delegated the planning for the divisions to the general managers, it called on a consulting firm to help in drawing up an over-all plan for the company. The cosulting firm was asked to study such problems as further diversification, the growth potential in existing divisions, and the prospects of competition from products and processes which might be introduced by other companies.

Specialists and Consultants

When the long-range planning task is added to the already crowded schedules of a company's executives, progress on the plans may be painfully slow. To alleviate this problem, several companies have set up a special staff, usually reporting at a high level in the company, or have retained a management consulting firm to prepare the plans. For instance:

The chairman of the board of Company D hired an economist to develop a five-year plan. The economist brought three assistants with him. This group conducted extensive interviews and investigations in the company and drew upon sources close to the industry, such as the trade association, investment bankers, and government agencies. Within about eighteen months, the economist made a four-hour presentation outlining a master plan to the board of directors, which is composed mainly of the top officers in the company. The meeting broke up after a brief discussion, and the chairman asked that each member of the board study the 450-page report written by the economist and his staff. At the time this article was written, six months had elapsed since the initial presentation, but discussion of the report had not been resulted.

The lesson of this case is clear. The master plan was supported by a mass of evidence and had been carefully reasoned. As a starter, it was more complete and embodied a greater range of ramifications than most plans developed in companies that have relied on existing line and staff personnel. Yet I suspect that nothing will come of it. The understanding and confidence in a plan that can come only from months of painstaking development by the managers concerned are missing. Unless the chairman of the board presses hard, none of the major proposition.. in the plan will ever be acted upon. And the chairman probably has a bad case of indigestion as he looks at his untouched copy of the big report, and thinks of the equally sizeable bill.

I do not deny that at certain stages a special staff or a management consultant may be indispensable to a company planning group. Rather, someone with technical knowledge or broad experience in a market or industry quite often can assist tremendously by bringing a fresh and objective point of view to bear. But specialists lose their advantage when complete responsibility for the planning is turned over to them, and unfortunately, many companies have foundered on this "easy" course of action. Part of the gain to be secured in long-range planning is the thinking-through that the company itself must do, without regard for whether it ends up as prices of paper with words and graphs on them.

The Starting Point

The type of management organization, the diversity of products, and the extent of previous budget and research activity are probably the most important factors in deciding how to pick a strating point for the planners.

For instance, a company organized into divisions with a relatively autonomous general manager responsible for a single product or related group of products may be able to begin, as did Company C, by asking each division to prepare a five-year plan. Implicit in such a request is the assumption that the division will continue to expand so long as a satisfactory return on investment can be earned. Home office management may even leave to the division manager the burden of presenting arguments as to what rate of return should be expected in his organization, although it will probably reserve the right of final decision.

Some home office coordination may be required if comparisons are to be made of one division with another or if uniform yardsticks are to be applied. One company, for instance, developed a "standard" outline for each division's representation:

The industry	Working capital
Our position	Return on investment
Competiton' activities	Location of new facilities
Sales forecasts	Manpower requirements
Present products	Management controls
New products	Pricing policies
Capital investment requirements	Appraisal of strengths and weaknesses

Special problem areas

If a company has had considerable experience with market research and budgeting procedures, the planning group may be able to start by setting five-year sales goals as did Company A. The point, however, is that sales and cost forecasting techniques are indispensable to this phase of planning. Unless the members of the planning group are familiar with such techniques and certainly many operating managers are they will probably be skeptical of the "crystal gazing" when first introduced to it. Because it is foreign to their own experience, the planning may seem to them like so much "guesswork."

Selection of Projects

For starting the work of the planning group, the most desirable kind of project is one which poses some operating questions, has long-term implications, and involves the operating experiences of several members of the committee. For instance:

If the committee sets out to formulate a plan for taking a new product from the research laboratory through the various stages of introducing it in a national market, the members can learn how to function effective as a group; and at an early point they may derive a sense of accomplishment which will give them more "steam" for the forays ahead.

Also, since the time span for the introduction of a new product may be two or three years or even longer, the committee will get some practice in setting up time-tables and in stating explicitly the action which needs to be taken at various stages. As an illustration. training assignments may be needed immediately if management personnel with proper qualifications are to be available three years hence, when the product reaches the market.

After working with one or two limited projects of this type, committee members, should be more ready to tackle a more comprehensive planning assignment, if it happens to be called for. Interesting enough, in this connection, one planning committee which has functioned successfully for several years has never in fact attempted to draw up a master long-term plan for the company's future. But look at some of the projects which have been undertaken:

Optimum size of main manufacturing facility (a major expansion is now underway as a result of the planning committee report).

Building versus renting home office space (a large office building has now been started).

Employee housing adjacent to main plant (this was undertaken as a company project and subsequently developed into a major rehabilitation project by the community).

Scholarships (a policy on contributing to educational institutions was formulated).

Employee stock purchases (a plan for acquisition of company stock by employees at all levels evolved).

Reappraisal of an existing product (production and sale of this product were discontinued as a result of the planning committee's recommendation).

Note that the decisions reached in each of these projects represent long-term commitments. Moreover, the chairman's insistence that the committee produce definite recommendations and put them in writing has resulted in a series of carefully documented statements; and as these seemingly unrelated recommendations are accumulated, a very useful background of sales, production, and financial data is being built for a possble over-all company plan.

Perhaps more important these studies have forced the planners to make more explicit the criteria which will guide the company's growth. For jnstance, in making a recommendation to expand its main plant, the committee found itself involved in long-term market forecasts for certain geographical areas. Once the commitment for expansion was made, the company was tied irrevocably to concentrating its marketing efforts in those areas.

The significant thing to keep in mind is that such "piecemoal" efforts would not be making a contribution to real planning if they focused on projects oriented toward operations. Unless such a focus is avoided, the committee may find itself falling into the role of supervising a sort of top-drawer suggestion box and never pushing on to the task of tackling long-range problems.

Within Real Limits

One good way to start, it seems to me, would be for the planners to make a study of the factors which will limit the company's growth in the future. This approach has the advantage of permitting a number of sub-groups to begin simultaneous exploration of questions vital to the planning activity, and in addition it encourages realism.

Take the sales forecast, for instance. Management falls too frequently into the trap of planning how the company will increase its share of the market with only slight recognition of what its competitors are doing. It is certainly understandable that this happens when the sales outlook is worked out by a committee of enthusiastic marketing men. But a planning group composed only partly of salesmen is more likely to be realistic on this point.

Again, shortage of capital may put a limitation on a company's growth, and so it is a good question to study. Even when management capital, other conditions may prevent the attraction of funds to the company. Shortages of production facilities place still another limitation upon growth, albeit a short-term one; and raw materials supplies may present a problem.

An important limitation to examine is management personnel. Planners seem to have a tendency to assume that an existing management organization can undergo unlimited upgrading and that the lack of capable, trained managers need never hamper a company's growth. The almost universal experience of managers when they come face to face with expansion, however, is that this is not true.

General Observations

As I review the experience of several different companies that have organized for long-range planning, a number of general points and suggestions stand out in my mind. I shall set them forth briefly by way of conclusion.

By-Products

Several valuable by-products can be derived from a long-range planning effort:

"Crystallization" of executive thinking is more likely to take place if planners are expected to produce recommendations, and especially if these recommendations are to be put in writing.

Committee investigations and deliberations are an excellent means of keeping the top executives informed about different parts of the business. Such a channed may be particularly needed in a company which has been growing rapidly, for oftentimes there is no systematic means for top executives to learn of developments in a new division, especially if its managers come to the corporation as a part of a smaller company. (Incidentally, new executives in a company might be appointed to a planning group as a part of their indoctrination in over all company problems.)

A planning group may find blind spots and potential problem areas which the regular management group might easily miss in a rapidly expanding firm. When given an over-all responsibility rather than a limited assignment, the planners should become skillful in catching up loose ends which are either being overlooked or perhaps even deliberately ignored.

The planning group may provide a company-wide sounding board for appraising the potential of new techniques. Linear programming, for example, may be introduced as a valuable planning tool for making decisions on plant location, production scheduling, and shipping patterns. However, the use of the technique requires the massing and interpretation of tata from many parts of a company. A planning group composed of managers with diversified backgrounds is better equipped to judge the usefulness of such a complex device.

Common Blind Spots

The planners may find it difficult to persuade sales managers to disassociate sales estimates for planning purposes from the estimates they set as goals for the sales force. The practice of setting sales goals higher than those which are reasonably attainable is so habitual for the sales executive that he unconsciously carries over his heady optimism into planning work. Moreover, the objective of expanding sales volume can become such an obsession that the costs of expansion are ignored. For example:

In one company, the sales representative on a planning committee insisted that a certain volume of sales was attainable, in the face of opposition from every other committee member. Only when he was confronted with the costs of production facilities needed to back up his goal, and asked to vote on a recommendation that this expenditure be made, did he finally suggest that the sales estimates be scaled downward.

As previously noted, planners tend too easily to assume that enough management talent will be available no matter how ambitious the expansion plans may be. If their record is marred by one mistake, it is their failure to recognize that tho "lead time" needed for building the management organization may be longer than that needed in adjust any other single factor to higher profit goals. Rather than the after-thought that is, oftentimes is, manpower planning should figure prominently in the conception of a master plan.

Moreover, top management must not expect immediate results from long-range planning. It requires a type of thinking which is strange and difficult for most line executives, whose training and experience have prepared them to deal with operating problems but not to prove too far into the future. Unlike some new undertakings where the cream can be skimmed at the start, effective long-range planning will start slowly and gain momentum as more and more data are gathered to throw light on the future.

Any problem which is so complex as to require that it be analyzed piecemeal, and the analyses regrouped for an over-all appraisal, is particularly difficult in the early stages. The long-range planners usually have few facts about other phases of the business that they must rely on the whosesale assumptions in order to make progress; forward thinking based on such assumptions is alien to most practical operating men. However, once they can point to a tangible recommendation which sparked a line of action that otherwise would not have been taken, interest in long-range planning is sure to grow.

"Inside Job" Needed

If line officers are given the responsibility for developing the plans, they will be more ready to support them once they are translated into the action stage. The planning function strikes so close to the heart of the management task that line managers are almost certain to become defensive and resist intrusion if the board or the chief executive hires a consultant or an economist to master-mind the planning.

In working and talking with executives about long-range planning, I have been surprised, but agreeably so, that so many have resisted the temptation to begin by hiring a staff of specialists to do the job, and instead have taken the more difficult course of depending on the existing management staff to do the spadework.

If given the primary responsibility, specialists have a way of introducing new techniques and ways of thinking strange to a company, and such a start on long-range planning may saddle it with a handicap which can never be overcome. By dependence on the people already in the company, management gains another advantage in discovering the strengths and weaknesses of existing departments. As indicated earlier, however, the consultant can often serve usefully by giving assistance to the executives in change of planning for instance, by providing new leads or by making special studies.

Conditions of Success

Good long-range planning is expensive in more ways than one. The plans are inevitably complex, and many risks must be assessed, A comprehensive plan in which everyone can exhibit confidence will require hours of discussion even after the time consuming collection of data has taken place. Management should not be led to believe that long-range planning can be added to the list of executives' tasks without making noticeable demands on their time. To have a set of plans based on less than thorough discussions and superficial investigations by the managers who design them is probably worse than to have none. Such plans are a dangerously shaky foundation for commitments of company capital.

At the start top management must give strong support to the planning activity. Not only is it time-consuming, but the kind of thinking needed is foreign to most executives, and the returns are difficult to predict. However, there is a brighter side of the picture. Unlike other activities calling for strong top-management support, the long-range planning function need not be perpetually parasitic. If the top company officer and the board of directors show by their interest and action that they value planning, and if the planners can make one or two solid contributions, the activity should become self-sustaining.

The development of a master plan for growth probably must be entrusted to executives very near the top of the organization. In today's competitive scene, so many factors must be considered that only men with real management breadth are capable of assigning proper weights to the many different considerations involved in charting a future course of action. The specialist with a departmental point of view can make only limited contributions to an over-all plan for the company. Another argument in favour of placing the planning at the top level is the fact that the planners must have access to confidential information and broad dissemination of such material in a company may provide dangerous leaks to competitors.

Finally, the planners should be near enough to the top to see their efforts as an influence on company policy. Planning has many frustrations, but the worst is to see top management making major commitments while failing to recognize or ignoring the long-term implications which the planning group could help to clarify.

❐

4

Business System

It is frequently difficult to emphsise adequately the need for good organizational structure because many of this incorrectly assume that every social unit and every firm is well organized. This is true because most of our wants are satisfied through cooperative and organized work with others.

When managers organize or reorganize parts of their firm's system, they must of necessity keep in mind their goals or objectives because these are the determinants of how the system is organized initially. Likewise, as goals and objectives change so must the organized system change in order to effectively meet these goals. Essentially most of our lives are spent working with organizations such as our families, clubs, churches, governments, or the business enterprises where we earn our livelihood. We satisfy most of our desires working through these and similar organisations. In fact, for many of us organization represents the only practica means we have for overcoming our individual limitations. Good organization enables us to achieve ends that could not have been obtained as efficiently or as effectively through our individual efforts. Organization is not an end in itself, but a means to an end. Through organized effort we accomplish things. The act of two boys pushing a car out of the mud affords a practical example of a simple organization designed to accomplish an objective, in this case, dislocating a car stuck in the mud. Kenneth C. Towe, when President of American Cyanamid Company, indicated that a sound form of organization is the answer to every business problem; that a poor organization could run a good product into the ground; and that a good organization with a poor product could run a good product out of the market. While this may be an overstatement of the importance of organizing, it does emphasize the important role it plays in any corporate undertaking. When Andrew Carnegie sold his vast holdings to the United States Steel Corporation in 1901, he sold not only his physical assets but the intangible asset that kept his empire effectively operating his organization. What he thought about his organization and the value he placed on good organization is indicated by his statement: "Take away all our money, our great works, ore mines and coke ovens but leave our organization, and in a few years I shall have re-established myself."

Organization has been given various interpretations. Many people, when referring to the organization of a firm's system, are actually referring to the personnel of the firm. This reference can be misleading because organization embraces a wider more comprehensive meaning than simply personnel. Perhaps one of the best known definitions of organization was first stated by. Oliver Sheldon: "Organization is the process of so combining the work which individuals or groups have to perform with the facilities necessary for its execution, that the duties so performed provide the best channels for the efficient, systematic, positive, and coordinated application of the available effort." Thus, organization concerns itself with combining and coordinating individual as well as group activities in an enterprise. In this sense, the organization structure can be thought of as the machine through which management works to accomplish its task. Organization integrates the various jobs of the enterprise into an effective operating system to provide for accomplishing the firm's objective; and management achieves this objective in the most efficient manner possible through this effective machine which we call organization.

Some of us lack an appreciation for the value of organization in the total managerial system, as well as a knowledge of how organization can be put to work to help attain greater productivity. So that we may better understand these aspects, perhaps it would be wise for us to look first at the basic forms most organization structures take, an after this discuss some of the more subtle aspects.

Although the types of organization employed by companies vary considerably, three fundamental, organization structures are commonly recognized. These are:

1. Line organization

2. Functional organization

3. Line an staff organization.

Each of these three will be discussed briefly, indicating its strong and weak points.

Line Organization

A line organization is characterized by a direct flow of authority from the top boss through the various executives down to the workers. There are no staff or advisory positions.

Because of its simplicity, members of the organization find no difficulty in determining to whom they report and who is responsible to them. No nebulous staff positions exist to confuse the workers. This makes for a simple and easily understood organization. In addition, this factor also makes for clarity in the division of authority and responsibility among managers. Because it is headed by an individual who is not limited by committees and staff, a line organization usually makes for quicker, easier divisions and is, as a result, much more stable. Obviously, with no expenses involving staff personnel, the line form of organization is less expensive from the standpoint of overhead costs.

The line organization does, however, present drawbacks. Specialization, for example, is frequently incidental, and the same tasks are often performed using different procedures and crude methods in different departments. Because it is headed and run by one man with no staff aid, a line organization can be seized by a strong individual and run on an arbitrary even dictatorial-basis. Obviously, if this leader and his associates happen to be stronger than they are wise, then their actions could easily damage even destroy the organization. In line organizations, provisions are seldom made to train, develop, and replace the top leaders. As a result, when the leader leaves or dies, a replacement is frequently difficult to find and the business suffers because the leaders in line organizations have no staff assistants, they are frequently overworked and mere fore, tend to lace unduly heavy reliance on their subordinate including the workmen. In many situations, this results in jobs being performed ineffectively.

Although the line organization concept is extremely important to modern business, a pure line organization is seldom found except in small compact enterprises. Its many disadvantages and inflexibility deter its use in larger complex undertakings.

Functional Organization

Functional organization, often called functional foremanship, was originated by Business System Frederick W. Taylor in an attempt to bring about a specialization of management. Taylor contended that a foreman could not be a specialist in .everything he was expected to do. Therefore, instead of having one single superior, as in the line organization, Taylor arranged for a group of "specialists" to boss the worker in the various aspects of the business. You will not that the office work is separated from the shop work, with the time an cost clerk, instruction card clerk, order of work and route clerk, and disciplinarian on the office level on the other hand, the gang boss, speed boss, repair boss, and inspector are on the hop level. The gang boss was responsible for setting up machines and moving jobs from machine to machine, whereas the speed boss instructed the men in maintaining the specified machine speeds and rates of production. The other men performed the duties their names would indicate. Thus, Taylor separated the mental and clerical functions from the shop or production functions.

One of the major advantages Taylor claimed for his functional organization was that each function was administered by a specialist. Expert advice was always available to the worker. This advantage, however, was often more than offset by the difficulties encountered in having eight bosses for each worker each boss telling the worker what to do.

This type of organization, employing the principle of specialization, is based on individual proficiency and specialized knowledge. Because of specialization, the employees in a functional organization can be placed and utilized more effectively, and their skills, as a result, can be developed more highly. The air of specialization is further emphasized by the division of mental and manual work. Finally, functional organization, by its very nature, Overcomes one of the main disadvantages of the line organization, that being the inefficiency of one-man control.

Despite these advantages, functional organization is practically never used today in its pure state. For one thing, it is difficult to establish and maintain properly because of its high degree of specialization. With changes in personnel, for example, the effective performance of a particular function often shifts, making an unstable organization. Indeed, many people point to this as a major criticism. Another disadvantage encountered in functional organization is that with a series of specialists in charge, control and coordination are difficult to attain. In other words, it tends to operate not as a total system but as a series of independent units. In addition, discipline is difficult to maintain. As you would suspect, locating and fixing responsibility is difficult in functional organization. In fact, responsibility and authority between the bosses must overlap somewhat because of the nature of functional organization, and this overlapping frequently provides the impetus for friction and disagreement between both workers and management. As a last disadvantage, many individuals point out that a functional organization develops specialists rather than all-around good managers. As a result, the organization frequently lacks good leadership.

Because of these disadvantages, pure functional organization is seldom found today. Various modifications and combinations employing the principles of functional organization, however, are frequently used in the organization structures of some of our most modern and advanced firms.

The Line and Staff organization. To utilize the advantages of both the functional organization and the line organization, the line and staff type of organization was developed. Essentially, the line and staff organization consists of the addition of functional specialists to the simple line organization previously discussed. Thus, the advantages of specialization are gained without the inherent disadvantages of Taylor's functional organization. In essence, the line portion of a line and staff organization serves to maintain stability and discipline, whereas the staff or functional portion serves to bring expert knowledge to bear on problems. By thus, combining these two forms of organization, we retain most of the advantages of the line and functional types of organization, and retain few of their disadvantages.

Line and staff organization does possess disadvantages, however. For one thing, the authority and responsibility of the staff with respect to the line supervisors may cause confusion if they are not clearly set forth. Out of this confusion can come many difficulties. Frictions and jealousies, for example, may develop between the line and the staff members over who has the authority to do what. Also, an aggressive staff member may at times irritate a shop foreman and even usurp some of his line authority. Finally, with a line and staff organization, it is possible for the line supervisors to depend too much on the staff, thereby losing their ability for original thought, initiative, and action.

Of these three types of organization, the line and staff is the most common in our business economy, particularly among the larger enterprises. Usually a small company starts out with a line organization. In this instance, the owner-manager hires, directs, and rewards his men. With a growth in his business, however, a stage is reached where he is physically and mentally unable to cope with the many problems of his business. At this point the manager turns to another person for assistance. Quite often this person is a staff man such as a record keeper, an accountant, or a personnel man. As the business continues to grow, other staff functions are added as the situation demands. These additions, evolving as a result of the company's needs, make for a change in the form of organization. As the business grows, the organization also continues to grow and develop. The more complex the company, the more complex the organization.

Perhaps a distinction should be made between the line and the staff components. In every business three functions have been found essential; the concern must be financed, product must be produced, and the product must be distributed. These three necessary components of an enterprise are often called the organic functions of industry. Although other functions such as personnel and engineering are helpful, they are not found universally in every organization and are not, therefore, considered absolutely essential.

The line components of an organization to those whose efforts directly affect the finance, manufacture, or distribution of the product or service. Thus, a salesman in the field and a shop worker making the product can both be considered part of the line organization. Their efforts directly affect the product; the worker, in its physical manufacture; and the salesman, in its distribution to the ultimate consumer. All other aspects except those directly affecting finance, manufacture, and distribution may be considered staff.

Staff is usually advisory in nature and has only the power to recommend. In its strictest sense, staff possesses no authority over the line. The purpose of staff is to be on tap for advice, but not on top authoritatively. The latter is a line function. Thus the legal adviser and the personnel director are usually considered staff. The work of these individuals has no direct effect on either the finance, production, or distribution of the product. the lawyer advises on legal matters which may mean the business can function legally, but his work has no direct effect on the product. The same is true of the personnel director. He may recruit personnel, administer tests, and aid in the placement of individuals, but his work is staff in that his work has no direct effect on the production, distribution, and finance of the item produced.

As a practical matter, however, staff positions in many plants are accorded the authority to command. This may come about because of the staff individual's exceptional competence in a particular field. A respected engineer, for example, might "suggest" to the supervisor in charge of the paint shop that stop dipping part in paint and spray it instead, and the supervisor would do as the engineer said even though it may be more expensive to spray the part. Or a staff man may be accorded the authority to command because the top manager has indicated that whatever the staff man says to do should be done when it pertains to his function or sphere of competence. A personnel manager indicating to a shop foreman how he should go about hiring an employee would be an example of this because the hiring procedures fall within the personnel function. One could argue, of course, that the personnel director has no real authority of his own but is merely speaking for the boss.

It may be well to note at this point that staff departments within themselves can be and often are organized on a line basis. The personnel department, for example, although a staff organization with respect to the overall firm, may be organized within the department on a pure line or a line and staff basis. Also, we should recognize that one major line division of a firm, such as the manufacturing division, can be made up of both line components and staff components. For example, in the manufacturing division of the Ford Motor Company there is a staff function known as "Production Programming and Control" whose function is to advise and recommend programming and control procedures to the manufacturing division. This staff office has no direct command over the basic manufacturing divisions, but. exists in the manufacturing line division to advise and render a service.

Committee organization is not in its strictest sense a type of organization. Instead, it is supplemehtary to the or line and staff types of organization. Essentially, in committee organization either an individual's position is assumed by a committee or a function of the enterprise is advised or directed by a committee rather than one person. Many churches, for example, are run by a committee variously known as a board of stewards, board of deacons, or the like. Conceivably, all positions in a company could be manned by committees. Such an organization structure would be highly improbable, however, and very unwieldy. In government, education, relegion and business, some uses of committees have been found to be both desirable and effective. The use of a committee is especially desirable in large complex corporate organizations where multifaceted problems are too big for one individual to handle effectively. In such instances, a committee may be appointed to advice the executive in the performance of his task. In this instance, such a committee would be part of the staff organization since it is only advisory in nature.

Types of Committees

Committees can be formal or informal in nature; advisory or managerial; permanent or temporary. The four types of committees most commonly found in industry today are: *(1)* the committee in control, *(2)* the coordination and discussion committee, *(3)* the investigatory and advisory committee, and *(4)* the dissemination and education committee.

The Committee in Control. This committee has the full power to act and usually assumes a position that could be manned by one person.

The Coordination and Discussion Committee. This type of committee is formed to discuss problems and give the executive in charge a wider base on which to make his decision. This committee has no power to act. It discusses and advises only. As a by-product of the discussion, coordination of the actions of the members is often effect.

The Investigatory and Advisory Committee. Formed to investigate the various aspects of a problem, this committee investigates and then advises an executive of its findings and recommendations. The executive or other indiyidual still retains his power to act.

The Dissemination and Education Committee. This type of committee is helpful in getting information about company problems, policies, and projects to the major individuals concerned. In addition it may well serve to indoctrinate new members in company procedures and give them an insight into the ultimate company organization and its preferences.

Committee Limitations and Uses

In any organization structure, the committee should be used with great care and discretion. A committee is a poor substitute for good organization, and should not be used to shift responsibility from one person to the several members of the committee. In appointing an individual to serve on a committee, management should realize that the committee member's work often suffers because of his attendance at time-consuming meetings. Another committee weakness is that its final action or recommendation often represents a compromised position and does not truly reflect the real feelings and opinions of the group. Because of these major weaknesses,many firms believe a committee should never be used in place of an individual manager unless a plural executive is absolutely required. Leadership is an individual matter and should not be relegated to group action.

Despite the above criticisms, however, committees can be used effectively. A committee, for example, can be especially good in rounding out plans and in pointing out discrepancies that an individual play have overlooked. Committees are often helpful in formulating objectives as well as in studying plans of organization. Since collective. judgment usually carries greater weight than the judgment of an individual, committees may be effectively used to appoint personnel to fill vacancies. In addition, some companies have found committees to be ideal arbitrators. Committees are especially good at innovation or "brain storming" as it is commonly known. Using this technique, individual members express new ideas about a product or problems in a brain storming committee meeting; these expressions and ideas, in turn, start other members of the committee thinking and their ideas also are communicated to the group. Out of the ideas and discussions that ensure a new concept or innovation may be born which is actually a product of the group and not of anyone individual.

Effective Operation

When a committee can be used appropriately to aid in accomplishing an objective, the committee's effectiveness can be improve considerably by observing a few fundamental rules. Most managers agree that the following are important for effective committee operation.

1. The objective of the commitfee should be well defined and the committee's authority should be clearly indicated. Each member should understand the committee's purpose and objective, otherwise, there is a tendency to wander from the subject. Whether its authority is decision making or deliberative should also be indicated.

2. The size of the committee should be such that it is not indecisive or too time consuming. It should, however, be large enough the provide the experience, discussion, and deliberation necessary for the problem at hand. The purpose of the committee plays an important part in determining its size; no fixed number of members, therefore, can be cited as an appropriate number. In general, however, the committee should be no smaller than five or six and seldom larger than fifteen or sixteen.

3. The membership of committee should be appropriate. If the individuals are to work together harmoniously, attention should be given to their business backgrounds and knowledge, the possible contributions that they can make in analyzing and solving the problem, and to their ability to work with other members of the group in a friendly cooperative manner.

4. An agenda should be prepared by the leader and distributed well in advance of the meeting for each member to study.

5. The committee's conclusions and recommen dations should be published, circulated to interested individuals, and a check made of the action taken as a result of its recommendation. The committee, thus apprised of the action being taken, is aware that its work and recommendations were not wasted but are being used as a basis for managerial action.

Developing an organization structure for a business, however, does not consist of simply choosing one of the types of organization structure previously discussed and using it. Organization planning and development is much more difficult than this. In fact, the final structure of an industrial organization results from a careful and detailed study and application of many organizational principles and practices. Let us, therefore, examine some of these principles and practices and see how they apply to building an organized system that will aid in achieving the objectives of the firm.

Principles of Organization

Irrespective of the size or type of business firm, a few rules of organization have been found to be universally applicable in developing its organization structure. These principles apply to an organization developed to run the corner grocery, a church, a hospital, or one of our industrial giants. Neither size, nor financial might nor type of firm has any effect on their applicability. Instead, experience has shown that in modifying or developing any type of organization structure, we should be certain to keep in mind the following basic principles of organization which have been developed over the years.

Consideration of Objective

An organization is a facilitating mechanism which enables us to accomplish things to achieve goals. The objective of an organization plays a large part in determining how quickly the structure should be developed, vlhat it looks like, its operating cost, and its permanency. Since this is true, what we want to accomplish through the organization should be kept clearly in mind while we are designing and setting up its structural system. For example, an automobile wreck involying several cars and detaining traffic may call for the quick assembly and organization of several persons to direct traffic and summon help. One person, perhaps a patrolman, will assume leadership and give instructions to the several individuals about traffic direction, and other problems. Speed in developing the organization is essential here. This speed and the temporary nature of the organization objective determine its structure.

Contrast this hastily developed organization with one set up to control, say, an international church or a large industrial corporation where permanency rather than speed of development determines to a large degree the structural development. Obviously the organization structure of each will be much more complex and will be developed more slowly; here, too, the objectives of each will affect the structure. For example, if it is decided that the corporation should add a new line of television receivers, obtain all its own raw materials, and expand its marketing territory, such objectives and their concomitant activities would necessarily affect the final structure of the organization.

Strangely enough, this fundamental principle of consideration of objective is often overlooked by individuals when they begin to group people and organize functions in any cooperative human endeavour. Frequently these organizers seem to be carried away by structural types and forms, and apparently forget the reason for the structure and lose sight of the total system. Since the objective of the endeavour does have an important bearing on the organization structure, we should have dearly in mind what we want to accomplish, the objective of the undertaking, before developing the organization structure. Once the objective has been clearly determined, we should then develop a structure that will help us reach this objective. An organization should never hinder the achievement of an objective; instead, it should be a facilitating mechanism that enables us to accomplish things more easily and effectively than we could have in an unorganized fashion.

Specialization

Specialization of labour is the concentration of one's efforts on a particular job or area of work. The more a person concentrates on a particular job the better he usually is at performing the job.

Specialization of labour, sometimes called division of labour, is basic to all collective organized efforts. Through organization a person's actions and responsibilities are narrowed to one or a few functions, enabling him to specialize on these few and thereby to increase his efficiency. Organization itself is nothing more than the outward expression of this universal law of specialization.

Effective organization must include specialization. Consider the organizational development of an expanding grocery store. Starting with a one-man operation, let us assume that business necessitates adding additional personnel. With growth into a supermarket, these persons are placed in charge of departments. One is responsible for canned goods; one is responsible for the fresh fruits and vegetables; and one is in charge of meats and dairy products. The manager has effectively organized his store with specialization of labour as an integral part of his organizational structure. Consider what type of organization would have resulted if, instead of organizing and specializing on the basis of departments, he had hired his clerks and instructed them to "help the customers." Confusion, poor service, and out-of-stock conditions would have existed.

Organizing by dividing work into specialized areas enables one to understand his job thoroughly and thereby be in a better position to improve his work. Specialization in organization also enables skills of varying degrees to be utilized more effectively. The work of every person in a firm, therefore, should be confined as far as possible to the performance of one or a very few leading or major functions.

In applying this principle of specialization, however, care should be exercised not to lose sight of the total operating system. While work or functions can be organized on a specialized basis, we must view each of these areas of specialization as it relates to the total operating system of the undertaking. Unless we do this, we may find that our final organizational structure is made up of a series of highly specialized units which are independently effective but which collectively do not operate as a total integrated system.

Delegation of Authority

Authority is the right to command or act and, as such, is a power over others. It is the basis of superior-subordinate relationships in the organization hierarchy, and in this sense, it empowers the supervisor to cause a subordinate to perform a task or take an action that is considered appropriate for achieving the objective of the enterprise. If you have the necessary authority, you can tell a person what to do, how to do it, and where it should be done. Thus every person in a managerial position is vested with the authority necessary to secure cooperation. This cooperation can be secured by personal leadership, by coercion, or by promise of social and/or economic gain or loss.

Often we hear of responsibility being delegated, but actually it is the power to act or command, *i.e.*, authority, that is delegated through the lines of authority established in the structure of the organization. Responsibility cannot be shifted, delegated, or assigned. Jobs, duties, and tasks can be assigned, but only authority can be delegated.

Delegation of authority is the key to organization. In fact, without delegation there would be no organization only one-man operations. This principle of delegation is the center or core of all the processes in formal organization. No one expects a president personally to finance, produce, and sell the firm's product, but he is responsible for seeing that a product is produced and sold; and the only way that he can accomplish this task is by a cooperative organized effort brought about through delegation. A major task of a top executive, therefore, is delegating authority to proper individuals in order to secure appropriate action.

This actual delegation of authority to take action or make decisions should be made to an individual who has the necessary knowledge and ability to take intelligent action, and who is as far down the hierarchy of the organization and as close to the point of action as possible. Stating it otherwise, authority should be as close to the scene of action as possible, thus freeing higher management for overall planning and decision making. Delegation can be accomplished more easily and quickly if clear-cut lines of supervisions and authority have been established. Clear-cut lines of supervision indicate who is responsible for what; they show who reports to whom; they indicate how functions of the organization are grouped. Such an organization setup makes for ease and efficiency in determining responsibility and in delegating the necessary authority.

Clear lines of authority, therefore, must run from the top to the bottom of the organization.

Lack of clear lines of authority and supervision may result in overlapping actions, in omissions of acts, or in improperly conceived job responsibilities and authority. Many organization systems fail because adequate provision has not been made for proper delegation of authority.

Parity of Responsibility and Authority

Responsibility literally means a charge for which one is responsible or accountable; it means accountability. With respect to the organization structure, responsibility may be defined as the obligation of a subordinate to a superior to perform a designated and assigned task or function. The key idea in this definition is that one is charged with an obligation. While authority to perform a job is delegated to an individual, he is held responsible for its performance and therefore responsibility is demanded of him. Since its would not be just to hold a person responsible for performing a task without first giving him the authority necessary to get the job done, responsibility should always be coupled with commensurate authority. Stating it otherwise, authority that has been delegated should always be coupled with responsibility, that is, appropriate action should be demanded from delegated authority. When a person has been given the authority to perform a job, he should be held accountable for its accomplishment. A supervisor, for example, should never be held responsible for the output of his department unless he has been given the authority to direct the actions of the individuals reporting to him.

Contrary to what many people believe, responsibility cannot be delegated or shifted. Parents, for example, are responsible for raising their children, and although they may hire maids or governesses and assign them certain tasks or jobs, the parents are still ultimately responsible. Likewise, in an organization a superior who is responsible for performing a task may delegate the authority necessary to perform this task to one of his subordinates. The acceptance by the subordinate of his assignment obliges him to perform the task;

however, this obligation does not relieve the superior of his responsibility: The responsibility of a superior for the acts of his employees is absolute. Whereas authority to command can be delegated, responsibility cannot.

Span of Management

By span of management we mean the number of individuals one supervisor directs. There is a definite limit to this number, which obviously determines, to a large extent, the number and the arrangement of the units of an organization. In a small firm every member may report directly to the president, but in a large company this would be impracticable. Indeed, an appropriate number of individuals must be grouped under one superior. The question, of course, is: "How many employees can one supervisor effectively direct?" If too few employees report to one supervisor, his time will not be used effectively. Also, there may be a tendency for him to over supervise and in effect make all the decisions for his subordinates. On the other hand, too large a number of employees reporting to one individual may well make for either ineffective or scant supervision.

Some experts say a maximum of five foremen should report to one superior and a maximum of ten to twelve employees should report to one foreman; however, no hard and fixed rule for the number can be established. Instead, the number of employees that can be supervised depends on the type of work being performed, how far apart the employees are geographically, whether all employees are performing the same jobs, whether the jobs are highly repetitive in nature, the training possessed by the employees, the supervision necessary, and similar considerations. If, for example, the work is highly specialized and all employees are performing the same task at one table, then the number that can be effectively supervised will be relatively large. However, if each employee is performing a different task in isolated areas and these tasks require careful supervision, then the number that can be supervised effectively will be relatively small.

In recent years the trend in span of management has been toward an increase in number. This is particularly true in retail establishments where an attempt is being made to reduce the number of levels in the organization so as to improve communications. As a result of increasing the span of management, one large mail order company reported a rise in morale, sales, and profit. This increase was attributed to the fact that the large number of employees reporting to the manager forced him to delegate authority to his subordinates because he could not personally supervise all their actions. Since he could not supervise them closely, the manager gave more careful attention to the selection of his subordinates; and this careful selection, in turn, made for the employment of higher caliber employees and lower turnover. This delegation also forced the employees to learn their jobs better and gave them a greater sense of accomplishment, a feeling of belonging, and made for high morale.

Unity of Command

Frederik W. Taylor's functional organization uncovered the difficulties involved when a person has more than one boss. In fact, receiving directions from several superiors may easily result in confusion, conflict, lack of action, and poor morale. Each member of an organization, therefore should be responsible to and receive directions from only one boss, his immediate superior. The plant superintendent or division manager, even though superior, should not give direct orders to a worker. A hospital administrator should not give direct orders to a floor orderly. Instead, such supervision should come through the worker's immediate supervisor. This practice keeps the supervisor apprised of all directives and prevents conflicting orders. It also enables the immediate supervisor to control his work and make adjustments where necessary. If it can be avoided, therefore, no one in any organization should report to more than one line supervisor; and everyone should know to whom, he reports and who reports to him.

Personal Ability

An organization is people and their proper selection and placement cannot be overemphasized. An organization structure reflects the abilities of the individuals in the structure, and the abilities of the members of an undertaking determine to a large degree the organization structure. This is not to say that an organization should be developed considering only the individuals who will make up the organization in the immediate future. It does mean, however, that in developing an organization, proper regard should be given to the personal ability of individuals assigned to various components. Assigning a job to an individual does not mean it will be accomplished any more than moving a mountain can be done by saying to the mountain "be thou moved." Individuals differ in capacity and ability, and these differences as well as personal limitations should be considered before placing an individual in an organization.

If you were given the task of appointing one individual to sweep a room and another to raise three million dollars for a worthy charity, you would give careful thought to the personal abilities which would enable each to achieve his objective. Although this is a far-fetched example, the same sort of careful thought should be given to selections and transfers of individuals within an organization.

Persons possessing the required ability are not always available to fill a particular vacancy, and if an individual in the company cannot be trained for the job, management often must go outside of the enterprise for the man. If the needed person is not available either inside or outside of the firm at the time he is required, it is not considered good practice to use a "second best" person; instead many companies modify their particular organization structure temporarily so as to redistribute the work among other individuals until such time as a qualified person is available.

Communication

Inasmuch as an organization is developed to aid in accomplishing an objective, a good communications sub-system is necessary if all employees are to know what to do to aid in reaching this objective. In fact, one of the most immediate and costly results of poor organization is the breakdown of intra-organizational communication, and the resulting loss of an integrated operating system. Despite the fact that lines of authority provide ready-made channels of communication downward and upward, they are often used solely to pass directives downward and never as a means of communicating attitudes, feelings, or ideas upward. Using lines of authority solely as channels for transmitting orders often results when busy administrators do not want to be bothered with the "small" ideas of their supervisors. Frequently when the supervisors are finally heard, their ideas are either ignored by the administrator or given a superficial appraisal. This same difficulty in communication may also be true at the worker level. Ideas or attitudes expressed by a worker to his foreman often stop there, particularly if they might reflect discredit on the foreman's organization. Such blocks in communication occur all up and down the lines of authority in great many organizations.

A supervisor is chosen and placed in a position of authority because his superior has confidence in his ability to get the work done. This confidence in a subordinate plus free two-way communication are the two factors that unite an organization into an effectively operating system. Despite its importance, however, many organizations are formed with no apparent though given to free two-way communication, especially upward communication. Some companies have established two lines of communication upward; one through the regular lines of authority; the other through the appointment of a non-supervisory individual, often called a counsellor, to serve as a connecting line between the workers and upper-level management. Suggestion systems are also useful. Where a labour-management agreement has provided for a prescribed grievance procedure, this procedure may be employed as an upward channel of communication. Reducing the number of levels of authority also aids in the flow of upward communication.

Though not as difficult to establish a upward communication, downward communication also presents problems. If good communications downward are to exist, management must first of all have something good, sound, and worthwhile to communicate in the way of policies, beliefs, and principles of management. Although films, booklets, bulletins; and other printed and visual aids may be used, greatest reliance should be placed on personal, face-to-face communications, using the organizational lines of authority as the channels of communication.

Combination of Line and Staff Functions

Line and staff functions should not be combined in one individual or department where separation of the functions is possible. Line functions, as we indicated previously, are those which directly affect the finance, production, or distribution of the product or service. Staff functions are those that aid the line or are auxiliary to the line functions. Because confusion of authority could result from having two such functions combined in one individual or department, line and staff functions should be separated where possible to do so.

Regulations

Rules and regulations aid in the proper operation of the enterprise, because they enable each supervisory individual to have a better understanding of his authority, responsibility, and scope of action. Therefore, a complete statement of the operating objective of an enterprise as well as the responsibility and authority of each supervisor should be formulated and issue as a set of operating rules and regulations. Such rules and regulations should be available in writing to all personnel in the organization. They may be broad or specific, even detailed enough as in methods manuals to describe precisely how each task in a business is to be carried out. The amount of detail, however, depends on the extensiveness of the organization. Written rules and regulations are valuable to a firm because they represent the law of the organization they define the authority which certain individual have over particular functions.

Flexibility

An organization is formed to achieve an end. The environment in which the organization exists and the individuals who make up the organization are constantly changing. Most people think of an organization as a static entity; therefore, they draw a chart and say, "Here is our organization." This is usually unrealistic inasmuch as the chart actually represents a picture of how the organization was.

Organizations change because of technological changes, economic changes, personnel changes, or changes in the objectives of the company. To cope with these and still reach its objective, an organization must be flexible. Flexibility, however, does not mean haphazard aimlessness. Instead, it consists of the ability to bend and blend before experiencing any serious setback. An organization possessing flexibility withstands minor pressures, but gives way to the demand for genuine change, permitting either expansion or contraction without seriously altering the basic functions of the various segments of the structure.

Job Assignment

Logical groupings of related jobs and functions should be made in developing the organization structure. For example, all work pertaining to the financial aspect of a firm could well be placed in one section. Such a grouping could include the activities pertaining to payroll, vouchering, budget preparation, and similar jobs. In addition, it is often desirable to have the responsibility for each of these jobs assigned to specific individuals, with these persons in turn reporting to the leader charged with the accomplishment of the overall finance function. insofar as possible, only one leading or major task should be assigned to anyone individual. This restriction of job assignments is another way of implementing the principle of specialization previously mentioned. Although this objective of logically relating work assignments cannot always be achieved, its desirability is obvious, and such groupings should be effected wherever possible.

Structural Balance

In a balanced organization, each function of the structure should be large enough to accomplish its objective but not overly developed in relation to all other functions of the organization so that the "tail wags the dog." In an automotive firm, for example, the product research and development section should be large enough with respect to all other aspects of the firm to design and engineer a desirable product, the sales division should be adequate to the task of marketing the output; and the finance section should be large enough to meet the requirements pertaining to that function. Without such balance, the objective of the organization cannot be achieved economically and effectively. An unbalanced condition may result in a firm when an individual in an executive leadership capacity is partial to a specific function because of previous review training or experience. In such instances where an unbalanced condition has developed, the cost of maintaining the oversized division cannot be warranted by the returns to the company; the organization structurally is not in balance; and functionally, the organization is not as effective as it could be.

In the process of forming a new organization structure or of reorganizing an existing one, the principles and practices discussed above should be considered. Obviously, however, the consideration of these principles, rules, and types of organization structures will not in itself result in the development of a new organization. Instead, a new organization structure must be visualized and developed on a step-by-step basis. Although no series of rules can be given that will assure the development of an effective organization, this objective can be approached in a systematic fashion without too much difficulty. Many persons have found the following steps to be quite helpful..

1. Determine clearly the objective of the enterprise. This was listed as the first principle organization because a clear definition of the objective determines the type, stability, structure, and permanency of the organization. The objective of an organization determines the basis organization characteristics.

2. List the areas of activity by main division and subdivision. This physical listing of activities should be complete and will in itself suggest areas for regrouping and consolidation of work. Products, tools, and processes should be considered as possible areas within which to regroup the activities listed. As far as possible, similar functions should be combined into one position.

3. Determine the ideal structure to accomplish the desired activities irrespective of availability of funds or personnel. Each of the regrouped and consolidated activities determined under step 2 are to be studied and an "ideal" organization structure developed to carry

out these functions, taking into account, of course, the principles previously discussed. This ideal structure may represent the long range or ultimate organization, and because no consideration has been made of available personnel or funds, implementing it may not be possible or practical immediately.

4. Make a detailed survey of available personnel from the point of view of capacities and abilities. List all personnel currently in the organization as well as those available from outside the organization. Indicate clearly their capacities and limitations.

5. Revise the "ideal" organization in light of the available personnel and funds. In step 3 the best organization structure for achieving the objective was determined and in number 4 the practical aspects of available personnel were ascertained. This last step, therefore, consists in reconsidering and changing the "ideal" organization to fit the reality of available personnel and dollars. This determines the current working organization.

Following these five steps not only develops an organization structure to fit current realities, it also sets forth an ideal organization in step number 3 that serves as a model and guide towards which the working organization can develop and progress as personnel and other conditions make such development possible. Again, it should be emphasized that the principles and considerations of organization previously discussed should be kept in mind in developing this structural setup.

An organization conceived and developed along the principles of organization, as well as one which adheres closely to the other considerations of organization covered previously, will more than reward its leaders and its members. Not only will the objectives be achieved more easily and quickly, but the physical operation of the organization will be greatly enhanced. Good organization typically:

1. Establishes responsibility and prevents "buck passing"
2. Provides for easier communication.
3. Eliminates jurisdictional disputes between individuals.

4. Helps develop executive ability.
5. Aids in measuring a person's performance against his charges and responsibilities.
6. Aids in equitable distribution of work functions and/or personnel supervision.
7. Permits expansion and contraction without seriously disrupting the structure.
8. In times of change, it affords movement in the direction of the "ideal" organization.
9. Makes for closer cooperation and higher morale.
10. Points out "dead-end" jobs.
11. Delineates avenues of promotion.
12. Prevents duplication of work.
13. Makes growth possible with adequate control and without literally killing top executives through overwork.
14. Aids in wage and salary administration through forced job analysis and description.

❒

5

Organization Functions

MEN have always acted in groups to perform work which is beyond the capacity of one individual. In industry and commerce, we say that organization is concerned with the relationships between individuals and the work which they perform.

In small business enterprises or departments, these relationships between individuals and work are simple. The chief, who has first-hand experience not only of the work but also of all his employees, whom he knows by name, finds it possible by himself to balance the needs of the work with his knowledge of the abilities of his people to carry it out. All the facts are known to him, and his decision, therefore, as to groupings of work is often speedy and sound, usually subconscious and almost automatic. This kind of personal organization, where work is completely co-ordinated by one person in terms of a limited number of other persons, reveals no systematic pattern. Things are arranged as the chief finds it most convenient from day to day. It is impromptu and spontaneous.

As the small business enterprise expands in numhers employed, its organization begins to assume a certain pattern. It becomes formalized. The work itself must be divided and subdivided to meet new requirements. The different contributions of individuals to the total work of the enterprise become more definite, more specialized, and more permanent in character.

First-hand operational knowledge in terms of work and individuals is no longer entirely in the possession of a sole chief; it is obtained by consulting others. In this way the problem of relating work and individuals gradually passes beyond the capacity of one person. He finds it necessary to delegate his authority to others who have replaced him in the possession of first-hand operational knowledge.

In the largest enterprises of all, organization, the structure of the undertaking, becomes extremely complex. The collection of facts alone, both with regard to suitable divisions of work and the responsibilities which meet the needs of each division, becomes a specific investigation which may have to be undertaken by more than one person. Presentation of these facts and the inferences drawn may pass through an advisory body before providing a basis for policy decisions by the board of directors.

Organization, whether of small, medium or large enterprises, is a process which, in spite of the many analytical techniques it uses, has also an intensely pessonal aspect. In dealing with people exact knowledge is often impossible. There must be a balancing of individual judgements.

The organization of any enterprise may be liked to a tree, with its roots, its main trunk, its larger branches, its smaller branches, and its individual leaves. One can label parts of the tree, yet at the same time recognize that no one tree is the same as another. Each is at its own stage of growth; each must be tended in a different way and by different means; one may need pruning more than another. Above all, each is a living organism.

The identification of stages of growth is no easy matter. Most enterprises have their roots in the past, some several generations ago. An accurate appreciation of an enterprise at any stage of growth is impossible without knowledge of the history of its industrial background and how it has evolved.

Origin of Organization Study

One of the benefits to be gained from a study of organization is the discovery of what time and effort can be saved and made available for other work. Such a study can be of considerable value even if the personnel of an enterprise are good, as it enables their abilities to be matched more carefully with the requirements of particular jobs and faulty relationships between individuals and work can be rectified.

It is only in the twentieth century that serious attempts have been made to deal with the subject of organization analytically and to apply general principles to building up the structure of industrial enterprises. This work originated with Frederick Winslow Taylor (1856-1915), an American engineer whose tomb carries the inscription "the Father of Scientific Management." About the beginning of the twentieth century, Taylor investigated the relationships between a foreman and his work. He discovered that so much was demanded of the foreman of that period that it was impossible for all his work to be done as efficiently as it might be. As a result of his studies, Taylor recommended that the work of a foreman should be divided amongst several individuals. He classified the foreman's activities into eight groups; these again were divided into two levels which he called "Planning" and "Performance"; the foremen cocerned with planning were situated in the planning room.

The single foreman was superseded in this way by eight different men, each with special duties. They are, as Taylor says, "the expert teachers who are at all times in the shop helping and directing the workmen." The duties he allocated to the so called "Shop Disciplinarian" were, broadly, those allocated today to a personnel officer.

The real importance of Taylor's work lies in the fact that, for the first time, problems of industrial organization, the existence of which had not previously been recognized, were subjected to detailed analytical investigations. Since his time the investigation of facts and evidence about the relationships between individuals and work has been continued through such activities as method study, work measurement, work simplification, organization and methods, etc. Under any of these names an attempt is made to discover exactly what work is at present being done and how it is being done, as a basis of comparison with ideas as to how such work might be done better and more efficiently.

Work Study

As far back as the beginning of the nineteenth century Robert Owen in Britain was interested in problems of layout, in the need for new methods to provide better working conditions for his workpeople, and in making provision in the time allowed for doing a particular job for the effects of fatigue and for the necessary rest periods. He recognized the importance of the human element in industrial work involving machinery.

The scientific development of work study owes a great deal, however, to the pioneering work at the end of the nineteenth and beginning of the twentieth century of the Americans—Frederick W. Taylor, Henry L. Gantt, and Frank and Lillian Gilbreth.

Taylor concentrated his attention on the best way to do a job and what constituted a fair day's work. He introduced the technique of time study. In his study of a particular job he broke down the cycle of the operation into small groups of motions called elements. Each element was timed separately because he realized that the total time to do a particular job gave no indication as to where time was wasted or used inefficiently, whereas when the individual elements were timed the operation was broken down in a way that could be easily studied.

Gantt, in addition to producing a chart to give a continuous picture of the progress on a particular job, developed incentive schemes, and stressed the importance of the human element in any study of work.

The Gilberths developed the techniques of motion study. They held that most manual work could be broken down into a few simple motions which are repeated over and over again. These primary motions they named therbligs (a simple anagram of their own name), and symbols were devised for recording them. They distinguished seventeen elementary movements or groups of movements into which all types of human activity could be divided, but since their time the number has been increased to eighteen. They also investigated the problem of fatigue and its elimination, and suggested ways of eliminating "needless fatigue".

The difference between the approaches of Taylor and the Gilbreths is brought out by the two terms that they introduced, namely time study and motion study. Taylor was mainly interested in the time factor, whereas the Gilbreths were mainly concerned with devising the most economical methods and the most effective layout of work space, followed by the motion study.

Interest in work study has grown rapidly in recent years, and it has been shown that its scope extends far beyond the engineering field in which the original researches were made. Work study today is important in the office, and in retailing, as well as in the factory. For this reason the term work study is preferred to its American equivalent title of industrial engineering.

Work study is defined in British Standard 3138:1969 as: "A management service based on those techniques, particularly method study and work measurement, which are used in the examination of human work in all its contexts, and which lead to the systematic investigation of all the resources and factors which affect the efficiency and economy of the situation being reviewed, in order to effect improvement."

Two distinct yet interrelated analytical techniques are involved in work study, and these are known as method study and work measurement.

Method Study

The British Standards Institutions Glossary of Terms in Work Study (Btitish Standard 3138:1969) defines method study as: "The systematic recording and critical examination of the factors and resources involved in existing and proposed ways of doing work, as a means of developing and applying easier and more effective methods and reducing costs."

Method study is essentially concerned with finding better ways of doing thing, and it contributes to improved efficiency by getting rid of unnecessary work and avoidable delays.

The basic procedure of method study is to select and define the work to be studied, record all the relevant facts of the present method by means of charts, diagrams, and models, examine these facts critically and in sequence, and then to develop the most effective method of doing the work. After installation the new method has to be maintained by regular routine checks until it can be established as standard practice.

When this procedure is combined with the questioning attitude of mind developed by the method study approach, substantial improvements usually result. In particular, improved processes and procedures, improved layout and design, a better working environment and economy in human effort and reduction of fatigue have resulted from method study. Once it is decided that a particular job is necessary and that it is correctly located in relation to preceding or subsequent operations the way in which the workplace is laid out and the positioning of tools or parts to be assembled or papers to be handled can make a great difference in the time it takes to complete the operation. Method study is used to investigate the layout of the workplace and the movements made by the worker in doing the job. Having obtained all possible information on the methods used, the investigator analyses them and tries to eliminate unnecessary movements, This aspect of the job is called motion study. This is a scientific approach to the investigation of the movements involved in performing any activity, with the object of eliminating ineffective movements and thus utilizing energy, time and materials to the best advantage.

It does this by promoting rhythm and balance of posture, by attention to working conditions and by consideration of the workers' psychological and physiological make-up. Thus, they are able to achieve greater output without additional exertion.

Work Measurement

The basic technique of work measurement is defined as: "The application of techniques designed to establish the time for a qualified worker to carry out a specified job at a defined level of performance."

Work measurement assists method study by comparing times for alternative methods, and in the allocation of labour to jobs in proportion to the work involved so that an appropriate balance of labour is maintained.

Time Study

The technique of time study is defined in B.S. 3138 as: "A work measurement technique for recording the times and rates of working for the elements of a specified job carried out under specified conditions, and for analysing the data so as to determine the time necessary for carrying out the job at a defined level of performance."

The time study engineer is not only concerned with the actual time a job takes to do, but how long it should take. He has to assess the value of the operator's performance to differentiate between time which is essential to the satisfactory performance of the activity and time which is wasted or lost. Some operators put more into a job than the class of work justifies: components for aircraft require a high degree of finish that would be wasteful on garden tools, for example.

Motion and time study are interdependent: motion study improves the method, time study follows up by setting a time for doing the job when using the improved method.

Principles of Organization

In the course of investigation facts have been collected, classified and co-ordinated into theories. Various principles of organization have been developed underlying the correct formal relationships which should exist between work and individuals, and between individuals doing work of different kinds.

These principles are not, however, laws. While failure to observe them is always ground for inquiry, any attempt to apply fixed and universal rules to anything which is so largely dependent on the processes of human judgement as is organization would be misleading. The activities which must be performed in all manufacturing enterprises have much in common. But the methods by which they may best be grouped together in any particular situation involve so many variables that any attempt to produce a standard classification should be avoided. It is highly dangerous to attempt to apply to one undertaking a system of organization which is a slavish copy of another and ignores the individual characteristics of the second undertaking. There is no such thing as a typical or standard form of organization. It follows, therefore, that any of the examples quoted are merely illustrative, and do not attempt to lay down a prescribed method of organization to suit all cases. Organization must not be mass-produced.

Several techniques are used for the collection and presentation of the facts needed for a study of organization.

1. Job Analysis. This consists of determining the exact content of each of the positions in an undertaking to identify its component parts. What are the duties and the responsibilities attaching to the position? What are its relationships with other positions? In compiling job analyses the investigator may be able to economize in time and effort by using questionnaires. But a busy manager or foreman should never be asked to fill in a questionnaire without a preliminary interview to explain what it is all about. And usually, after the questionnaire has been filled in, the investigator will require a further interview to clear up doubtful points. Generally speaking, it is wisest to proceed by interview alone, the investigator filling up his own questionnaire and clarifying points of difficulty as he goes along. The result is usually known as a job specification.

2. The Flow Process Chart. As its name implies, this is a picture of a procedure. It shows in diagrammatic form all the steps necessary to achieve a given object. It may vary in scope from recording and classifying all the detailed movements necessary for a single process (its use in motion study) to all the responsibilities involved in a major operation, such as launching a new product, which may engage at some stage the majority of the executives and departments of a large-scale undertaking. It serves as a check on the information supplied by job analyses; by showing the organization in movement, as it were, it reveals omissions or overlapping responsibilities. Process charts are usually compiled from the information collected in job specifications; supplemented by special ad hoc inquiries.

3. The Functional Diagram or Functional Analysis. This is a statement, which may be in diagrammatic form of all the activities necessary to any purpose, arranged in groups on the principle of like with like. It is not concerned with positions or persons. In a particular enterprise the Sales Manager may, as a matter of convenience, be looking after the canteen or be doing some of the buying of raw materials. But, logically, buying has nothing to do with selling; it is a separate function. Running the canteen is an activity concerned with the well-being of those employed; again it has nothing to do with selling. It is part of the function usually described as personnel management. This grouping of activities ensures:

(a) That there have been no omissions: every activity which is necessary is included somewhere.

(b) That if considerations of convenience have led to illogical arrangements so that unlike activities are grouped, this is recognized as an aberration from sound principle only to be tolerated temporarily because of some historic or personal accident.

(c) That, ultimately, activities are arranged and assigned to individuals in groups which "hang together" and for which the specialized training is an adequate preparation (*e.g.*, in production engineering, accountancy, marketing, personnel management).

4. The Organization Chart. The position in an undertaking of those whose job it is to plan, organize, and control the work of others (the leaders of groups of various sizes) is defined in the organization—the formal structure or pattern of responsibilities and duties and their interrelation. An organization chart is an illustration of these responsibilities and the relationships of the various members. It shows in diagrammatic form the lines of authority and responsibility and the distribution of functions in a section, department or undertaking.

The larger the size of the operation covered by the chart, the less detail should be given. It is a mistake to try to show too much on an organization chart; detail should be filled in by subsidiary charts or subordinate units. Organization charts should not be used to try to show the relative status of individuals in different departments. Status can be indicated by titles or symbols; if attempts are made to include it in the organization chart it will confuse the proper grouping of functions. If the organization of any undertaking cannot be presented in a clear, balanced diagram it is an indication that there is confusion in the actual arrangement of functions and authority. An organization chart is never a complete description of an organization as it cannot show all the complexities of human relationships. It needs to be supplemented with lists of duties and responsibilities (job specifications) and statements of relationships (procedures).

The Main Functional Division

Organization is not an end in itself but a means by which policy, operational and administrative problems can be solved in accordance with the aims of an enterprise. Duties may be grouped in accordance with a number of different methods and all of them may be, and commonly are used at various levels in an enterprise, or in combination within a single department or section. There is no one system of organization which is superior to another; it all depends on the situation. The problem is to determine which or what combination of the various methods is appropriate both to an undertaking as a whole and to each part of that undertaking. It is more important that everyone should know what the organization in fact is, than that it should be theoretically perfect. Uncertainty about authority and responsibility always causes trouble.

The main business of an industrial enterprise may be grouped into six main divisions, each having a distinct function, no matter by whom it may be exercised. These divisions are:

1. Purchasing.

2. Production.

3. Marketing.

4. Development.

5. Personnel.

6. Finance and Clerical.

The exercise of each of these functions involves planning, organizing, directing, co-ordinating and controlling.

In a very small enterprise these main divisions of activity may be in the control of one person only, who acts at the same time as executive and supervisor of a few people in his employment.

The small enterprise expands. The executive finds that he cannot do everything himself. He must engage someone to look after the sales side entirely. Production demands more attention and more planning. He must take on new employees to meet growing demands. With further expansion and the consequent need for subdivision of activities; each of the main functions already named can be broken down further. Examples of the subdivision are:

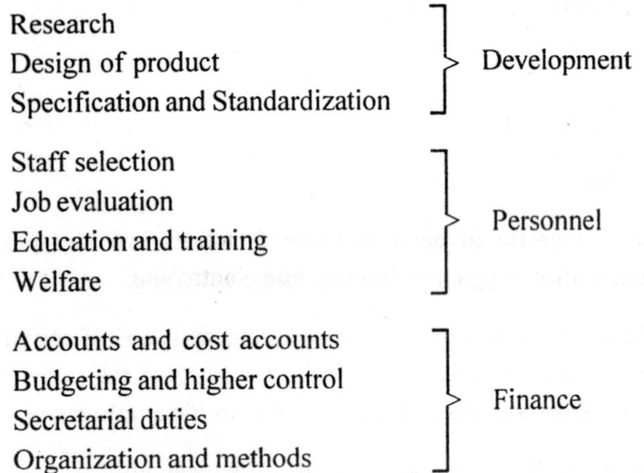

Little of importance can be achieved in modern industrial enterprises without some such arrngement of distinct and specialized functions. F.W. Taylor wrote: "The work of every person in the organization should be confined as far as possible to the performance of a single leading function," The analysis of the distinct functions into elements and the grouping of these elements so that each job is within the capacity of the individual is one of the basic principles of organization.

Co-ordination of Functions

All the activities which are embodied in a function must be supervised: someone must be responsible for them. The functions are sub-function are co-ordinated by having delegated to them certain authority. This is divided into levels according to divisions of work. Levels of authority should be as few as possible.

Authority

The delegation of degrees of authority to individuals enables each employee to know to whom he reports and who reports to him. It is one means of securing co-ordination. It is important, especially in routine matters, that power to act should be delegated to those possessed of the necessary operational knowledge.

According to the method followed in grouping activities, authority in formal organization is of three different kinds, involving three different kinds of relationship.

There is the usual relationship of superior to subordinate, where the superior's authority is direct and his responsibility is general. This relationship, which may be called a "line" relationship, occurs wherever superiors have direct subordinates, regardless of the kind of work on which they are engaged. A chief specialist's relation to his specialized subordinates or a high executive's relation to his personal assistant is still a line relationship.

But the specialist, though he may deal with people all over the undertaking on his special subject, cannot have direct authority over other peoples's direct subordinates. If he attempts to exercise such authority he upsets the chain of command. His authority must be indirect, *i.e.*, exercised through the line superior of the individual çoncerned and limited strictly to his special subject. This relationship may be described as a "functional" or specialized relationship.

The authority of an "assistant to" an executive is neither line nor functional. The "assistant to" has no personal authority whatever; he is merely the representative of his chief, exercising his authority. The chief does not delegate to him responsibillty for discharging certain tasks but merely for seeing that the chief's wishes are correctly interpreted in detail by those to whom he has delegated certain specific tasks, and that conflicts of authority are avoided. Consequently, he cannot give verbal orders to his chief's direct subordinates or to their subordinates. He can,. of course, issue a written order by virtue of his office: that is his chief's order. As he has no authority he cannot discharge any task on his own responsibility; his authority accompanies the resposibility and he engages his chief's responsibility. But he has a duty to advise his chief to the best of his ability. This relationship is known as a "staff" relationship.

These three relationships can be shown in a simple table:

Relationships in Organization

Relationship	*Authority*	*Responsibility*
Line	Direct	General
Functional or Specialized	Indirect	Specialized
Staff	Representative	Advisory

A great deal of confusion has been caused in the discussion of organization by the idea that there are only two relationships—staff and line. This arises from the fact that the word staff is sometimes used ambiguously both of functional or specialized relationships and of true staff relations. Some writers on business management have failed to note the difference between these two relationships. An "Assistant too" or "Secretary to" an executive is not a specialist.

It is still not uncommon to find enterprises where only line authority exists and where the line supervisor directs the activities of a group of subordinates, some of whom are functional. Such instances generally do not provide for good specialization or for efficiency. Again, it may be that a specialized supervisor may also have direct authority within the production function with equally serious effects on efficiency.

The distinction between these three kinds of authority and the resulting relationships is one of the cardinal features of management. In the past, and even today, where these principles are misunderstood, overlooked or regarded as only of academic interest, there is manifest a lack of co-operation, personal squabbling, and waste of time and effort.

Responsibility

A good system of organization matches authority with a corresponding delegation of responsibility and duties. Such matching follows what is known as the Principle of Correspondence.

All responsibilities and duties should be classified and grouped before allocation. Care must be taken that such a grouping of activities comes within an individual's mental capacity and does not overstrain his span of control. One superior cannot supervise effectively more than five, or at the most six, direct subordinates whose work interlocks.

Responsibilities and duties should be clearly stated in writing—often a difficult task too frequently avoided. They should be fully understood. Such a procedure prevents shortcircuiting of authority, and enables staff to exercise their initiative within clearly defined limits.

Committees

A feature of organizational structure is the extensive use made of committees to help in the co-ordination of staff and work. If used properly, these committees can fulfil a useful role. Some committees may make specific investigations into particular problems, such as wages structures or the education and training of apprentices; others may even make or recomend policy decisions at regular intervals. The number of such committees, however, should be kept to a minimum. Members of a committee, especially the chairman, should be fully aware of the correct conduct and procedure at meetings.

Organization in Theory and Practice

At best, organization is a compromise in which the personal qualifications of the individuals available must play an important part. In making these compromises, however, it is desirable that the task shall not be considered merely as a matter of making A responsible for the actions of B, C and D, but of linking together like activities which logically should be placed under unified control. Personalities are only one of the factors to be considered in designing organization. To ignore all the others will almost certainly result in illogical development; disruptive re-adjustments will have to take place whenever key men leave.

There is little doubt that, from a long-term point of view, the activities to be performed must be a dominant consideration. They are permanent and not contingent upon the continued association with the enterprise of particular individuals. Because man is mortal the personnel of an undertaking is by nature transient.

To build too much upon the strengths and weaknesses of existing personnel inevitably leads to re-orgnization if these individuals leave. The very theory of the corporate business is that it has an existence as an entity apart from those who may be managing its affairs at any given moment. Its strength lies in the fact that its success is not dependent upon the continued survival of anyone individual or group of individuals.

On the other hand, from the short-term point of view and at any given period in the existence of an enterprise, it is the personalities of those who are serving it at that moment which supply the driving force and guidance necessary to make the enterprise a living organism capable of accomplishing its objectives. Its personnel may not be ideal or perfectly adaptable to its needs. But it can discard "key" men only at its peril. The organization must be designed in terms best calculated to utilize their strengths while protecting the enterprise front their weaknesses.

Automation and Organization

Since the beginning of the second half of the twentieth century many enterprises have passed through a period of organizational change induced by social, economic and technical changes. Of particular interest is the impact of automation.

Before discussing its influence it is necessary to define automation for it is another word that has acquired more than one meaning in popular usage.

Automation is a development of mechanization, although it is quite distinct from it. Automation is much more than mechanization for whereas the latter means the development of machines to replace human labour, automation involves a substitute for nerve and brain as well as muscular activity, which means the development of machnies to control other machines. It is this additional feature, the ability of the machine automatically to control its own actions, that characterizes automation equipment.

Automatic control increased rapidly with the development of electronic devices. They can plan and control the operation of a machine tool with high precision; they can detect faults in a processed part, and by means of a closed-loop circuit (widely known as "feed-back") can communicate the error to the machine and adjust its operation so as to correct the fault; they can integrate the work of individual machines; the more complex of them can choose between alternative decisions or courses of action according to the instructions given to them; finally, they extend the possibilities of remote control.

In its widest sense, automation embraces all forms of mechanization that involve the linking, co-ordination and control of simple industrial processes. It applies to:

(a) automatic machining;

(b) automatic process-control in the "process-industries" such as petroleum, chemicals, beverages, food, cement, fertilizers, paper, plastics, and parts of the iron and steel industry; and

(c) automatic processing of data such as the use of electronic digital computers for clerical operations.

A typical example of automatic machining is the transfer machine for the machining of the cylinder block of a motor car engine. The cylinder block must be planned, milled or broached. The cylinders must be bored. Valve guides must be drilled and valve seatings bevelled and ground. Bearings for crankshaft and cam shafts must be machined. Various flats for mounting auxiliary equipment must be milled and bolt holes drilled and tapped. All these are carried out by a sequence of machining operations in automatic machine tools, the block passing automatically from station to station between each stage of machining, until finally it leaves the transfer-machine and is conveyed mechanically to the assembly-line.

It will be readily appreciated that it would be uneconomic to complete a whole sequence of operations and reject the finished work because of a fault due to the first of them. With automatic transfer there must be automatic inspection involving the problems of how to effect it and how often and where to apply it. Again there is the problem of breakdowns. Nothing works perfectly. A tool tip may wear or break. A press die may wear or be damaged. Is a whole sequence or transfer line to become immobilized because of a halt at one single point? When tools wear out or machines break down there is loss of production time. "down-time" as it is called, and this can be extremely serious since there are many points on the line at which stoppages can occur. Clearly it is important to keep the down-time to a minimum by increasing flexibility.

The transfer-machine illustrates well the problem of technical inflexibility in automatic processes. The time taken by each of a series of consecutive operations by a machine on the same component will differ from operation to operation for obvious reasons. The time spent at each station will be decided by the largest individual operation. At all other stations the tools will not be used to full capacity. If the larger operations can be speeded up the line will work more efficiently and output will rise.

Automation also increases the importance of maintenance as a function of production, and emphasizes the need for preventing faults, as distinct from repairing them, thus to minimize the number of stoppages, and for the analysis of the performance of machine-tools to provide the basis for future policies of maintenance. The need for a high and constant rate of output from automatic processes makes it imperative that there should be rapid and effective communication between the machine-minder, maintenance staff and technical specialists in the event of a machine's breaking down, and also between the various technical specialists who set up the plant and correct faults in its operation. When faults need to be remedied quickly, the machine-minder may have to draw on his own knowledge of the equipment or process and call in the right specialist without going through the chain of authority on the line. It would seem, therefore, that the line and staff principle may not be the most suitable for automatic plants. This is one of the modern problems of organization resulting from automation.

❐

6

Production Policy

PRODUCTION functions involve the transformation of a set of inputs to predetermined outputs in accordance with the objectives of the organisation. Production management encompasses the design, implementation, operation and control of system made up of workers, materials, capital equipment, information and money to accomplish some set of objectives. Following are the major production/operations policy decisions with their determinants:

1. ***Process Planning and Job Design.*** Forecast of demand, product engineering, production technology, labour force, design stability.

2. ***Raw Material and Work-in-progress Inventory.*** Forecast of demand, cash flow, supplier reliability.

3. ***Facilities Layout.*** Medium and long-range forecast of demand and stability of product line production technology physical facilities constraints, safety considerations.

4. ***Plant Location and Capacity.*** Long-range forecast of the size and location of the market, capital structure, environmental conditions, state of operations and logistic system production technology.

5. ***Planning of Aggregate Output.*** Short-range forecast of demand finished goods inventory level, cash flow, employment policy, plant capacity, state of production/ operation system at the time of decision.

The basic objective of policy decision in the area of production operations is the effective utilisation of organisational resources.

PURCHASING POLICY ISSUES

Having discussed the production policies bearing on vertical integration, production process, plant size and capacity and maintenance of facilities, we may now turn to the basic purchasing policy matters. While examining the question of vertical integration we have already explained the relevant factors that may influence decisions to produce raw materials, components and, parts for the final product, and the extent of backward vertical integration possible under various circumstances. What about supplies and services? Should a company make or buy its requirements of containers, stationery, transport services, water and power supply and such other items? Secondly, how should vendors be selected for procuring the supplies? Thirdly, what kind of policy decisions should govern the coordination of production purchasing and sales?

Policy on Vendor Selection

All companies regardless of the extent of vertical integration have to make purchases of certain materials and supplies as well as services. This is because of the various constraints—mainly financial and managerial—which make downstream integration impracticable beyond a stage. Wholesalers have to buy the factory stores and supplies, if not raw materials, for the final product, or for components and parts to be produced. Assuming that a number of dependable outside sources of supply exist, it needs to be decided:

(a) by what criteria should the company choose the suppliers to deal with?

(b) how many suppliers (vendors) should a company make purchases from-several of them, or one or two of them.

Maintenance and Replacement Policy

If the existing plant capacity and service facilities are well maintained, there are distinct advantages, and management can accordingly decide on plant capacity to be initially created. Depending on personal preferences of the executives and the philosophy of management, determining the attitude toward up-keep and maintenance, the policy may be one of high level conditioning of work environment, or a discriminating policy with deliberate decisions to provide for proper maintenance of only those facilities which are of critical importance like production, and stores. But just fixing things up is not good maintenance. Machines and equipments, plant services (power, gas, water, swears, pumps, fire protection), transportation facilities, and buildings (roofs, walls; floors, fixtures and fittings) need repairs. The importance of preventive maintenance is recognised in all workplaces for several reasons. Breakdowns stop production, make men and machine idle, cause lost production, and put orders behind schedule. It helps to reduce repairs, particularly those caused by breakdown of machines in use. The cost of maintenance cannot be kept too low. Preventive maintenance cost may be fairly high but the corresponding pay-off may justify the same. One way of holding down maintenance costs it to have trouble-free machines-machines that are designed to be trouble free, or which provide for built in detectors and gauges to reveal trouble spots before failures occur. Operations Research techniques like the 'queuing or waiting line theory' may also be useful to balance the need for maintenance staff and the maintenance work involved.

Whether to repair or replace machine parts and equipments which have worn out is a decision related to the maintenance of facilities. Obviously it should depend on the cast involved.

GOVERNMENTS APPROACH TO LOCATION

The Government can tackle the problem of concentration of industry by following two approaches:

(i) Positive approach-encouraging establishment of industrial units in the backward areas; and

(ii) Positive approach restraining the establishment of industrial units in the concentrated areas.

Negative Approach. The negative approach includes certain deterrents (*i.e.*, restrictions and disincentives) designated to prevent establishment of new units in concentrated areas. The State may introduce the following deterrents:

(a) Absolute prohibition to set up new industries in particular areas may be followed. For instance, the Industrial Policy, 1977 stated that no more licenses should be issued to new industrial units within certain limits of the cities having a population of more than ten lakhs and urban areas with a population of more than 5 lakhs.

(b) Enhanced rates of local taxes may be introduced. A levy may be imposed on the industrial units in the concentrated areas which may be spent for the benefit of units in the backward areas.

(c) Licensing policy may be so designed that it discourages new units in highely developed regions.

Positive Approach. The adaptation of positive approach is likely to give more satisfactory results as compared to the negative-approach. Under this approach, the State provides certain incentives for the establishement of industrial units in the selected areas. These incentives may take the following forms:

(a) Provision of public utility services in selected areas. These services include electricity, water, gas, transport and provision of socio-economic lamenities like recreation, education, health, etc. In addition, the Government has also extended certain ancillary economic facilities in these areas like institutions for importing technical knowledge to the workers.

(b) Providing adequate and cheap financial facilities directly by the Government or through the financial institutions. Establishment of industrial estates in industrially backward regions and liberal issue of licenses on a preferential basis for industrial units in backward areas.

(c) Granting of direct and indirect subsidies, granting of income tax exemption to the units set-up in backward areas and giving assurance by the State to purchase the products of the industrial units established in backward areas.

Considerations Regarding Buy Decisions

Research studies have shown that make-or-buy decisions are sometimes made on the basis of insufficient data and faulty evaluation of implications resulting in huge wastes from making what could be more advantageously bought. Whether it is the production of containers and packing materials, or printing of forms, circulars and notices, or securing factory and office supplies, or transportation service, if there is no dependable source of procuring the items, obviously the buying option is ruled out. Dependability or reliability of supply should be naturally considered in terms of quantity, quality and timeliness of availability. Thus, for instance, the inadequacy of public power supply has led to the installation of power generators by many companies in certain States.

In general, a decision to make should follow whenever the expected cost savings provide higher return on the required capital investment than can be obtained from employing the funds in an alternative investment bearing the same risk. Thus, few firms, if any, consider making the items of office stationery (pencils, writing paper, and hundred other items) worthwhile. Likewise, setting up of printing press to print office forms, circulars and notices may not be worthwhile for most firms since there may not be enough printing work to ensure economic use of the printing machine.

Identifying and estimating the relevant costs of manufacturing a product or creating a service facility require the following aspects to be noted:

1. Labour costs should be projected the light of such factors as the effect on the existing labour force, availability of the type of labour needed, probable labour cost trends, etc.

2. Imputed interest costs have to be taken into account when large investment are involved, which can be done by discounting the future cash flows;

3. Sunk cost (*i.e.*, costs otherwise incurred on creating facilities) have a value depending on whether the same can be utilised by the firm for other internal purposes rented, or disposed of;

4. Fixed costs seldom remain unaffected, particularly the managerial costs. The planning and supervision of any new operation may divert present managers from other responsibilities or require additional supervisory personnel. These costs are somewhat difficult to measure and are often ignored;

5. While calculating the differential cost of making and buying, the purchase cost should include the net supply price plus freight and incremental handling cost;

6. Projecting the cost of raw materials needs consideration of the type and quantity of materials required, probable market trends, availability of reliable suppliers, freight, order size, discount, etc.

7. Risk of long-term investment creates a bias in favour of buying. The risk element may be recognised by adding a premium to the rate of expected return;

Apart from the saving in cost and return on capital investment, there are several non-cost factors that also need to be considered. In favour of making, there may be such factors as:

(a) maintenance of labour already employed,

(b) idle facilities,

(c) tax considerations,

(d) desire to maintain secrecy of process,

(e) poor quality of supply,

(f) instability of supply.

On the other hand, in favour of buying there may be considerations, such as:

(a) special services rendered by outside suppliers,

(b) scope of wider selection,

(c) fluctuation in requirements due to uneven production of end products,

(d) possibility of passing on the risk of investment to suppliers,

(e) lack of capita,

(f) lack of managerial experience.

CHOICE OF PRODUCTION PROCESSES

Along with the policy decisions on production activities policies need to be formulated also on production processes. Following are different aspects of the choice, *viz.*,

(1) Division of Labour. The volume of production and the extent of standardisation of products determine whether and how far line operations could be sub-divided and entrusted to different operatives. Divisions of labour has been the characteristic features of large-scale manufacturing works since the industrial revolution. Routinisation of operations is known to produce monotony, boredom, lack of motivation and low morale due to 'anomie' (aloneness among many). Job enlargement is recognised now as a superior means of securing higher productivity and efficiency.

(2) Policy on Mechanisation and Automation. Technological advances over the last half a century have enlarged the scope of mechanisation and automation in many industries; *e.g.*, the use of tractors and harvesters in agriculture, automatic spinning and weaving in textile mills, packing and packaging of products, loading and unloading of cargo, automatic signalling in the railways, assembly line operations, etc.

(3) Choice of Technology. The technology to be used is uniquely given in the case of certain industries (products). Airlines may use aircrafts of different types to service particular regions. On the choice of technology depends the devisions regarding equipment, personnel methods of operation and organisation. In the service organisations, too, the process to be used may require a choice to be made out of different alternatives.

(4) Size and Location of Production Units. For large enterprises, the decision with respect to the size of plant needs to be examined with two alternatives in view, *viz.*,

(i) Large size with centralised location, and

(ii) Dispersal of operating units with small size of plant capacity.

MARKETING STRATEGIES OR LEADING INDIAN COMPANIES

Plans and policies related to marketing have to be formulated and implemented on the basis of the 4 Ps of the marketing mix, *i.e.* product, pricing, place (distribution), and promotion. The major issues and decisions relate to these marketing mix factors. Questions such as; what types of products to offer? to offer at what prices? through which distribution channel? and, by the use of which promotional tool? have to be answered. We discuss each of the marketing mix factors below.

(A) Product Policy

Product denotes the goods and services that an organisation-offers to its target markets. Plans and policies related to the product and market need to be formulated and implemented on the basis of characteristics such as quality, features, choice of models, brand name, packaging, etc. Strategies dictate the manner in which product and market characteristics would be defined. Thus, competitive strategic may be implemented by stressing on high quality, better and more features. The growth strategy of Bajaj Auto has the quality of its vehicles as a prominent factor. The product policy of Reliance is to offer high fashion fabrics of new varieties and design. Not only consumer goods companies but industrial products manufactures may also have to consider the product characteristics, as mentioned above, to set marketing plans and policies. Thermax offers a service franchise scheme to implement its marketing policy for boilers. This policy is based on the thinking that if service is assured in a competitive market, sales will follow. In this manner, product and service characteristics help a company in implementing its strategy just like a strategy guides the formulation and implementation of product plans and policies.

(B) Place (Channels of Distribution Policy)

Place (or distribution) is the process by which goods or services are made available to the customers. Distribution plans and policies address themselves to issues such as, the channels to be used; transportation, logistics, and inventory storage management; coverage of markets; etc

The use of distribution plans and policies in the marketing function as well as strategy implementation is important. The success of market-oriented strategies, specially in competitive environment, rests on the efficiency and activeness of the distribution system. Several companies realise this importance and make efforts to use their distribution systems strategically. For instance, Foods Specialities Ltd. (FSL) has a conscious policy of regarding the retailer as an important link in the distribution system. It offers better margins, facilities support to its retailers. In contrast, Glaxo-its competitor in the baby foods market-failed to react favourably to retailers demand for better margins during the 1970s as a result of which its popular brand Farex lost out to Nestle's (now FSL) brand Cerelac, a competitive disadvantage that still exists.

Marketing Plans and Policies at Atlas Cycles

Atlas Cycles, traditionally for over three decades, had relied on a marketing policy built around the product attributes of durability and reliability. But during the 1980s, its leadership position was seriously threatened by competitors, mainly Hero Cycles, which offered their products with new features and lower prices. Since

1985, Atlas Cycles has had to rethink its marketing plans and policies as it has decided to adopt a growth strategy.

The major aspects of marketing plans and policies are described below:

> *Product.* Based on stringent quality control newer models such as Atlas Goldline, Atlas Goldline Super, Funfleet (in the sports cycles category), and Atlas Concorde Pro.-10 have been introduced, Several new features, such as front wheel reflector, better handle, new chain cover, and mascot on front mudguard were added to create Atlas Goldline. Atlas Concorde Pro-l0 is a high-tech model with an imported 10-gear system and a new set of seats, handle grips, reflectors, etc..
>
> *Pricing.* Atlas Cycles markets its products on the basis of a premium pricing policy, *i.e.* its models are priced higher than those of its competitors. All the marketing policies revolve around the question: how to maintain competitiveness, market share, and leadership position with higher-priced products?
>
> *Promotion.* The advertising policy at Atlas Cycles is built on two central tasks to adopt a proactive approach to highlight the genuine "quality" leadership of Atlas products; and to find ways to project the market leadership of the company through contemporary and technologically superior products.
>
> *Distribution.* Dealers in the bicycle industry-like those in several other industries-have a major influence on the brand choice. Distribution policies at Atlas Cycles are centred on the approa :h of maintaining a close relationship with dealers arid convincing them of the high quality of products that justifies a premium pricing policy.

In this manner, Atlas Cycles attempts to implement its strategies of modernisation and competitive stability in a market which is increasingly becoming more quality and status conscious.

(C) Promotion Policy

Promotion deals with marketing communication intended to convey the company, and product or service image to prospective buyers. The promotional mix consists of four activities: advertising, personal selling, sales promotion, and publicity.

Promotional plans and policies have to consider the basic question of what promotional mix to adopt so that promotional activities can be used to implement strategies.

The increasing competitiveness in several industries in India has prompted companies to adopt promotion as a strategic tool. The availability of the medium of television has encouraged small companies making products like Vicco creams, Lijjat Papad, Pan Parag, Promise toothpaste, Nirma and several others to adopt a promotional policy of using TV advertising extensively., The nature of product/industry also determines the type of promotional tool used. The promotional policy of Lohia Machines for LML Vespa Scooters currently rests on using safety as a unique selling proposition as scooters are considered as vehicles mainly for the middle class men. Eureka Forbes has adopted a deliberate sales promotion policy of door-to-door selling, and demonstrations at exhibitions for its home improvement products.

(D) Pricing Policy

Price denotes the money that customers pay in exchange for goods and services. It is important to the seller because it represents the returns of efforts. To a buyer, price is the value that is assigned For instance, HCL has based its marketing policy on low-priced copiers and competes with its rivals, mainly Modi Xerox, by claiming a better price-performance relationship of its products. This is done through a promotional policy of comparative advertising. Prices are often used as a determinant of market segmentation, which in turn becomes the basis for creating different models of the same product. The market for soaps, for instance, is divided into premium and popular segments representing the high-priced and low-priced soaps. A segmentation of this type has implications for all the factors in the marketing mix, apart from pricing and helps in implementing marketing policies such as market penetration or partial retrenchment from markets.

PRODUCT LIFE CYCLE

Marketing managers plan for creating new products and recreating the image of existing products. The question is why they do so? Product life cycle concept provides the answer. The concept informs the managers that sooner or later a product will die. If a business enterprise is to be an ongoing entity, it must develop new products or improve on its established ones. What is product life cycle, then? Product life cycle refers to the stages from conception to death in the life of a product. William Shakespear spoke of seven ages of man from birth to death. Like human beings, products also pass through several distinct life stages, each of which generates unique problems and opportunities and calls for special strategies. The product life cycle is made up of five phases: introduction, incubation, growth, maturity and decline.

(1) Introduction. After testing, a product enters the introduction, stage during which the public is acquainted with the merits of the new product and acceptance is gained. Since the product is new to the public and customers take time to shift from the existing products, sales and profits are at a low level. Sales begin to build up as the prospective customers learn of the product from advertising and other promotional avenues. The rum may even incur losses at introduction stage since heavy expenses in overheads are involved and also because of the risk attached with product's acceptability in the market.

(2) Incubation. In this phase, a rum conceives the idea of a product, develops the 'Product on a limited scale and tests its profitability before finally deciding to introduce it in the market-place. Conception of ideas, Creation or development and testing of the product involves huge investments in Research and Development (R & D). Therefore, at this stage of a product's life, the firm will have lots of expenses to incur but no profits. The diagram shows that in incubation phase, the profit line is sinking below the axis.

(3) Growth. If the product is accepted by potential buyers, it usually enters a rapid-growth stage. Sales volume and profits rise rapidly as new customers give the product a try and the early buyers go for repurchasing it. The product may gain reputation by word of mouth, advertising or acceptance by opinion leaders. Due to greater sales, the firm bothers less about promotion costs. Price remains high during growth stage to recoup heavy introduction losses. During later growth phase, prices are lowered as other competitive firms introduce similar products to exploit the market opportunity. The rum should try to prolong the growth period as much as possible to take advantage of rising profits.

(4) Maturity. Growth rates remain stable during maturity period, but eventully decline as the backlog of potential buyers is exhausted.

Competition is tough and pressure to reduce price forces some firms to get out of the market. The maturity stage usually lasts longer than the introduction or growth phases. Customers develop loyalty to certain brands on the basis of their personal liking and sales for a particular product are mostly limited to the customers who are satisfied with that product. Prices are lower and comparatively stable among competitors. Attempts are made to increase sales by advertising with new phrases or slogans, developing new uses of the product, making slight improvements in the existing product and concentrating on those potential buyers which might have been left out earlier.

(5) Decline. In the decline phase, the product starts fading and something else begins to shine the product gradually loses a sizable number of customers without replacing them. Both sales and profits go down steadily and films reduce promotional expenditure as they begin to accept the product's fate. Many firms leave the market and only few firms produce the product. Safety razor and electric shavers replace the straight razor, colour television supplants black and white and slode rules are exchanged for cheap pocket calculators.

FACTOR TAKEN INTO ACCOUNT TO DECIDE THE LOCATION OF PLANT

One of the important problems of launching an industrial enterprise is the choice of suitable location which will help in minimisation of production cost and maximisation of profit. In order to select an optimum location, the promoters must carefully study the impact of the following factors:

(1) ***Availability of Raw Materials.*** The availability of the required quality and quantity of raw materials at a reasonable cost is an important factor for determining the location of an industrial unit in most of the industries, the cost of raw materials forms more than 50% of the total cost of their products. The impact of raw materials on location depends upon their nature and the source of their deposits. Generally, ubiquities like wateclay, and sand which are found a all places have very little influence on location. That means the place of production would be fixed independently. But in some cases materials of ubiquitous nature may so very in quantity and quality that they are in fact regarded as fixed. For, example, paper manufacturing plants require a regular supply of a large quantity of pure water and they are, therefore, located near the banks of the rivers.

(2) ***Transport and Communication Facilities.*** Transport services are required for assembling of material and distribution of products. While selecting the location it should be seen that transportation facilities are easily available at reasonable rates. The junction points of waterways, roadways and railways have the tendency to become industrial centres because of this reason only. If an industrial unit is directly linked with the means of transportation, its transportation costs are lower. Besides transportation, communication services also play an important role in the location of industrial units.

(3) ***Proximity to the Market.*** Industrial units using non weight losing raw materials tend to locate near the markets because

of so many advantages. A manufacturer can improve his customer relations and render rapid services to his customers. Industries producing perishable commodities and those producing for a local market are also drawn towards the market. Because it would reduce the cost of transport in distributing the finished products.

(4) ***Labour.*** Every plant requires an adequate supply of labour with appropriate skill. Weber deduced that an industrial unit will deviate from the point of minimum transportation cost to the cheaper labour centre if the additional cost of transportation at the new centreis more than compensated by the savings in labour cost. But this hypothesis has lost it significance in the recent years because of many reasons. Labour is easily mobile and there is a level of minimum wages fixed by law below which an industrial concern cannot go. Moreover, certain in industries are capital intensive and they require less labour.

(5) ***Finance.*** Finance is the life-blood of any industrial venture. Availability of adequate funds at low rates of interests is an important factor influencing industrial location. But in these days capital has become a highly mobile factor of production. Despite this fact, availability of funds at cheaper price is an important consideration. For instance, there are State Financial Corporations in various states which offer loans at a very low rate of interest if the entrepreneurs start their projects in the specified areas.

(6) ***Power and Fuel.*** An adequate supply of power and fuel is an important factor for the un-interrupted operations of any enterprise. In the initial days of industrial revolution, industrial units were located near coal deposits because coal was the major source of power and fuel and was of weight losing nature and quite bulky. But with the introduction of other sources of power like electricity, gas, oil etc., the power factor has become more mobile. This has helped in dispersal of industries. The industrial units

which mainly depend on electric power tend to shift from a place if they do not get its regular supply.

(7) ***External Economics.*** Sometimes industrial units are located in those centres where other industrial units are already located. It is because of the fact that transportation, warehousing, banking communication and other services are easily available. Secondly, the raw materials may be easily available at cheaper rates. For instance, by-product of one unit may be the raw material for another.

(8) ***Personal Factor.*** Personal preference and prejudice of an entrepreneur may also play an important role in the choice of location. For instance, Mr. Ford started manufacturing motor cars in Detroit because it was his home town, and Lord Nuffield selected Cowley because the school in which his father was educated happened to be for sale. The success of the entrepreneur in such a location depends upon his extra personal efforts.

(9) ***Climatic to Considerations.*** Natural and climatic considerations like level of ground, topography (hilly and rocky surface) of a region, and drainage facilities influence the location of industries in certain cases. For example, cotton textile mills require a humid climate. The humid climate of Mumbai offered greater scope for the development of cotten textile industry. But the development of artificial humidification and air-conditioning has reduced the importance of climate to some extent. Entrepreneurs do not prefer to locate their units in hilly and rocky areas because of increase in transport cost.

(10) ***Government Policy.*** In planned economies, the role of government policy with respect to location of industry is crucial. In India, the Central Government follows the policy of balanced regional development of the country which is necessary from the point of view of defence and social problems like slum, disparity of income an wealth

and optimum use of resources. In order to implement this policy, the Government encourages industrialists to invest their money in backward areas by giving various tax incentives in the form of remission of excise duty or sales tax. Government also offer certain non-tax incentives like loan at cheaper rates, factory sheds, etc. to attract the entrepreneurs.

SELECTION OF THE SITE

The promoters of an industrial unit are confronted with the problem of choosing the exact site after deciding the area of location. While choosing the site, the following factors should be taken into consideration:

(a) Site is well connected with various modes of transport.

(b) Raw materials are available easily.

(c) There was facilities for disposal of polluted water and other waste material, if there is any.

(d) Municipality rules and regulations allow the construction of building suited to the plant.

(e) The site has good surroundings. There should be no congestion of traffic.

(f) Labour is easily available.

(g) The size of the plot has scope for expansion.

(h) Certain essential service organisations like post office, bank and warehouse exist near the site.

The guiding principle in the fixation of exact location for the plant is that it must result in the lowest unit cost in producing and distributing a product. For this purpose, industrialists will determine and compare the total cost per unit of product at various sites. The elements of total cost are transportation costs, costs of material and fuels, cost of power and water, cost of plant site and building, rates and taxes, and labour and administrative costs. Besides these economic factors, there are other considerations which are the matter of judgment rather than mathematical calculation. For instance, personal or historical factors may compel an industrialist to choose a particular site.

The total cost per unit of product varies according to the site chosen. Some industrialists are inclined towards cities while others towards the villages. The site in the city is associated with many benefits like availability of transport and communication, repair and maintenance facilities, facilities for disposal of effluent and water and presence of subsidiary services like education, health and recreation. But land is very costly and rents are high in cities or urban areas. Moreover, there is over-crowding congestion of traffic, noise and dust in these areas. That is why, some industrialists decide to move away from urban complexes. Rents, rates and taxes are very low in villages and semi-urban areas.

It is the policy of the Government to have dispersal of industries so that there is balanced regional development in the country. Government provides many services and supplies raw materials at subsidised rates in these estates. The disadvantage caused by non urban siting are more than compensated by the facilities and subsidies provided by the Government. It is significant to point out that financial institutions also encourage the setting up of new plants in semiurban or rural areas. The licensing policy of the Central Government is also guided by the consideration of balanced regional development. In practice, an industrialist is not so free to choose the location and the site for his project.

Government Policy on Industrial Location. In a planned economy like India, location of industries is an important factor in the creation of a climate for the balanced economic growth of various regions. In the absence of regulation of industrial location by the Government, industrialists are generally attracted towards the places where the industries are already developed. They do so because they will get a large number of external economies from those places. The private entrepreneurs decide the location by keeping in view the economic considerations only. They do not think in terms of social cost-benefit.

Concentration of industries gives rise to problems of housing, transport, health and other social services. It gives rise to congestion of traffic, overcrowding and other problems also. Concentration of industries at particular places takes place at the cost of other areas. Thus, backward areas remain backward. Moreover, concentration of industries is not equitable because people living near the industrial places will enjoy many benefits of industrial development including employment opportunities.

The basic policy followed by the Indian Government after independence in regard to location of industries is the achievement of balanced regional growth of the country. Balanced regional development is a vital part of India economic planning. Different ways have been followed to achieve balanced regional development of different regions in the country during the Five Year Plans. The industrial policy statement made by the Government from time to time have also given due recognition to the fact that balanced growth of various regions has an important impact to generate employment, to remove poverty and to increase the standard of living of the people.

GOVERNMENT'S APPROACH TO LOCATION OF INDUSTRY

The Government can tackle the problem of concentration of industry by following two approaches:

(i) Positive approach—encouraging establishment of industrial units in the backward areas; and

(ii) Negative approach—restraining the establishment of industrial units in the concentrated areas.

Positive Approach. The adaptation of positive approach is likely to give more satisfactory results as compared to the negative approach. Under this approach, the State provides certain incentives for the establishment of industrial unit in the selected areas. These incentives may take the following forms:

(i) Provision of public utility services in selected areas. These services include electricity, water, gas, transport, etc.

(ii) Provision of social-economic amenities like recreation education, health, etc. In addition, the Government has also extended certain ancillary economic facilities in these areas like institutions for imparting technical knowledge to the workers and marketing organisations for the benefit of localised industries.

(iii) Giving assurance by the state to purchase the products of the industrial units established in backward areas.

(iv) Providing adequate and cheap financial facilities directly by the Government or through the financial institutions.

(v) Establishment of industrial estates in industrially backward regions. The main objectives of industrial estates is to enable a large number of small scale units to have the advantages of common services and other facilities. Being located near one another, they may also be able to use the goods and services of others.

(vi) Granting of direct and indirect subsidies. Direct subsidies may be in the form of price subsidisation, supply of raw materials and machinery at Low prices, etc. Indirect subsidies may be in the form of reducing the cost of certain services to offset the influence of unfavourable factors.

The negative approach includes certain deterrents which have not proved to be so effective in practice. To prevent excessive concentration of industries in certain areas, the State may introduce deterrents like enhanced local taxes. A levy may be imposed on the established industrial units for the benefit of new units in the backward areas. The State may also follow absolute prohibition to check excessive concentration of industries in particular areas. Licensing policy may be introduced to achieve balanced regional growth.

PRICING METHOD IN BUSINESS POLICY METHOD

The method or technique of price fixation depends upon the pricing objectives and policies of the final. The basic methods, based on costs, used by business concerns are:

(1) Cost Plus Pricing

Cost plus pricing is the most pervasive pricing method used by the business enterprises. Under this method, the cost estimate of the product is made and a margin for profit is added to it to determine the price. The basic philosophy behind this approach is that the sale pricing of a product must cover its cost and bring about a reasonable margin of profit. The margin is known as mark up and that is why, cost plus pricing is also known as 'mark up pricing'. The simple formula used in cost plus pricing is:

Selling Price = Unit Total Cost + Desired Unit Profit

Several different concepts of cost component may be used in cost plus pricing. In general cost means either actual, expected or standard cost. Actual cost usually means historical cost for the latest available period. It reflects recent wages and material prices and overhead charges at the current output rate. Expected cost is a forecast of actual cost for the pricing period on the basis of expected prices, output rates and efficiency. Standard cost is a conjecture as to what cost would be at some normal rate of output and with efficiency at some standard level. In practice, cost is determined on the basis of estimates and cost experience. Formulas for cost plus pricing differ widely among industries and even among firms within an industry. This variation is probably due to differences in accounting practices.

The size of the markup depends upon competition, distinctiveness of the product, habit of custom of the market and some vague notion of a reasonable profit. Some big organisations determine the average markup on cost necessary to obtain a required rate of return on their investments. Under this policy pricing starts with a planned rate of return on investment. To translate this rate of return into a per cent markup on cost, it is essential to estimate a normal rate of production and its standard cost. After this, the ratio of invested capital to a year's standard cost of normal production is computed. This is called capital turnover. Multiplication of capital turnover by target rate of return gives the markup percentage to be applied to the standard cost.

Merits of Cost Plus Pricing. Cost plus or full cost pricing helps in achieving reasonable return on the amount of capital invested. It discourages the manufacturers from cut-throat competition. It is the safest method of pricing. The manufacturer will sell those products which can give him sufficient return.

Inadequacies of Cost Plus Pricing. Cost plus pricing has been criticised by many authors on the following grounds:

(a) It ignores the level and nature of demand.

(b) It fails to reflect competition in the market.

(c) It presumes a fixed margin of profit. But in practice businessmen increase their margin of profit when they expect good demand.

(d) The firm using cost plus pricing never knows how much a customer is will ling to pay.

(e) Cost plus pricing may not deliver goods particularly when there is idle plant capacity. In such a case, marginal costing may be useful.

(f) In practice, businessmen use rules of thumb to determine the markup on the cost of the product.

(2) Marginal Cost Pricing

Marginal costing and break-even analysis are the important tools for determining the price of a product. They are very helpful techniques when a firm has full knowledge about the demand and revenue conditions in the market. Costs of production are divided into two parts, namely, fixed cost and variable cost. The fixed cost remains fixed up to a certain level of production and variable cost keeps on changing with the change in the number of units produced. Marginal cost is the amount of money at any given volume of output by which aggregate cost is changed if the volume of output is increased or decreased by one unit. It represents the variable cost per unit up to a certain stage of production. Marginal costing is quite helpful when a firm is confronted with the problem of quoting the price of its products.

(3) Break-even Analysis

Break-even analysis uses market demand as a basis for price determination and also considers cost of production. It involves developing tables and/or charts which are useful to determine at what level of production the revenues will equal the costs assuming a certain setting price. It establishes relationship among cost of production, volume of production, profit or loss, and sale. It determines the break-even point which represents the volume of sale at which costs (fixed and variable) are fully covered. Sales at levels about the break-even point will result in a profit on each unit. Output at any stage below the break-even point will result in a loss to the seller.

Break-even analysis is the most sophisticated pricing technique which takes into consideration both fixed costs and variable costs. It uses market demand as the basis of price determination. Break even point (BEP) which represents the volume of production at which there is no profit and loss can be calculated by the following formula:

$$\text{BEP} = \frac{\text{Fixed Costs}}{\text{Selling Price per Unit} - \text{Variable Cost per Unit}}$$

$$= \frac{\text{Fixed Costs}}{\text{Contribution}}$$

Suppose, Fixed Costs = Rs. 1,60,000

Variable Cost = Rs. 6 per unit

Selling Price = Rs. 10 per unit

$$\text{BEP} = \frac{1,60,000}{10-6} = 40,000 \text{ units}$$

The vertical scale represents cost and revenue and the horizontal scale represents the sales. The fixed cost line is drawn horizontally through the fixed cost point and the total cost line is drawn from the inter-section of the fixed cost line at the left vertical scale. The sales line is drawn through the zero point on the left scale. The total cost line represents the total cost of production and the sales line shows the amount of revenues (rupees in lakh) at various volumes of sales. The point at which the total revenue line and the total cost line intersect is the break-even point.

Evaluation. Marginal costing and break-even analysis are not free from limitation. These techniques assume a single product which is not possible in practice. They also assume that all the costs can be divided into two categories only, *i.e.*, fixed and variable, but there are certain semi-variable costs also. Therefore, it is not easy to find the marginal cost of a product. Break-even analysis is a theoretical tool to know the volume of production at which profits could be maximised. In practice, the determination of the price is not so easy. Despite these limitations, marginal costing can prove very helpful. It can help in taking the decision whether to continue production or stop production. During depression, the management of a firm may decide to keep on marketing its products at the prevailing market price which is more than or equal to the variable cost because fixed costs have to be incurred whether there is any production or not.

In this way we conclude that full cost pricing is the most widely used pricing practice followed by the business enterprises. Under this method, the price represents the cost of the product plus a certain markup representing a reasonable profit. Deviation from full cost pricing takes place to clear old stocks, to get Government orders, to utilise idle capacity, and to meet depression. Many enlightened businessmen use marginal costing to determine the prices of their products when the demand is lower and there is idle plant capacity. In such a situation, it is advisable to maximise contribution towards variable cost and fixed cost rather than stop production.

PLACE OF ADVERTISING PUBLICITY AND SALES PROMOTION IN THE BUSINESS

It has already been observed how competition in the market makes it absolutely necessary for manufacturers to think of new and unfamiliar uses for their products or to find out new buyers for their products. Demand creation is, therefore, almost as important as meeting the existing demand. Both demand creation and catering to the existing demand require some means by which consumers—existing as well as potential—are informed about the availability of the product. Of the various means and devices employed to perform this essential function, advertising is easily the most outstanding and the most far-reaching approach.

To the layman, advertising is nothing more than the "use of bright ideas, stunts and slogans to popularise goods which appeal to the great body of ordinary consumers." But in believing so the layman is not merely missing the importance of advertising in the modern world, but is also confusing it with mere propaganda. Propaganda is employed to spread some ideology or doctrine.

Some firms would send their travelling salesmen round to canvass for their products from door to door. Shop windows were tastefully and attractively decorated so that the products could catch the eye (and the heart) of the customers who happened to pass by. A businessman would write to those consumers who are known to him or else would ring up to inform them that a certain product in which they would possibly by interested is available. All these efforts of the producers or sellers were directed towards informing the possible customers about their products or services. Underlying all of them was the desire to promote sales. But they could achieve their objectives within certain limitations. A travelling salesmen can call on a limited number of consumers or retail shops. Not many people may really care to notice the goods on display in show windows. The businessman may know a small number of persons whom he may contact personally to pass on information concerning his products. Thus sales may be promoted on a rather small scale by such means. It need hardly be pointed out that these techniques of sales promotion do not fully meet the requirements of the mass production industries of the modern times. When goods are produced on a mass scale, their sales can be effectively promoted only by those means which can be used to inform the largest possible number of possible consumers about certain goods which can meet certain requirements of theirs. In the modern sense, therefore, advertising has to be understood as a mass selling technique. The older devices of window-dressing, personal salesmanship and personal call can serve the purpose of small business only, though even there they may be used to supplement advertising rather than to supplant or replace it. The needs of the growing number of large-sized concerns established to cater to national and international markets can be met only by the technique of advertising through various media of mass appeal and mass communication.

Objects and Purposes. In the foregoing paragraph, the informative aspect of advertising has been stressed. Though the basic purpose of advertising is to bring the advertised product as well as its features and uses to the notice of consumers, has begun to be used for a number of other allied purposes now.

(i) The existence of intense competition has given rise to what may be described as competitive advertising. In other words, advertising is undertaken these days not only to inform people about a product, but is used to maintaing the demand for an existing product and to add to existing demand by weanin people away from rival products in the market. To take a concrete case, when the bottlers of Coca-Cola found a strong rival in Pepsi Cola, they changed the tone and emphasis of their advertisements and began to emphasize that only 'it is real'.

(ii) It follows from the above that advertising may be used with a view to preparting ground for a new product that is proposed to be introduced in the market. Most of the cinema advertisements are designed to serve this purpose. But the time the film starts its run at a theatre the people are already prepared to receive it. That explained the gate-crashing and the heavy rush at the box-office right on the opening day of the picture.

(iii) Advertising is used as a means to demand creation. Many needs of the people are the creations of advertising. Actually, advertising seeks to channelist the surplus incomes of the people towards those products which are not included among the basic necessities of life. In this process, it makes people conscious of the need for something without which they had been living so far. This consciousness is turned into a desire, and an ardent desire, when the advertisement continues to rub to the need for such a product.

(iv) Large-scale advertising is often undertaken with the objective of creating or enhancing the goodwill of advertising company. This, in turn, increased the market receptiveness of the company's product and helps the salesman to win customers easily.

In short, advertising aims at benefiting the producer, educating the consumer and supplementing the salesman. Above, all, it is a link between the producer and the consumer.

Advertising is non-personal communication. It is communication that is paid for. The sponsor is usually identified. He is conveying news or promoting ideas, goods or services to a specific group of people. He buys space or time in media which would reach them. He may resort to advertising with any or all of the following in mind: speed, economy, impact, convenience. Advertising is one channel of information for consumers. They get to know about new products, product improvements price changes, packaging innovations, special credit terms, new uses for the product and so on from the advertising columns.

"Publicity", in its restricted sense, is communication favourable to a company in the editorial part of media, be it press, radio, film or TV. Publicity is not paid for though the message that are printed or broadcast may have been inspired by the company concerned. This may be done through press conferences, which do cost money-invitation cards, telephone calls, tea or more elaborate fare for journalists, hire of hall where the conference is held, an information kit for the invites and so on. Sometimes transport is hired to take a party of journalists to a function or a plant. Special interviews and press releases (with or without supporting brochures) are other methods adopted. Often photographs are taken for pictorial coverage in media and these also cost money. Since the messages appear to emanate from the editor-who is regarded as an objective person unlike the sponsor of an advertisement—they command more credibility with the reader or the viewer or listener. But publicity messages are controlled by the editorial staff. These people-not the advertiser—will decide when themessages will appear, how much space or time will be devoted to them, and how they will be presented. Editors will seldom repeat the same story. Advertising, on the other hand, is controlled by the advertiser.

"Sales promotion" would cover three groups: salesmen, dealers and consumers. Training of salesman (in the case of technical salesmen—as in the case of pharmaceuticals or engineering goods-this can be expensive and time-consuming), conferences of salesmen, salesmen's kits, prizes for the best performers and so on are meant to cover the first group. Their morale, and enthusiasm are of immense value to a company. Some companies make the annual conference of safe men some thing of a gala affair, and often wives are invited. Sales promotion among dealers takes a variety of forms. Trade letters, house journals for the trade literature on products, displays and competitions, "mystery customer", schemes, painting of sign-boards, gifts like diaries, demonstrations, film shows, parties and conventions are some of these.

Value of Advertising. The importance of advertising is realised on all hands. In fact, advertising has already become such an integral part of our life that we never feel the need of pausing to consider its value and importance. There is no doubt about the fact that in the absence of advertising, our lives would have been lived very differently. Such being the place of advertising in our life, it will be worthwhile to consider some of the important advantages of advertising here.

1. Advantages to Manufacturers

There is justification in the adage, "it pays to advertise" because of the following advantages of advertising accruing to manufacturers:

(a) ***Increased Sales.*** The chief object of the manufacturer in advertising his products is to promote the sale of his products. Goods produced on a mass scale are marketed by the method of mass persuasion through advertising. By repeating advertisements, the manufactures are not only able to retain existing markets but are also able to expand the markets both by attracting more people to their products as also by suggesting new uses for them. Advertising acts as an aid to selling.

(b) ***Lower Costs.*** Advertising provides a spure to the sale and increases the turnover tremendously. This is advantageous in two ways: on one side, the selling costs including the cost of advertising get spread over a large volume of salts, thus lowering the average cost of selling; while on the other side; higher turnover necessiates high volume of production, thus lowering the average cost of production per unit.

(c) ***Steady Demand.*** Advertising has led to the smoothening out of the seasonal fluctuations in demand for many products. The manufactures are generally trying to discover and advertise new possible uses of which a seasonal product may be put. The innovation of cold tea and cold coffee for the use during summer has helped in increasing

the demand for these beverages even in that season. The same may be said for refrigeration.

(d) ***Greater Dealer Interest.*** The retailers who deal in advertised goods are materially assisted by advertising in the performance of their functions. Advertising creates demand which every retailer gets an opportunity to share with others. The retailers have not to bother much about pushing up the sale of such products. So they evidence more interest in advertised products.

(e) ***Quick Turnover and Smaller Inventories.*** A well-organised advertisement campaign creates a highly responsive market thereby facilitating quick turnover of the goods, This, in turn, results in lower inventories in relation to sales being carried on by the manufactures.

(f) ***Supplementing Salesmanship.*** Advertising prepares the necessary ground for the efforts of the salesmen. When a salesmanship its a prospect, he has just to canvass for a product with which the consumer may already have been familiarised through advertisements. Thus, the salesman's efforts are supplemented and his task is made easier by advertising.

(g) ***Creation of Goodwill.*** By constantly associating the name of the manufacture with certain standards of quality, advertising builds a fund of goodwill for him. Goodwill thus created is a valuable asset not merely because it enables him to get more and more of repeat orders for his existing products but also for the reason that the manufacture can introduce new products in the market with confidence. The Godrej concerns have been able to sell the whole range of products ranging from oils to-soap and from locks to typewriters mostly on the strength of their goodwill.

(h) ***Encouragement to Better Performance.*** Advertising gives the employees that feeling of pride in their jobs and the

products they produce or help to produce, which is basic to high morale. It can, thus, inspire executives and workers to improved performance. Moreover, an advertiser may have built up a vast fund of goodwill which will serve as assurance of security to the employers. This will also serve to boost up the morale of the men working in the manufacturer's organisation.

2. Benefits to Consumers

(a) ***Facility of Purchasing.*** Advertising makes purchasing easy for the consumers. Moreover, the resale prices (prices at which the goods are to be sold by the retailers) are generally fixed and advertised. Thus, advertising offers a definite and positive assurance to the consumer that he will not be overcharged for the advertised product. The consumer can make his purchases with utmost ease and confidence.

(b) ***Improvement in Quality.*** Goods are generally advertised under brand names. When a person is moved by the advertisement to use the product he proceeds on the hope that the articles of the particular brand will be better than the other brands of the same goods. If his experience confirms his expectation, a repeat order can be expected. Otherwise, the sales may rise very high once but may drop down very low subsequently when the consumer's confidence in the quality of the product is shaken.

(c) ***Elimination of Unnecessary Intermediaries.*** By advertising his goods, a manufacturer may seek to establish direct contacts with the consumers. In this process, the number of middlemen whose profits increase the price and reduce the manufacturer's margin of profits may be considerably reduced. This will mean large profits for the manufacturer and cheaper products for the consumers.

(d) ***Education of Consumers.*** There is considerable truth in Sir William Leverhulm's remark that advertising is an

educational and dynamic principle. Advertising aims at educating the buyers about new products and their diverse uses. In this process, it introduces new ways of life to the people at large and prompts them to give up their old habits and inertia. Advertising thus paves the way to better standards of living.

(e) ***Consumer's Surplus.*** Advertising increases the utility of given commodities for many people. It points out and emphasizes the qualities possessed by certain goods and leads consumers to appreciate more strongly the utility of such goods. As a result, the consumers may be willing to pay even more for certain products which appear to have higher utility to them. If these products are available at the original lower prices, there will naturally be a certain amount of consumer's surplus in terms of increased satisfaction or pleasure derived from these products.

3. Benefits to Society

(a) ***Encouragement to Research.*** The manufacturers will undertake research and discover new products or new uses for existing products only when they are assured of sufficient profits. Advertising provides this assurance and thus encourages industrial research with all its advantages.

(b) ***Substaining the Press.*** When advertising made its beginning, advertisements generally occupied some odd nooks and corners in the newspapers. The present situation is just the reverse. The newspapers, periodicals, journals, may the whole press, look to advertisements for support and sustenance. In the absence of income from advertising, the newspapers have to be produced at a higher cost and may not be able to keep themselves free from party pulls and pressures from business lords.

(c) ***Encouragement to Artists.*** Men of talent, including artists, story writers, announcers, etc., get an opportunity to do some creative work while earning their livelihood through

the designing of advertisements and the use of ideas in advertising various products.

(d) ***Change in Motivation.*** Advertising has radically changed the basis of human motivation. While people of earlier generations lived and worked mainly for bare necessities of life, the modern generation works harder to supply itself with the luxuries and semi-luxuries of life. Advertising has brought to the notice of the masses, numerous products which are more than mere necessities and has created in their minds a desire to possess them. Thus, the motive force of fear (or going without the bare essentials of life) has been replaced by desire (for more and newer products).

(e) ***Glimpse of National Life.*** Advertising does provide a glimpse of a country's way of life. It is, in fact, a running commentary on the way the people live and behave and is also an indicator of some of the future trends in this regard.

(f) ***Higher Standards of Living.*** Advertising leads to a rise in the standards of living, not only through the education of the buyers but also through greater consumption, increased production and a larger volume of employment.

Advertising in a Developing Economy. One sometimes comes across questions such as: Has advertising any role to play in a developing economy? Does its aim, *viz.*, promoting mass consumption and increased sales, not conflict with the aims of a developing economy? A developing economy aims at accelerating the rate of capital formation by means of encouraging savings and thrift. It has to make its production available for export to earn foreign exchange to be able to pay for its imports of capital goods and essential raw material. At first sight, advertising and a developing economy appear to be working at cross-purposes.

It is admitted that squandering is undesirable from the national point of view as savings are reduced. Nevertheless, one must always be chary of providing or implanting a hope and an expectation of better home, food or clothing if incentive to earn by hard work is to be retained. This incentive is crucial to successful implementation of any plan for economic development. It is here that advertising has a role to play. Advertising nourishes the consuming power of men. It creates wants for a better standard of living. Even otherwise, advertising is very well suited for selling the idea of saving. The advertising done by commercial banks and the Life Insurance Corporation of India is a case in point.

Advertising comes to the aid of a developing economy in promoting exports as well. 'Export or Perish' is the slogan of such economies. However, success in exports requires at least two things—first the prices must be competitive and second, the commodities must be of good quality. There are some who think that advertising expenditure raises the cost and price of the articles and thus regard advertising as "a mill-stone round the neck of a product" which checks its sales. But his notion is not well-founded. It has been the experience of all advanced nations like the U.K. the U.S.A., Germany, Japan, etc., that increased internal sales are necessary to lower the average costs or prices. It is also confinned by our own experience in the field of bicycles and sewing machines which we have been able to export because of low costs made possible by wider domestic market. Moreover, advertising sharpens competitive selling.

The last, but not the least, justification for advertising in a developing economy which, though poor, wants to spread literacy among its people, is that advertising makes it possible to drop the same thought into a thousand minds at the same time. In the absence of advertising, the hundreds of regional language publications would fold up for want of advertisements.

Objections Against Advertising. Advertising has also been subjected a number of objections mainly because it has been misused by some people to serve their own ends, overlooking the business interests. An examination of some of the forceful objections will be of interest.

(a) ***Multiplication of Needs.*** It is said that advertising compels people to buy things they do not need. Human instincts, like desire to possess, to be recognised in, the society, etc., are provoked in order to sell products. Sometimes, various types of appeals are advanced to arouse interest in the product. Sentiments and emotions are played with to gain customers.

(b) ***Misrepresentation of Facts.*** Through misrepresentation of the benefit a product will give, goods of no real value are sold. Tall claims are made by the advertisers to tempt people to take such actions as go purely to their advantage and cause tremendous loss to the consumer. Even adulterated food and medicines are marketed, which by no stretch of imagination can benefit anybody. By sheer exaggeration of facts, demand for the merchandise advertised is created without much difficulty even when the commodities carrying greater worth or satisfaction are already therein the market.

(c) ***Increased Cost.*** There is a great deal of controversy as to whether advertising leads to increase in the cost which the community has to pay for a product. In a sense it is true since expenses on it form a part of the total cost of the product. But at the same time it would be wrong to infer that if the advertising costs were cut down the goods would necessarily be cheaper. Advertising is, no doubt, one of the items of costs but it is a cost which brings savings in its wake on the distribution side. On manufacturing side, it is one of the factors that make large-scale production possible and anyone would agree that large-scale production leads to lower costs.

(d) ***Consumers Deficit.*** While advertising leads to increased satisfaction from commodities already in use, it also creates discontent in the minds of many people who are tempted to purchase/some commodities but are not able to do so because of insufficient purchasing power. Such discontent is obviously not very desirable from the point of view of society, particularly if it affects a large majority of people. But it is important if it acts as a spur to social change.

(e) ***Wastage of National Resources.*** A more serious objection against advertising is that it is used to destroy the utility of goods before the end of their normal period of usefulness. Now models of automobiles with nominal improvements are, for instance, advertised at such high pressure that the old models have to be discarded long before they become useless, Not that merely, the most-advertised products are delicate, fragile and brittle. In the U.S.A., there is evidence of a marked decline in the quality and durability of cars, furniture, rugs, television sets, refrigerators, etc. That appears to be the way in which the increased demand created through advertising can be sustained. The same is true of dresses, furniture and other products. From the points of view of the community it is a waste of resources.

STARTGIC PLANNING TO MEASURE THE SIZE OF THE BUSINESS

There has been a tendency of the business firms towards increase in their size in order to achieve economies in production, marketing, finance and management. In practice, different firms operate at different levels of operations. This is an important reason which explains that different firms are not able to operate with equal efficiency. Many economists have attempted to explain the size of a business firm which every business firm should try to achieve. These important concepts about the size of business unit which must be distinguished are: *(i)* Representative Firm, *(ii)* Equilibrium Firm, and *(iii)* Optimum Firm. These concepts are discussed below:

(i) ***Representative Firm.*** Alfred Marshall introduced the concept of representative firm. A representative firm is a model firm in an industry and it can be used as standard of reference, because it works under average conditions and at average efficiency. A representative firm is one which has had a fairey long life and fair success, which is managed with normal ability and which has normal access to the economies, external and internal, which belong to the aggregate volume of production, account being taken by the class of goods produced, the conditions of marketing them and economic environment generally.

Marshall meant a representative firm as one working under average condition and at average efficiency. It is an average firm with normal success. It is the size towards which every firm in an industry tends to grow. Such a firm can be found by undertaking a broad survey of the firm in an industry. The concept of representative firm is too abstract to be of much practical utility. There are many firms which started on a large scale from the very beginning and there are many firms which started on a small scale and do not find it profitable to expand even after a long period. Thus, a representative firm need not unnecessarily be an optimum firm. An optimum firm as the lowest average cost of production per unit of output in the given conditions of technique, knowledge and organising ability. A representative firm has a long period average concept and the optimum firm is the most efficient one.

(ii) ***Equilibrium Firm.*** The concept of equilibrium firm was developed by A.C. Pigou. Pigou was of the opinion that an equilibrium firm is one, which has reached a stage where there is no urge or incentive to expand further. In other words, the owners of the business firm are satisfied with its profitability and do not want any further expansion or contraction in its size. It may be pointed out that according to economics, a firm is in equilibrium when marginal revenue is equal to marginal cost and at this level of output.

The concept of equilibrium firm is imaginary and divorced from reality. Equilibrium firm can be achieved only under perfect competition. But in real life, perfect competition is not found. It is only under perfect competition that the size of equilibrium firm is equal to the optimum size. The idea of optimum firm is a relative concept and keeps on changing depending upon the techniques of production and organising ability. But equilibrium firm is to be found only under perfect competition which is a theoretical state of affairs.

(iii) ***Optimum Firm.*** A business unit may be launched on a small scale and then expanded gradually. With the increase in the scale of operations, it can enjoy various economies in regard to production, marketing, financing and management. But it must not be presumed that these economies will be available in increasing measure with every growth in the scale of operations. The law of diminishing return applies after a certain level of production. In other words, a point will come beyond which further expansion of business operations may lead to inefficiency. This point indicates the optimum size of firm.

The optimum size denotes the size of a firm at which there is maximum efficiency in operations. Efficiency will be reduced whenever the size is reduced below the optimum level or expanded beyond the optimum level. The concept of optimum firm was developed by E.A.G. Robinson.

Implications of Robins on's Definition. An analysis of the concept of optimum firm shows that it has the following implications:

(a) Average cost per unit and not the total cost should be minimum.

(b) White calculating the average cost of production per unit, all long run costs must be included. Average cost means total cost divided by the aggregate output.. The total cost should include not only direct costs like those of materials and labour but also indirect costs like depreciation, administrative overheads, distribution overheads, etc.

(c) Lowest average cost of production is emphasised and not the maximum profits. We are concerned only with the relations of cost to size while ignoring the question of maximum profitability because when there is monopoly, the prices need not coincide with average cost and maximum profit may be earned by charging a higher price.

(d) Optimum size is a relative concept. It is not something absolute, static or fixed. It changes with the changes in the techniques of production, efficiency of management, mode of financing, and so on.

(e) There is fullest possible utilisation of the available technological potentials.

Assumptions. The concept of optimum size is based on the following assumptions:

(a) The market is sufficient to absorb the whole production of at least one firm of optimum size.

(b) There is perfect competition in the market.

(c) The establishment of the optimum firm will being part the result of conscious decisions by businessmen who are considering how they most profitably cap invest their resources; in part it will be the product of the forces of competition, which tend, as a rule, to eliminate the inefficient and encourage the efficient firm.

Criticism. The concept of optimum size has been criticised on the following grounds:

(a) The market may be limited and may not be able to absorb a large number of firms of optimum size.

(b) It is very difficult to determine the optimum point, because it keeps on changing with every change in production and techniques of organising ability.

(c) The assumption of perfect competition is not satisfied in practice. The price differs in different markets because of slight product differentiation, knowledge gap, etc.

Inspite of the above criticism, the concept of optimum size draws the attention of the businessman to reduce the average cost of production through the use of the available techniques of production and organising ability. It also induces the businessman to think consciously of achieving the optimum size by consider ngthe impact of various forces on the size of :he firm.

Technical Forces

According to Robinson, technical forces fix a minimum scale of operations. They do not fix maximum scale beyond which growth will lead to progressively increasing average cost per unit. If other considerations require a scale larger than the technical optimum, the technical scale of production can be increased by the mere multiplications, until it coincide with that scale which those other considerations would demand. In other words, in every industry and for every method of production within each industry, there is more or less a fixed minimum size of plant below which production is technically impossible or economically unprofitable.

Technical optimum is attainable usually by a large sized business unit because technical forces operate mostly in favour of increasing the size of firms. The technical forces are the factors which influence the process of production. The important technical forces making for technical optimum unit are:

(i) Division of Labour. A large scale firm can reap great advantages of specialisation and division of labour. Through division of labour, the manufacturing process may be split into small operations which can be taken over by machlnes specially designed for the purpose. Division of labour can be used only by a large sized firm which can afford to install machines. Adam Smith gave three reasons for the increase in the quantity of work which in consequence of division of labour, a given number of people are capable of performing:

(i) It increases dexterity in every workman.

(ii) It saves time which is commonly lost in passing from one piece of work to another.

(iii) It facilitates invention of a great number of machines which enable one man to do the work of many.

(ii) Integration of Processes. A large sized firm can achieve economies by the integration of processes. Integration of processes involves designing a large machine to take over what was previously done by a series of munual or less mechanical operations. That means the process of division of labour is reversed so that fewer rather than more processes of manufacture are required to do the job. The integration of processes may be horizontal to vertical. Vertical integration consists in the combination of one stage of production with the other previously by separate stages of production under control of a single firm. An increase in the size of the mechanical unit gives an increase of efficiency and if greatest technical efficiency is to be achieved. The size of the firm must be sufficient to use largest mechanical unit necessary to utilise its full capacity. A small firm can also operate efficiently by obtaining access to some of the technical economies of large scale production through vertical disintegration. Where some given process requires a scale of production considerable greater than the small firms in an industry can achieve, this process tends to be separated from the main industry, and all the small firms to get this particular process performed for them by an outside specialist firm.

The size of optimum technical unit will be larger in those industries in which the productive machinery is physically very large as in steel making, ship building, etc. and in those in which the final product is highly complex as in the case of manufacture of typewriters, watches, motor cars, etc. On the other hand, optimum technical unit will be smaller where the product is both small and simple and the productive process is routine and standardized, as in the case of baking of bread. The technical costs of production are likely to fall as more and more is produced upto a certain point as a result of economies, butthey are likely to remain constrained after a point, where the economies of further growth are compensated by the increased costs.

Financial Forces

The stability and growth of the firms depend to a large extent on their ability to procure capital required for the conduct of their business. Firms having no assured access to financial facilities are unable to expand and may ever find it difficult to stay in business. They ability of the firm to raise the capital necessary for its activities is an important factor for the efficiency of business.

Financial forces favour the larger firms. A big firm can raise more funds easily on easy terms because of its reputation. It can expand its business easily. The financial cots per unit go on decreasing as more and more output is produced. However, the amount of capital required is largely influenced by the nature of the industry. Some firms have to start on a very large scale and so they need huge amount of capital. In these cases the joint stock company form of organisation with limited liability has become popular. The size of the company gives an impression of solidarity and security to an investor. Big companies are also favoured by the financial institutions and the commercial banks. There are certain limitations of big firms also. Greater investment involves increased risks, and there may be misuse of funds.

Marketing Forces

The optimum size in respect of marketing operations is attained by a firm through the conduct of its marketing operations on sufficiently large scale consistent with production capacity and sales potential. According to Robinson, marketing forces are concerned with both buying and selling. There are difinite economies in large scale buying and selling. The importance of efficient buying of materials can hardly be exaggerated. A large firm has more bargaining power as compared to the small firms. It can afford the services of purchase experts. Economies in the form of lower prices, higher discounts, lower transport charges, etc., are also obtained. On the selling side also, there are many economies. A large firm can afford elaborate and expensive sales organisation and can employ good sales persons. It can undertake marketing research and make use of advertising.

There are two points which go against a large firm and favour a small firm:

(a) Mistakes committed in buying or selling by a large firm may prove very costly and even difficult to rectify in some cases.

(b) If organised markets and distribution channels are available, a small firm would have no disadvantage as it can make use of these services.

Channel of Distribution

Whether a firm will sell its product or service directly to the consumers or make use of intermediaries (middlemen) for the purpose constitutes a major policy issue. For certain service organisations, direct sale to consumers is invariably called for, like, for instance, civil airways, banks, consultancy firms, passenger and freight transport services. But for most manufactures of goods, selection of the channel of distribution involves a choice of great significance For one thing, on channel decisions depend the firm's pricing decisions, advertising decisions and sales force decisions. Pricing decisions depend upon whether it chooses wholesalers or retailers for distribution of its products; the firm's advertising decision depend upon the degree of co-operation from the agencies in the channel of distribution; the sales force decisions also depend upon whether the firm chooses to sell to retailers or uses its own representatives. Secondly, the significance of channel decisions lies in that they involve long-term commitments to and dependence on other firms.

Channel decisions refers to the managerial decision on the selection of the most suitable route for distribution of goods from the producers to the users. Following are the important reasons which place channels decision in policy decision areas:

(a) If the choice of channels is proper, fluctuations in production may be reduced. The manufacturer can obtain data regarding sales and stock of the middlemen and exercise control wherever he feels necessary. The stability of production will help to ensure steady employment and proper budgetary control.

(b) The channels chosen involve the firm in relatively long-term commitments to other firms or middlemen. The relations between the manufacturer and the middlemen depend mainly on the choice of appropriate channels of distribution. Therefore, it is necessary that channels decisions are taken with great care.

(c) The channels selected for the firm's product affect every other marketing decision like pricing, promotion, physical distribution and the cost involved in the use of trade channels enter the price of the product that the ultimate consumer has to pay. If the costs of trade channels are very high the firm may draw public criticism.

CHOICE OF CHANNELS OF DISTRIBUTION

The choice of a suitable channel of distribution is an important marketing decision. The importance of this decision arises from the following considerations:

(a) An appropriate selection of channels can reduce fluctuations in production. The stability of production is important both for reasons of stable employment and proper budgeting of costs and revenues.

(b) The costs involved in the use of a channel or channels enter the price that the ultimate consumer has to pay. A proper decision in this regard may enable the management to cut on these costs and reach a wider market.

(c) The relations between the manufacturer and middlemen depend to a great extent on the choice of appropriate marketing channels. The manufacturer wishes the middleman to sell as much as possible at the lowest margin of profit while every middleman is interested in maximising his profit. A reconciliation of these conflicting interests can be brought out only through a rational decision regarding the choice of marketing channels.

(d) The decision regarding an appropriate channel or set of channels has a bearing on the other marketing decisions like pricing, product-line and promotion. This means that thoughtlessness on the part of the management in regard to the choice of suitable channels can affect adversely the whole marketing mix comprising various elements of the firm's offering to the consumers.

Channel Decision. A rational decision regarding the choice of the appropriate channel (s) of distribution can be taken only after all the relevant factors are taken into consideration. The procedure for the purpose will depend upon the nature of the product. Specifically, the procedure for established products will be different from that followed for new products. Also the factors or criteria on which a decision is made may be quantitative and qualitative. Here we shall concern ourselves first with the criteria for the choice of channels for existing products. Of course, the goals underlying the criteria are; *(a)* maximum geographical coverage of the market, *(b)* maximum promotional efforts, and *(c)* minimum costs.

The choice of a suitable channel of distribution which can be utilised for canalising the flow of existing products from the producers to the ultimate consumers is generally governed by the following eight factors:

(1) The Type of Product. The peculiarities of the product influence and determine the number of middlemen through whose hands the products will pass before it gets into the hands of the consumers.

(a) Servicing Required. Products like automobiles and sewing machines which require servicing, expensive handling equipment, or instructions before use also pass through the hands of a few middlemen. Fashion goods generally require direct selling since their special features have to be explained to the consumers effectively. Retailers may not do this very well.

(b) ***Seasonal Character.*** If a commodity is in seasonal demand there may be no need for middlemen.

(c) ***Perishability.*** As arule, fewer middlemen are required for selling perishable goods and commodities. Most of the bakery products and food products, generally, pass through only one middleman—the retailer—and may in many cases be sold directly by the producer.

(d) ***Unit Value.*** Generally, producuts of lower unit value and high turnover are distributed extensively through indirect channels, *e.g.*, hosiery goods, cosmetics, etc.

(e) ***Bulk or Weight.*** Where the movement of goods involves heavy freight and poses problems of transportation, limited channels may be employed. Selling may be mostly direct in such cases.

(2) Consumers or Market Considerations. The consumers influence the choice of the distributive channels in the following ways:

(i) ***Geographical Location.*** If most of the consumers using a particular product (say, bread) live in the same city or locality as the producer, the producer can sell his products through his own salesmen. On the other hand, if the consumers are large in number and are scattered over a wide area, the producer will have to depend upon wholesale and retail channels for the sale of his products.

(ii) ***Consumer or Industrial Market.*** The purpose for which the product is purchased by consumers also influences the choice of channels of distribution. If a product is used for an industrial purpose, direct purchase from the manufacture will suit the consumer better and the manufacturer will adopt direct selling.

(iii) ***Order size.*** The size of orders received and the volume of goods supplied to individual firms will influence the channels used to reach them. A food products manufacturer will sell directly to large grocery chains because the total volume of business makes this channel economically feasible.

(iv) ***Number.*** If the number of consumers is small as in the case of bulky and expensive machinery, the manufacturer can employ his own sales force to sell directly to the consumers. If, however, there is a large number of consumer interested in a product, the producer has to make use of the services of wholesalers and cannot afford to employ sales staff for direct selling or even deal with the host of retailers. Cigarettes and other consumer goods belong to this category.

(v) ***Consumer Buying Habits.*** The channel policies are affected by the buying habits of consumers and industrial users, the amount of effort the consumer is willing to expend, the desire for credit, the desire for after-sales service etc.

(3) Size and Structure of Manufacturing. The larger the producer, the more profitable it may be for him to htablish direct contact with consumers through his own sales force. A small producer, on the other hand, finds it more profitable to rely on indirect channels making use of wholesalers and retailers. Also, if the manufacturing is widely dispersed geographically, in relation to the demand, the greater will be the necessity of using indirect channels, particularly wholesalers. This is so because the wholesalers will have to collect products from a wide area. Further the width or the range of the product-line also determines the broad pattern of distribution that a firm will adopt. If a manufacturer deals in a wide range of products, he will tend to serve the retailer directly eliminating the wholesaler because it is more convenient for the retailer to purchase from as few a sources as possible.

(4) Company Considerations. The character of the firm making the choice of channels of distribution will also affect the channel policies of firms. Some of the important factors in this regard are:

(i) ***Financial Resources.*** A financially strong firm will have a tendency to set up its own channels rather than depend upon middlemen.

(ii) ***Experience and Competence of Managemant.*** Where the management lacks marketing know-how, it may prefer to depend upon indirect selling through middlemen.

(iii) ***Reputation.*** Firms with established goodwill can usually make their own choice of middlemen and enter into advantageous agreements with them.

(iv) ***Desire for Control of Channel.*** A manufacturer may establish a short channel just because he wants to control the distribution. Moving closer to the final customer affords the manufacturer greater opportunity to gather current market information and control the freshness of the product and its retail price.

(5) Structure of Retailing. The structure of retail trade in a product has also an important bearing on the choice of channels. One important aspect of this factor is the number of stores selling mainly the product in question. Generally, if there are many such stores, the manufacturer will like to make use of the available retail channels instead of selling direct to the consumers. Also, retailers will be used for marketing a product if the retail stores provide convenience of shopping to the potential consumers.

In short, the important considerations relating to the structure of retailing are:

(a) Services provided by retailers.

(b) Availability of desired retailers.

(c) Attitude of middlemen toward manufacturer's policies.

(d) Sales volume possibilities.

(6) The Customary Channels. In cases where an established network of channels exists, the manufacturer may make use of such customary channels. For example, if washing soap is being marketed through grocers, a manufacturer may find that selling it through general merchants does not add substantially to the sales volume. However, the firm must be on the look out for new channels and should explore them and experiment with them.

(7) Selectivity of Distribution. An important decision in regard to the choice of channels is the one relating to the number of middlemen to be used. Three alternative policies are available to the manufacturer:

(a) Extensive distribution means that the manufacturer is willing to make use of any and all distributive outlets prepared to handle his product. A good example is provided by cigarettes. In following this policy, the manufacturer may use an independent wholesaler through whom he can reach all the retail outlets, or he may sell direct to the large retailers and reach the rest of the market through wholesalers.

(b) Selective distribution means that the manufacturer will select from among the available outlets rather than use all of the outlets. The purpose of this policy is to provide the channels chosen with large enough sales to keep them selling the manufacturer's product in satisfactory way. This may increase the sales at reduced distribution costs and bring forth better co-operation from the dealers. The manufacturer may be able to achieve a good measure of control overdistribution through this policy. On the other hand, it may happen that this market coverage is weak in that potential customers are not able to find his product because it is being marketed through selected channels.

(c) *Exclusive distribution.* This implies that grant of sole selling right for a product in a certain territory to a middleman under a contractual agreement. Generally, the middleman acting as the sole distributor for a territory does not handle competing products. The benefits and drawbacks of this policy are extension of those arising from selective distribution.

(8) The Profit Criterion. After the qualitative criteria indicated above have been applied and a broad choice regarding the type and number of channels made, the next step will be the use of the quantitative criterion in the form of estimates of profit. This means that estimates of demand, revenue and costs for each channel should be prepared and compared to make the final choice regarding the channels of distribution. The sales volume potential differs considerably channel by channel and the costs tend to move indirect relationship to the directness of the channel. As we move progresssively from a direct manufacturer-to-user channel to the most indirect channel through one or more independent wholesalers, the cost of distribution tend to become progressively lower. At the same time, the manufacturer's control over his products also gets reduced thus limiting the sales that might be achieved. The net gain from a comparison between these variables will be the criterion for the choice of a channel.

❐

7

Personnel and Financial Policy

PERSONNEL management is primarily concerned with human resources with the organisation. Therefore, policy issues in the areas of personnel management should be concerned with:

(a) manpower planning, recruitment, selection and placement;

(b) training and developments of manpower;

(c) transfer, promotion, demotion, and separation;

(d) working conditions and employee service;

(e) communication consultative and negotiation;

(f) human and social implications of change in the internal organisation and methods of working of economic and social change in the community at large. The basic objective of personnel policies is to ensure adequate and effective manpower at the right to implement the strategy. Besides the organisation has to formulate policies in other areas which can support the implementation of basic strategy through the performance of main functions. Such areas may be research and development, legal, and public relations;

(g) terms of employment, methods and standard of remuneration.

The significance of personnel policy in strategy implementation hardly needs any elaboration. Both physical and human resources are crucial to the achievement of strategic goals. The basic objective of personnel policy in an organisation is to ensure consistency of action and equity in its relations with employees. These policies constitute the basis for sound personnel practices. They provide the yardstick by which implementation of strategic plans and programmes can be appraised. Besides, personnel policies are an integral part of the whole policy structure of an enterprise. Any weakness in personnel policy may thus weaken the other functional policies.

The close interrelation between the quality of personnel and strategic management requires the top executives to be concerned with the following policy issues.

RECRUITMENT POLICY

The appropriate match between strategic goals to be achieved and the kind of people employed require two different but related aspects of staffing to be examined.

On the one hand, there is the necessity of recruiting and maintaining the required number of work people and on the other it is retired, experienced persons available for employment and others employed in other organisation but seeking a change for better prospects. External recruitment obviously provides a wider choice from among personnel to select those with skill, training, education and experience required by the firm. For a firm which needs personnel for implementing growth strategy, the process of recruitment from external sources must be planned well in advance. The problems of external recruitment consist of the relatively higher turnover of new recruits and the demoralising effect of outside recruitment on the existing work organisation.

Sources of Recruitment

A. Internal sources Internal sources refer to the employees currently working in an enterprise. As and when a post falls vacant, someone already working in the enterprise is transferred or promoted to it.

While a promotion or transfer does not result in any increase or decrease in the number and kinds of persons working in the enterprise, it may leave a significant effect on this working of the departments effected by it.

B. **External Sources**

(i) Advertisements, Personnel Consultants, and Jobbers and Contractors.

(ii) Employment Exchange and Educational Institutions.

(iii) Field Trips, Miscellaneous.

CHARACTERISTICS OF A GOOD TRAINING AND DEVELOPMENT POLICY

A good training policy must be based on the following principles:

(1) Relevance to Job Requirements. To be effective, a training programme must be related to the requirements of the job for which it is intended. For this, a thorough analysis of each job is essential.

(2) Allowance for Individual Difference. A good training programme should take into account the difference in ability, learning capacity, interests and temperamental and emotional make-up of trainees.

(3) Determination of Training Needs. Training needs of employees should be determined carefully and the methods chosen for the purpose should be effective.

(4) Management Support. Top managers should actively support all training programmes. It is in the nature of subordinates to look to their superiors for an indication on what to support and what to ignore. It is futile to expect subordinates to be serious about their training of their bosses themselves are indifferent about it.

(5) Suitable Incentives. There should be provision for suitable monetary and non-monetary incentives to motivate trainee, so that they take training seriously.

Compensation and Supplementary Benefits. Policies with regard to wage and salary administration and policy on supplementary benefits are vital components of personnel policy because it is mainly on the basis of satisfactory compensation schemes that company is able to attract and retain capable personnel. In the absence of sound policy with respect to the compensation structure, wages and salaries are likely to be based on personalised arbitrary decisions and thus fall short of the essential elements of adequacy and equity in compensation plans. A satisfactory policy frame is invariably conducive to high morale and minimum frictions among individuals and groups of employees. For, apart from the adequacy of the level of compensation, inequities in the pay structure happen to be the most common causes of dissatisfaction and grievances among employees.

The basic issues to be resolved while formulating the compensation policy are those relating to:

(a) Incentive pay;

(b) Recognition of relative efficiency of performance;

(c) The internal structure of compensation or internal alignment of pay for different job so as to ensure that pay rates are equitable;

(d) The level of pay and its adequacy.

PROMOTION POLICY

Promotion refers to the advancement of an employee to a higher job involving greater responsibility, more pay and better status. It is the movement of an employee to a position of better remuneration, higher status and greater responsibility. A there in crease in pay or working conditions without an increase in status and responsibility is called upgrading or dry promotion. Demotion is the opposite of promotion.

The policy of filling vacancies at higher levels through promotion of lower level employees has several advantages:

(a) Employees have an opportunity for improving their status and earnings. Promotion, therefore, improves the motivation and morale of employees.

(b) It improves the quality of performance. Reduction in waste and indiscipline results in lower costs. "The company that has no recognised promotion policy likely to have frustrated and restless employees as they have no opportunity for advancement."

(c) It creates sense of royalty among employees. By satisfying the basic urge for advancement, it reduces industrial disputes, labour turnover and absenteeism.

However, all higher level vacancies need not necessarily be filled through promotion. Sometimes, lower level staff may not be fit for promotion. Moreover, recruitment from outside brings new blood and independent thinking. The basic aim should be to obtain the best possible personnel irrespective of where from they come.

Basis of Promotion—Merit *vs.* Seniority

There are two bases of promotion, *i.e.*, seniority and merit. Employers generally favour merit, while employees and their unions prefer seniority as the basis of promotion.

Seniority means length of recognised service. It is counted from the date of joining the organisation or from the date of confirmation. Seniority can be calculated in several ways. It is lost due to certain events. *e.g.*, frequent absence from duty.

Seniority is the oldest and most widely used basis of promotion. Promotion on the basis of seniority is justified of following grounds:

(a) It is an objective basis. It prevents favouritism and arbitrary action as there is no room for discretion or prejudices.

(b) It is very simple and practicable as seniority can be measured easily and accurately.

(c) It reduces labour turnover as employees try to remain in the firm to accumulate seniority.

(d) Every employee has a definite idea at all times of his place in the group. He feels secured and develops a sense of loyalty to the organisation. Promotion based of seniority is reward for loyalty.

(e) Seniority is acceptable to trade unions and gives a feeling of satisfaction to employees.

(f) Length of service is an approximate measure of experience and ability.

If a man has been in service for a long time he ought to be better than a newcomer, unless he has been dodging work. Seniority also fits with the cultural expectations for social customs of India.

Seniority as the sole basis of promotion has, however the following demerits:

(a) Rules for the accumulation of seniority have to be laid down with particular reference to the impact of suspension, lay-off, strike, discharge, etc.

(b) Employees with longer service are not necessarily more compete to Seniority overvalues experience and premium on merit.

(c) Rigid adherence to seniority makes it difficult to recruit and retain capable personnel.

(d) It lowers the morale of ambitious and meritorious employees as they get no recognition. When less competent lose interest in efficiency.

(e) The quality and quantity of work suffers as employees try to stick around and do not make full use of their capabilities.

(f) Seniority pro des performing and inefficiency, as no differentiation is made between efficient and inefficient employees.

Advantages refers to the efficiency and ability of an employee. Promotion on the basis of merit has following advantages:

(a) It provides a powerful incentive to work hard and make continuous improvement in efficiency;

(b) Ambitious and hard working employees are duty rewarded. They feel satisfied and contributed maximum to the success of the organisation.

(c) There is an overall improvement in operations and the profit of the enterprise.

Merit has been criticised due to following limitations:

(a) Employees feel insecure and become discontented.

(b) The morale of employees is low when they find that their juniors are promoted before them it causes frustration and loss of interest and loyalty for the organisation. Moreover, merit does not indicate an employee's promotability. An individual may be quite competent for the present job, but his overall personality may not be suitable for higher positions.

Thus, neither absolute seniority nor exclusive merit is a sound basis of promotion. A sound promotion policy should be based on a judicious balance between the two. In practice, seniority is given more weightage but merit should also be given due consideration. None of the two should be exclusive criterion for promotion. Seniority can be the wedding factor when two persons are equally meritorious. Similarly, out the two equally senior employees the more competent one should promoted first. If senior-most employee is incompetent to do the job well junior employees with merit should be promoted.

Essentials of a Sound Promotion Policy. A sound systematic promotion policy should consist of the following:

(1) The report of each employee should be prepared by his supervisor but subject to the approval of the departmental head.

(2) Promotion policy should be based on job analysis to define job requirements. Employees should know clearly what is expected of them in higher jobs, so that they can prepare themselves for advancement

(3) Accurate and uptodate records of seniority and merit should be kept. All employees should be kept informed of their record and opening for promotion.

(4) Objective and systematic plans of performance appraisal should be set up to identify promotable employees. This is necessary to avoid unfairness in promotions.

(5) Lines of promotion should be clearly defined. For each job a schedule of jobs to which promotion can be made should be prepared.

(6) The basis of promotion should be clearly defined. The relative weight to be given to merit and seniority should be specified.

(7) The policy management regarding filling of vacancies through promotion or from outside should be clearly stated.

Industrial Relations Policy

The personnel policies and practices of a rum in many ways are influenced by the state of union-management relations. To what extent the basic philosophy of top management *vis-a-vis* their human resources is subordinated to the bargaining power of employee union depends upon the company's policy with regard to:

> The nature of relation with the union, recognition the support of the union organisation, the scope of collective bargaining and settlement of industrial disputes. Ideally, harmonious relation between management and employee union should develop on the basis of mutual co-operation. But company executive are often inclined to adopt a policy of belligerency toward union activities. This approach is born out of strong dislike and mistrust of the union by the executives, who

refuse to recognise the union as a bargaining agent, of when forced to negotiate, do it grudgingly with a horse-trading approach. With a hostile attitude to management toward the union, the relationship is inevitably vitiated by mutual suspicion, and there is increasing militancy on the part of union leaders.

Characteristics of a Good Transfer Policy

To be effective the transfer policy should possess the following characteristics:

(1) If a transfer is going to result in any change in the rate of remuneration this should be made sufficiently clear.

(2) It is quite likely that requests for transfer to the same job, or to the same shift are received from many employees. In such cases a decision should be taken in keeping with the predetermined policy.

(3) There should be accurate and complete job description of the jobs to which transfers are under consideration. Requirements as to training of the new jobs should be clearly laid down. Also the workers to be transferred should be clearly informed about the time during which they are supposed to adjust themselves to the requirements of their new jobs.

(4) How a transfer is going to affect the seniority of the person concerned should be spelt out in clear terms.

(5) If transfers become necessary because there is surplus of labour force in one department of unit and shortage in another it should be ensured that workers in their new positions are not given completely new kinds of jobs.

(6) Responsibility for recommending and approving transfer should be clearly defined.

(7) The departments or units within which transfers have to be made should be decided in advance.

Features of a Good Personnel Policy

Every enterprise should relate its personnel policy to the economic, legal, social and technological factors present in the society in which it operates. This means it has to keep on adjusting and adapting personnel policy to suit and change in these factors.

A good personnel policy should possess the following features:

(1) ***Proper Communication.*** It should be properly communicated to those for whom it is intended.

(2) ***Acceptability.*** It should enjoy acceptability among the people for whom it has been formulated.

(3) ***Intergative.*** It must fully take into account the differing amenities, capabilities, interests, desires, aspirations, beliefs and tempramental make-up of the people for whom it is intended.

(4) ***Uniformity.*** It should be uniformly applicable to all members and units of the enterprise.

(5) ***Flexibility.*** It should not be so rigid and inflexible that it can not be adjusted and adapted to changes in economic, legal, social and technological factors.

(6) ***Responsiveness to Prevailing Trends.*** Personnel policy should be adjusted to the prevailing norms and trends in ways. For example, if the current thinking is in favour of involving in the management process the policy should be against.

(7) ***Protection of the Interests of all Parties.*** It should take into account the interests of all parties associated with the enterprise, *i.e.*, workers entrepreneurs, consumers, government and the community.

(8) ***Precision and Certainty.*** It should be clear to the point and complete in every respect. It should not lead to varying and conflicting interpretations.

(9) ***Promotion of Enterprise Policies.*** It should fit into the basis of overall policies of the enterprise.

(10) ***Stability.*** Even though personnel policy has to be consistently adjusted and adapted to suit any changes in economic, legal, and technological factor, it should be reasonably stable and permanent.

Considerations in Procuring Long-term Finance

It has been observed that the management of a company can use different method for raising finance for different periods and purposes. The methods of financing can be classified, on the basis of the term for which the funds are required, into the following categories:

(i) ***For Long-term Requirements.*** Issue of shares, issues of debentures; Assistance from special industrial Finance Institutions; and ploughing back or reinvesting of retained earnings.

(ii) ***For Medium-term Requirements.*** Issue of preference shares; issues of debentures, assistance from Special Industrial Finance Institutions; receiving public deposits; and Borrowing from commercial banks.

(iii) ***For Short-term Requirements.*** Borrowing from commercial banks; trade credit; instalment credit; accounts receivable financing; and customer advance.

(A) Issue of Shares

A Issue of ownership securities of shares is the most important method of raising long-term finance for permanent investment in the companies. Funds raised from issue of shares provide a financial floor to the capital structure of a company. A share may be defined as unit of measure of shareholder's interest in the company. The share capital of company is divided into a large number of equal parts and each part is individually known as share. According to Section 86 of the Companies Act, 1956, a public company limited by shares can issue two types of ownership securities *viz.*, equity shares and preference shares. An independent private company can issue deffered shares as well.

Perefence Shares. Section 85 (1) of the Companies Act defines preference shares as those which carry preferential rights as to the payment of dividend at a fixed rate either free of or subject to income tax, and as to the repayment of capital. Thus, preference shareholders enjoy two preferential rights over the other category of shares. *Firstly*, they are entitled to receive a fixed rate of dividend out of the net profits of the company prior to declaration of dividend on equity shares. *Secondly*, the assets remaining after the payment of debts of the company under liquidation are rust appropriated of returning the capital contributed by the preference shareholders.

Preference shares may be classified into following categories:

(i) ***Convertible and Non-convertible Preference Share.*** If the preference shareholder's are given a right to convert their shares into equity shares with a fixed period of time, such shares will be known as convertible preference shares. The preference shares which cannot be converted into equity shares are known as non-convertible preference shares.

(ii) ***Redeemable and Irredeemable Preference Shares.*** Redeemable preference shares are those which in accordance with the terms of their issue, will be repaid on or after a certain date. The preference share which cannot be redeemed during the life time of the company are known as irredeemable preference shares.

(iii) ***Cumulative and Non-cumulative Preference Shares.*** The holders of cumulative preference shares are entitled to arrears of dividend on their shares to be paid out of the profits of subsequent years, if in any year the dividend on them cannot be paid. Thus, they are sure to receive dividend on the preference shares held by them for all the

years out of the earnings of the company. If in a particular year they are not paid the dividend, they will be paid such arrear in the next year before any dividend can be distributed among equity shareholders. But the dividend on non-cumulative shares does not, accumulate if dividend is not paid in any year.

(iv) ***Participating and Non-Participating Preference Shares.*** The holders of participating preference shares are entitled to a share in the surplus profits if they remain after paying dividend to preference shares and equity shares. Thus, participating shareholders obtain return on their investment in two forms: *(i)* fixed dividend; and *(ii)* share in surplus profits. The preference share which do not carry the right to share in the surplus profits are known non-participating, preference share.

(B) Equity Shares

Under the Companies Act, shares which are not preference shares are called equity shares. They are also called ordinary shares. Equity shares provide intial capital on permanent basis to the company. Equity shareholders are the real owners of the company and they bear the risk of business. They get dividend only after the dividend on preference shares is paid out of the profits of the company. At the time of winding up, equity capital can be paid back only after every claim including that of preference shareholders has been settled. Since equity shareholders bear higher risk, they also stand a chance of getting higher dividend if the company's earnings are higher.

Equity shareholders control the affairs of the companies as they have the voting right in the general body meeting of the company. They eject the board of directors of the company and frame policies of the company in general meeting.

(C) Issue of Debentures

Debentures are creditorship securities which provide funds to the company on loan basis rather than on capital basis. A debenture may be defined as an acknowledgment of a debt by a company. The debenture holders are entitled to periodical payment of interest as fixed rate and are also entitled to redemption of their debentures as per terms of debenture issue. The debentureholders are the creditors of the company. Their rights depend upon the type of debentures issued by the company A company may issue the following types of debentures:

(i) ***Convertible and Non-convertible Debentures.*** The convertible debentures can be converted into equity shares of the company after the expiry of specified period. But non-convertible debentures cannot be converted into equity shares. In the recent years, the practice of issuing debentures which are partially convertible into equity shares has gained momentum.

(ii) ***Redeemable and Irredeemable Debentures.*** In case of redeemable debentures, the companies reserve the right of paying off the principle on or after a particular date. In case of irredeemable or perpetual debentures, the company does not fix any date by which they should be redeemed and the holders of such securities cannot demand payment from the company so long as it is a going concern.

(iii) ***Registered and Bearer Debentures.*** In case of registerd debentures the name of the debenture holder is entered in the debenture certificates and books of the company. They can be transferred by filling in the transfer deed. But bearer debentures can be transferred by mere delivery without any notice to the company. Debenture coupons are annexed with the such debenture certificates. The bearers of the debenture can fill in the coupons and claim interest after sending them to the company. But in case of registered debentures, the company pays interest to the registered debenture holders.

(iv) ***Secured and Unsecured Debentures.*** Secured debentures represent the fixed or floating charge on the assets of the

company. When the particular assets are charged by way of security, it is known, as fixed change. Such debentures are also known as mortgage debentures. When the charge is created assets which are of general nature like stock, it is called a floating charge. Under floating change, the company is free to deal with the property forming the subject matter of the charge until, the said charge become fixes default of company in paying the interest of some other event stipulated in the deed of charge. Unsecured debentures, also known as simple or naked debentures, do not carry any charge or security on the assets of the company.

RETAINED EARNINGS

The use of retained earnings as a method of 'self financing' is commonly used by the established companies. It is also known as 'ploughing back of profits'. Under this method, the undistributed or retained profits of the company are used to finance the requirements of the company. The main feature of this method is that it is an internal source of finance. Every good company does not distribute its entire earnings in the form of dividend but rather retains a part of it every year. Such a policy helps the company to build up reserves which can be used for financing expansion programmes.

The practice of 'ploughing back of profits' is influenced by many factors. *Firstly*, it depends upon the net profits of the company. If a company has earned huge profits in a particular year—its capacity to retain profits will be higher. *Secondly*, dividend policy of the company determines the extent to which profits can be retained for ploughing back. For instance, if a company follows a policy of declaring a consistent rate of dividend every year, it will not be able to retain much if in a particular year it earns less profits. *Lastly*, the age of the company affects the policy of ploughing back on profits. New companies generally do not retain much profits because of their desire to satisfy their shareholders. But an older company can declare less profits for distribution to shareholders and retain the major portion of its profit for reinvestment in the business.

Determinants of Retained Earnings. Once the importance of retained earnings is realised, it may interesting to know the extent to which a company can go or it. The amount of retained earnings is determined by a multiplicity of factors the most important among which are earnings of the company tax laws of the Government and dividend policy of the company.

(i) ***Earnings of the Company.*** The amount of profits earned by company is a basic factor determining the amount of retained earnings, greater the amount of profits, greater can be retained earnings. Clearly no retained earnings are possible if there are no profits. The amount of profits that a company would earn, is in turn, dependent on a numbers of factors including the demand and supply competition and price positions in the market, cost of production and distribution etc. Given the amount of profits, the size of a company's retained earnings should be decided in the light of purposes for which it is needed. The purposes may be to meet any known liability which may arise in future, to finance growth and expansion, to keep dividends at a uniform lever and to meet unknown contigencies or losses in future.

(ii) ***Dividend Policy.*** If a company adopts a generous dividend policy, it would have lesser amount of net earnings left for retention of earnings. On the other hand, a conservative dividend policy is conducive to good accumulation of corporate savings. Although management is not legally bound to declare any dividend on company's share capital certain amount of dividend might become necessary due to naked conditions. A highly conservative policy of dividend can create feeling in the investor's mind that equity investment is not attractive. Besides, the prices of shares of a company following this policy may go down. On the other hand, a liberal dividend policy may not allow the company to carry out its expansion programme for want of sufficient funds, especially when external financing is

difficult and costlier. The proper policy on retention of earnings would be one which strikes a balance between the two-fold objectives of enterprise growth, shareholder's satisfaction.

(iii) ***Tax Laws.*** The volume and rate of taxation on corporate income also influences the amount of retained earnings. In spite of huge profits that a company may earn its net earnings may be very little of the volume and the rate of taxation is very high. In our country the taxation policy of the Government hardly gives any encouragement for retention of earnings. A high rate of taxation has been preventing the business undertakings from ploughing back a desirable amount of profits for their growth and development. There is an urgent need to change the taxation policy of the Government and give positive incentive for corporate savings.

Utility of Retained Earnings

Retention of earnings is of great utility to a company primarily because it is a good source of finance. Besides, the retained earnings are useful for the shareholders and the society at large. We shall discuss the utility of retained earnings from these three angles:

(i) ***Utility from Shareholder's Viewpoint.*** If a company can benefit by the retention of earnings, the shareholder's can also gain by this practice in the long run since they are the owners of the company. In fact, retained earnings invested in profitable projects increase the value of company and ultimately the wealth of its shareholders. The market value of shares of such a company goes up. The shareholders can take advantage of high share prices by selling their holdings in the open market. Alternatively, they can retain their shares and benefit in the long run by the growth of the company.

(ii) ***Utility from Company's Angle.*** The retained earnings are of great importance to a company. The retained income or reserve acts as a shock-absorber A concern with large reserves is well armed to fight out depressions and seasonal changes in demand. Secondly, retained earnings enable a company to follow a stable dividend policy and add to its credit in the market. Thirdly, the company can finance the different types of projects for expansion and modernisation through retained earnings without having to borrow from outside. Internal financing is very economical method of financing. If the company were to issue debentures or raise a loan for this purpose, it will naturally have to pay a fixed rate of interest irrespective of profit, and return the amount after some time. Similarly, if more shares are issued, dividend will have to be paid on them. But if the reserves are used for this purpose, no such obligation is incurred. Fourthly, the undistributed income can be used for discharging such obligations as the redemption or retirement of debentures and others debts. Lastly, the reserves can also be utlised to maintain company's operating efficiency when the company is not able to make enough provision for depreciation and obsolescence due to which its efficiency is being adversely affected.

Dangers of Excessive Retained Earnings

Though a reasonable amount of retained earnings is useful for enterprise growth, excessive retained earnings may prove to be dangerous owing to various reasons:

(i) All over-enthusiastic policy of retained earnings may create dissatisfaction among the shareholders. They may be led to think that the directors are ignoring or even damaging their interest by paying a rate of dividend lower than that can be paid out of the available profits.

(ii) If the accumulated reserves are used for the issue of bonus shares, it may results in over-capitalisation later on.

(iii) The management may not always use the retained profits to the advantage of the shareholders *e.g.*, the funds may be invested in other concerns under the same management, bringing little gain to the shareholders.

(iv) By continuous ploughing back of profits over a long period of time, company may grow into a monopoly. This is more likely to happen when other companies find it difficult to raise funds from the market while an existing concern continues to grow on the strength of its internal resources.

(v) It may give the management an opportunity to manipulate the share values. By withholding profits, lower dividends may be declared. When the share values fall in the market, the management. Play take them up at reduced prices. The rate of dividend may, then be increased out of the past profits and the management may dispose of the shares at a profit.

(vi) Prof. Pigou thinks that excessive ploughing back entails social waste, because money is not made available to those who can use it to the best advantage of the community, but is retained by those who have earned it.

From the foregoing discussion, it is clear that the retention of earnings is a policy of undoubted merit for financing the long-term requirements of business enterprise. But it is necessary that the management follows a bold, though cautious, policy in this regard.

FACTORS AFFECTING CAPITAL GEARING

The following factors must be considered while determining the ratio of different securities or sources of capital:

(1) Cost of Financing. The cost of raising finance by tapping various, sources of finance should be estimated carefully to decide which of the alternatives is the cheapest. Prevailing rate of interest, rate of return expected by the prospective investors and administrative expenses are the various factors which affect the cost of financing. Generally, cost of financing by issuing debentures and preference shares is less particularly when the equity shareholders expect higher dividend and the other companies in the field are paying higher dividends.

(2) ***Flexibility of Financial Structure.*** A good financial structure should be flexible enough to have scope for expansion or contraction of capitalisation whenever the need arises. In order to bring flexibly , those securities should be issued which can be paid off after a certain number of years. Equity shares cannot be paid off during the life time of a company. But redeemable preference shares and debentures and public deposits can be paid off whenever the company feels necessary. They provide elasticity in the financial plans. They are generally not issued in the initial states of the company since they involve payment of fixed rate of dividend or interest every year. Fixed income securities are issued when the company is financially sound and it feels that it will be able to earn more than rate the interest or dividend to be given on such securities.

(3) ***Exercise of Control.*** The control of a company is entrusted to the board of directors elected by the equity shareholder. The equity shareholders have the voting right which can be exercised in the general body meeting to direct the board of directors of the company. But the preference shareholders possess veryfunited voting right and the debenture holders have no voting right. If the board of director and shareholders of a company wish to retain control over the company in their hands, they may allow to issue equity share to public. In such a case, more funds can be raised by issuing preference shares and debentures.

(4) ***Trading on Equity.*** The word 'equity' refers to the ownership of the company. Trading on equity means taking advantage of equity share capital to borrowed funds on reasonable basis. It refers to the additional profits that

equity shares earn because of issuing other form of securities, *viz.*, preference share and debentures. It is based on the premise that if the rate of interest on borrowed capital and the rate of dividend on preference capital which are fixed, is lower than the general rate of the company's earning, the equity shareholders will get advantage in the form of additional profits. Thus, by adopting a judicious mix of debentures and preference shares with equity shares income on equity share can be maximised.

Trading on equity is an arrangement under which the financial management raises funds by issuing securities which carry a fixed rate of interest of dividend, which is less than the average earnings of the company, to increase the return on equity shares. If a company can earn much more than the rate of fixed dividend or interest, excess earnings will go to the equity shareholders and they would thereby earn a higher dividend per share than they would have without the use of gearing of capital structure.

Trading on equity has three limitations. Firstly when the earnings of the company are not sufficient to pay fixed return on all types of securities, the dividend rate is unduly depressed rather than accelerated. Secondly the company must have sufficient assets to offer them as security to lenders in order to borrow on a large scale. Lastly, trading on equity is profitable for company which is likely to have regular, stable and certain earnings.

(5) ***Types of Investors.*** The shape of capital structure is also influenced by the likings of the potential investors. Therefore, securities of different kinds and varying denominations are issued to meet the requirements of the prospective inverstors. Equity shares are issued to attract the people who have the desire to have a say in the management of the company. Debentures and preference shares are issued to attract those people who prefer security of investment and certainty of return on investment.

(6) ***Period of Financing.*** When funds are required for permanent investment in a company, equity share capital is preferred. But when funds are required to finance expansion programme and the management of the company feels that it will be able to redeem the funds within the life time of the company, it may issue redeemable preference shares and debentures.

(7) ***Capital Market Conditions.*** The conditions prevailing in the capital market also influence the determination of the securities to be issued. For instance, during depression, people do not like to take risk and so are not interested in equity shares. But during boom, investors are ready to take risk and invest in equity shares. Therefore, debentures and preference shares, which carry fixed rates of return may be marketed more easily during depression.

(8) ***Statutory Requirements.*** The structure of capital of a company is also influenced by the requirements of the states applicable to it. For instance, banking companies have been prohibited by the Banking Regulation Act to issue any type of securities except equity shares.

FINANCIAL POLICY

Financial aspect of business activities deals primarily with raising, administering and distribution of funds by the organisation for the purpose of business operations. Thus financial policies have three major dimensions:

(i) determination of the total amount of funds to be used by the organisation;

(ii) determination of what specific assets the organisation should acquire, or allocation of funds among various assets in an efficient manner; and

(iii) determination of how the needed funds should be financed or obtaining the best mix of financing with relation to the overall valuation of the organisation. Accounting policies will be established to deal with questions as how to treat inventories, which accounts to capitalise, and how to treat expenses and cost. These policies affect the organisation's appearance of success or failure. Thus major policy decisions in the area of finance and accounting are as follows:

(a) ***Level of Dividend Payment.*** Dividend payment history the stability of earnings; rate of growth and profit levels, liquidity positions, ability to borrow, debt contract restrictions, legal constraints.

(b) ***Capital Structure.*** Nature of business operations, nature of capital market, cash generation capacity, tax savings.

(c) ***Level of Working Capital.*** Uncertainty of cash receipts and disbursements, borrowing capacity, efficiency of cash management, volume of credit sales, reasonability of sales, credit policies.

The basic criterion in financial policies is that the funds needed are available at the right time and at the lowest possible costs.

DIVIDEND POLICY DECISIONS

Dividends represent that part of firm's earnings which is paid out to the shareholders. Dividend policy determines the division of earnings between payments to stockholders and reinvestment in the firm. Thus a proper dividend policy is tied up with the retained earnings policy. The dividend policies of companies are of great importance because they may affect thousand of shareholders just in one company. Dividend policy also influences the size of internal financing by a fifth The guiding principle in framing a company's dividend policy should be the maximisation of shareholder's wealth. The optimum dividend policy would be one which maximises the market value per share. However, some financial experts hold the view that dividend decision has the value of the firm. Therefore, we shall first examine the relationship between dividend decision and the value of the firm.

Relevance of Dividend Decision

There are two key theoretical view on whether or not the dividend decision is really significant influencing the value of the firm as measured by the, market price of its shares. According to one view, the dividends are irrelevant because the amount of dividends paid does not affect the value of the firm. The second viewpoint is that dividends are relevant and that the amount of dividend paid does have an impact on the value of the firm. The supporters of the first view argue that the value of a firm is determined by the earning power of the projects in which it has invested its money and not by the amount of dividends paid. Dividend decision only splits the firm's income between dividends and retained earnings. It is the investment policy of the firm which will determine its income level and, in turn, the net earnings available for dividend distribution. Given the investment decision therefore, the dividend decision has no effect on the value of the firm. If there are good investment opportunities, the firm will retain the earnings for financing them, resulting in long-term capital gains to shareholders. On the other hand, the firm will distribute its earnings to shareholders if it does not foresee adequate investment opportunities. Investors are indifferent to returns in the form of dividends or of capital gains.

Objectives of Dividend Policy

The firm's dividend policy represents a plan of action to be followed whenever the dividend decision must be made. Once the relevance of dividend decision is realised, the management should frame a dividend policy that best fulfils the find's overall objectives. The two major objectives possibly shaping the dividend policy of any rum are: maximisation of the shareholder's wealth the provision of sufficient financing. These object ve are interrelated and not mutually exclusive Obviously, shareholder's wealth can not be maximised if there are insufficient funds to finance profitable projects; a provision of source of funds is meaningless if these funds are not used for shareholder's interest. These two objectives are explained below:

(a) ***Wealth Maximisation.*** The dividend policy of a rum should aim at the general objective of maximising the owner's wealth. It should be formulated not merely to increase the share price in the short run, but to maximise the owner's wealth in the long-run. Of course, the shareholders may not fully appreciate such a dividend policy and may prefer immediate dividends to future dividends and capital gains since they do not have a perfect knowledge of the implications of certain dividend policies in the light of market forces. As a result, the share prices may drop in the market. It is the responsibility of the firm management to make the owners aware of the objectives and implications of dividend policy, so that the market reaction is favourable.

(b) ***Providing for Sufficient Financing.*** Another important objective of dividend policy is the provision for sufficient funds without which profitable investment opportunities cannot be carried out. In the absence of adequate finance, wealth maximisation objective would remain a sheer dream. One of the important sources of long-term financing is retained earnings. But larger the amount of dividend, lesser would be the retained earnings. Therefore, the management has to decide what shall be the proper ratio between dividends and retained earnings so that the twin objective of short-term interest of the shareholders and long-term gain expansion are realised. The firm can also go for external financing. But the market forces may not be favourable for that and internal financing may be the easiest and the least costly choice. The ultimate decision in this regard is dependent on a multiplicity of factors which we shall now study.

Factors Affecting Dividend Policy

The dividend policy of rum should be formulated after taking into acccunt the objective of wealth maximisation and provision for internal financing and a number of other relevant factors. Some of the determinants of dividend policy are as follows:

(a) ***Legal Rules.*** The various provisions of law imposed by the Government regulating corporate dividend provide the framework within which a company can formulate its dividend policy. Subject to certain statutory restrictions and the provisions of Article of Association, the directors are free to declare any amount of dividends. But there is a basic legal constraint that the dividend must not be paid out of capital, which in other words, means that it should only be paid out of profits. This rule is meant for protecting the interest of creditors and preference shareholders who may suffer because of reduced equity capital if the dividends are paid out of it. However, if the current year's profit are inadequate, the company can declare dividends· out of accumulated profits (or retained earnings) in accordance with the rules framed by the Central Government. The dividends should be paid in cash, though a company is not prohibited from capitalising its profits or reserves (retained earnings) for the purpose of issuing fully paid bonus shares. A company is prohibited from paying dividends while it is insolvent, *i.e.*, when its liabilities exceed the assets or when it is unable to pay its bills. Within these legal boundaries, however, the dividend policy is primarily influenced by financial economic factors.

(b) ***Liquidity Position.*** Another restriction on the payment of dividends is the liquidity position of firm determined by the level of its liquid assets including cash and marketable securities. Quite possible, the firm may have a substantial amount of earnings to declare dividend, but may not have a substantial amount of earnings to declare dividend. This situation may exist, for example, when a firm declares dividends out of retained earnings which are not held as cash and have been invested in plant and equipment, inventories and other assets. A growing firm usually has a pressing need for funds. In such a situation, the firm may choose not to pay any cash dividends. Of course, it is possible for the firm to borrow funds to pay dividends, but this may be a costlier alternative.

(c) ***Contractual Restrictions.*** Often the firm's ability to pay cash dividend is restricted by certain specific conditions in loan when the finances are raised from external sources. Generally, conditions prohibit the firm from paying cash dividends until a certain level of earnings has been achieved or limit the amount of dividends paid to a certain amount of percentage of earnings. Such restrictions are imposed by creditors to protect themselves from possible insolvency of the firm in case its cash position is weakened by the payment of dividends. The financial manager must keep in mind various contractual requirements while formulating the dividends policy. If these requirements are violated, the creditors may withdraw their money from the firm.

(d) ***Desires of Shareholders.*** Directors of company are not legally bound to declare dividends. But shareholders are the real owners of the company and they appoint the directors to act as their true representatives. Moreover, the response of shareholders to the firm's dividend policy facts the market price of share which, in turn, determines the value of the firm. Therefore, the directors should give due weightage to the desires of shareholders. The shareholders may prefer dividends to Capital gains if they have tax advantage by such a decision or they want to use the dividend receipt in certain-personal investment channels-other than those offered by the Company.

(e) ***Growth Prospects or Investment Opportunities.*** Growth prospects or investment opportunities is another important determinant of the dividend policy. The management of successful enterprise would like to expand its scale of operations and try to ensure the growth of the firm. But a growing firm needs an increasing amount of financial resources to invest in the profitable ventures. Since external financing may be costlier, a growing firm may decide to depend heavily on internal financing through retained earnings. Such a firm is likely to payout a very small percentage of its earnings as dividends.

(f) ***Access to Capital Markets.*** A large, well-established firm with a fair record of profitability and stability of earnings will have easy access to capital market and will face little problem in raising finance through external sources. On the other hand, a small firm would attract less investors since they may consider that their investment in such a firm would be risky. As a result, a small firm may not be able to pay much dividend as it must retain more of its earnings to finance its operations, whereas well-established concern can afford to pay a higher rate of dividend since it can easily meet its financial requirements through external sources. Access to capital market, therefore, has a significant impact on the dividend policy.

(g) ***Control.*** The management may be interested that existing shareholders should continue to retain control over the company. In that case, it would not be wise to raise finances through issue of fresh shares lest the control is diluted into the hands of new shareholders. Besides, raising additional finances through the issue of debenture or other forms of borrowing can increase the financial risk of the firm. Under the circumstances, the firm may rely more on internal financing or retained earnings and is likely to have lesser dividend pay out ratio.

(h) ***Profit Rate and Stability of Earning.*** Profit position of a firm is a very important factor that influences its dividend policy. A firm with a large rate of return on its investment will have larger profits and therefore, can pay more dividends to its shareholders as compared to a firm with lesser returns. Moreover, if the earnings are relatively stable and do not fluctuate time and again, a firm can predict what will be its future earnings. The unstable firm is not able to determine what will be its actual future earnings and, therefore, it is likely to plough back more profits to meet adverse future conditions.

(i) ***Inflation.*** Inflation has an indirect impact on the dividend policy of a firm in the sense that it increases the replacement cost of assets which are being depreciated every year at the book value. Funds generated from providing depreciation may be insufficient to meet the rising cost of assets which might become obsolete and have to be replaced in future. Consequently, to maintain the earning power of the firm the management should decide to reduce the rate of dividend and increase the proportion of retained earnings during a period of inflation. In short, it is useful for every firm to establish a general policy with respect to the payment for dividends to its shareholders. An appropriate dividend policy must be shaped by multiplicity of considerations including legal and contractual constraints, growth requirements and financial position of the firm, the interest of owners, and market considerations. The aim of the financial manager should be to bring about a balance among various factors.

TYPES OF DIVIDEND POLICY

There are several patterns of dividend payments and therefore, there may be a number of possible dividend policies. Three of the more commonly used dividend policies are : Constant dividend per share, constant percentage of net earnings and small but regular dividend per share plus extra dividend.

(a) ***Constant Dividend Per Share.*** Many companies have attempted to establish a reputation for payment of annual dividends of a regular and fixed amount per share, irrespective of business conditions of profitable or unprofitable operations. Some companies that have a policy of constant dividend per share change it occasionally to a higher or lower depending on the changed conditions, but such shifts are infrequent and usually are followed for several years before another new rate is established. It is easy to maintain this policy when the earning of company are stable. However, if these are side fluctuations in the earnings pattern, it is difficult to continue with such a policy.

(b) ***Constant Percentage of Earnings.*** Some companies follow the policy of declaring a certain percentage of earnings in the form of dividends and retaining the rest as a reinvestment of earnings. With this policy the amount of dividend per share will not be fixed but win fluctuate in direct proportion to earnings. For instance, the board of directors may decide that one-half of the earnings should be distributed each year and the remainder should be retained. Management would like this type of dividend policy because dividend are linked with the earning, power of the company more earning more dividend less earnings less divided. A company is automatically able to provide for certain amount of retained earnings in profitable years as per this dividend policy.

(c) ***Small but Regular Dividend Per Share Plus Extra Dividend.*** This dividend policy is a variation of the constant dividend per share policy. Under this policy, the regular fixed dividends per share are board of directors announces an extra dividend the share as special distribution in the periods when earnings are higher than normal. This policy is particularly suitable for those companies that experience cyclical shift in earnings. The policy has the credit of maintaining shareholders confidence in the company by regular dividend payment without giving them false hopes of increased dividends every year but giving them due share of the additional profits in the periods of prosperity.

FINANCIAL SOURCES IN A BUSINESS

Every company requires funds for investment in the form of fixed capital and working capital. While estimating the need for funds, the period for which they are required is also to be ascertained. Funds may be required for long-term, for medium-term and for short-term period. It is the period of finance which determines the source or sources of finance to be tapped and the method of financing to be used. The term 'source' implies, the agencies from which funds are procured and the method of raising finance is linked with period for which funds are required and it deals with the mode of raising finance.

Sources. According to the length of the period for which funds are required, sources of raising finance may be classified as follows:

(a) ***Long-term Finance.*** It is required for investment fixed assets like land, building, plant and machinery, and for financing extension programmes. Long-term funds are raised for a minimum period of 10 years. The following are the sources of long-term financing: *(i)* shareholders; *(ii)* debenture holders; *(iii)* financial institutions; and *(iv)* retained earnings.

(b) ***Medium-term Finance.*** It is required for investment is working capital and for repayment of assets. It is raised for a period ranging from more than one year and less than ten years. The following are the sources of medium-term financing: *(i)* debentureholders; *(ii)* financial institutions; *(iii)* public deposits, and *(iv)* commercial banks.

(c) ***Short-term Finance.*** It is required for meeting the short-term needs of working capital. Its period is 12 months or less than 12 months and it can be raised from the following sources: *(i)* public deposits; *(ii)* trade credits; and *(iii)* commercial banks.

Methods. It has been observed that the management of a company can use different methods for raising finance for different periods and purposes. The methods of financing can be classified, on the basis of the term for which the funds are required, into the following categories:

(i) For Long-term Requirements

(a) Issue of shares

(b) Issue of debentures

(c) Assistance from special industrial Finance Institutions

(d) Ploughing back-up reinvesting of retained earnings.

(ii) For Medium-term Requirements

(a) Issue of preference shares

(b) Issue of debentures

(c) Assistance from Special Industrial Finance Institution

(d) Receiving public deposits

(e) Borrowing from commercial banks.

(iii) For Short-term Requirements

(a) Borrowing from commercial banks

(b) Trade credit

(c) Instalment credit

(d) Accounts receivable financing

(e) Customer advance.

ISSUE OF SHARES

Issue of ownership securities of shares is the most important method of raising long-term finance for permanent investment in the companies. Funds raised from issue of shares provide a financial floor to the capital structure of a company. A share may be defined as a unit of measure of a shareholder's interest in the company. The share capital of a company is divided into a large number of equal parts and each part is individually known as a share. According to Section 86 of the Companies Act, 1956, a public company limited by shares can issue two types of ownership securities, *viz.*, equity shares and preference shares. An independent private company can issue deferred shares as well.

PREFERENCE SHARES

The Companies Act defines preference shares as those which carry preferential rights as to the payment of dividend at a fixed rate either free of or subject so income tax, and as to the repayment of capital. Thus, preference shareholders enjoy two preferential rights over the other category of shares. Firstly, they are entitled to receive a fixed rate of dividend out of the net profits of the company prior to declaration of dividend on equity shares. Secondly, the assets remaining after the payments of debts of the company under liquidation are first appropriated for returning the capital contributed by the preference shareholders.

Preference shares may be classified into following categories:

(a) ***Cumulative and Non-cumulative Preference Shares.*** The holders of cumulative preference shares are entitled to arrears of dividend on their shares to be paid out of the profits of subsequent years, if in any years the dividend on them cannot be paid. Thus, they are sure to receive dividend on the preference shares held by them for all the years out of the earnings of the company. If, in a particular year they are not paid the dividend, they will be paid such arrear in the next year before any dividend can be distributed among equity shareholders.

(b) ***Participating and Non-Participating Preference Shares.*** The holders of participating preference shares are entitled to a share in the surplus profits if they remain after paying dividend to preference shares and equity shares. Thus, participating shareholders obtain return on their investment in two forms: *(i)* fixed dividend; and *(ii)* share in surplus profits.

(c) ***Redeemable and Irredeemable Preference Shares.*** Redeemable preference shares are those which in accordance with the terms of their issue, will be repaid on or after a certain date. The preference shares which cannot be redeemed during the life time of the company are known as irredeemable preference shares.

(d) ***Convertible and Non-convertible Preference Shares.*** If the preference shareholders are given a right to convert their share into equity shares within a fixed period of time,

such share will be known as convertible preference shares. The preference shares, which cannot, be converted into equity shares are known as non-convertible preference shares.

Evaluation. The issue of preference shares has the following benefits:

(a) The management can retain control over the company by issuing preference shares to outsiders because the preference shareholders have only restricted voting rights.

(b) Preference shareholders are entitled to a fixed rate of dividend which enable the equity shareholders to get higher dividend.

(c) The preference shares attract funds from those investors who prefer safety of their investments and a fixed rate of return on their investment.

(d) Preference shares do not impose heavy burden on the company because they carry a fixed rate of dividend.

(e) A company can raise finance for a long-term without creating any charge over its assets.

(f) Redeemable preference shares may be issued to bring flexibility in the financial structure of the company as they can be redeemed whenever it is desired.

There are certain limitations of raising funds by issuing preference shares. The investors may not like these shares because preference shareholders have restrictedly noting rights only. The issue of preference shares is costlier than the issue of debentures because these shares have to be given a rate of dividend which is higher than the prevailing rate of interest on debentures.

EQUITY SHARES

Under the Companies Act; shares which are not preference shares are called equity shares. They are also called ordinary shares.

Equity shares provide initial capital on permanent basis to the company. Equity shareholders are the real owners of the company and they bear the risk of business, They get dividend only after the devidend on preference shares is paid out of the profits of winding up, equity capital can be paid back only after every claim including that of preference shareholders has been settled.

Equity share capital has certain drawbacks also. If the equity shares are issued excessively, it may result in over-capitalisation which may be difficult to cure. In such a case, the company will also lose the benefit of trading on equity. Since the control of the company is with the equity shareholders.

ISSUE OF DEBENTURES

Debentures are creditorship securities which provide funds to the company on loan basis rather than on capital basis. A debenture may be defined as an acknowledgement of a debt by a company. The debentureholders are entitled to periodical payment of interest at a fixed rate and are also entitled to redemption of their debentures as per terms of debenture issue. The debentureholders are the creditors of the company. Their rights depend upon the type of debentures issued by the company. A company may issue the following types of debentures:

(a) ***Secured and Unsecured Debentures.*** Secured debentures represent the fixed or floating charge on the assets of the company. When the particular assets are charged by way of security; it is known as fixed charge. Such debentures are also known, as mortgage debentures. When the charge is created assets which are of general nature like stock, it is called a floating charge. Under floating charge, the company is free to deal with the property forming the subject-matter of the charge until the said charge becomes fixed by default of company in paying the interest or some other event stipulated in the deed of charge.

(b) ***Redeemable and Irredeemable Debentures.*** In case of redeemable debentures, the companies reserve the right of

paying off the principal on or after a particular date. In case of ill irredeemable or perpetual debentures, the company does not fix any date by which they should be redeemed and the holders of such securities cannot demand payment from the company so long as it is a going concern.

(c) ***Registered and Bearer Debentures.*** In case of registered debentures, the name of the debenture holder is entered in the debenture certificates and books of the company. They can be transferred by filling in the transfer deed. But bearer debentures cash be transferred by mere delivery without any notice to the company. Debenture coupons are annexed with such debenture certificates. The bearers of the debentures can fill in the coupons and claim interest after sending them to the company.

(d) ***Convertible and Non-convertible Debentures.*** The convertible debentures can be converted into equity shares of the company after the expiry of a specified period. But non-convertible debentures cannot be converted into equity shares.

❒

8

Corporate Structure

THE concept of corporate planning has in recent years gained wide currency in management literature. Its connotation is somewhat overlapping with the concept of strategic planning. It is, therefore, necessary that the scope of corporate planning and strategic planning should be clearly understood.

Simply stated, corporate planning is comprehensive planning process which involves continued formulation of objectives and the guidance of affairs towards their attainment. It is a systematic and disciplined exercise designed to help indentification of the objectives of an organisation or corporate body, determination of appropriate targets, and formulation of practical plans by which the objective could be achieved. It is undertaken by higher management for the firm as whole on a continuous basis for making entrepreneurial decisions systematically and with the best possible knowledge of their probable outcome and effects, organising systematically the efforts and resources needed to carry out the decisions, and measuring the results of these decisions against the expectations through systematic feedback.

The object of corporate planning is to identify new areas of investment and marketing. Initiating new projects, new courses of action, and analysing past experience are the subject-matter of corporate planning. Thus, it implies *(a)* the imposition of a planning discipline on the present operations of the business, and *(b)* a reappraisal of the business and of the direction in which it should be heading. The essence of corporate planning lies in the application of the company's resources and competencies to the most profitable uses. Innovation is the core of such planning. At the same time it ensures that managers are continually measuring their performance against the company's long-term profit and market objectives, evaluating alternative methods of reaching the goals, and keeping in touch with changes in the market and in technology.

The comprehensive nature of the corporate planning process lies in that operational planning, project planning and strategic planning are its constituents. These are now examined as follows.

It is essential for every business firm to manage its ongoing operations efficiently to keep the business afloat in the market with which it is familiar. Operational planning is necessary so as to ensure that changes in the market situation for the existing product line do not adversely affect the earnings for the firm. Thus, operational planning involves study of the market conditions for the existing range of products to maintain and improve the position of the firm in the face of competition. It is essentially a short-term exercise and deals with the existing product, market and facilities. The degree of uncertainty in operational planning is of a low order; the time span of discretion is short; choice of alternatives is relatively simple. But the firm can ill afford to ignore long-term changes in the product markets. It has to look for new markets for the existing product, develop new products, create a market for the same, and utilise the existing facilities and expertise to meet new requirements. Considerations such as these characterise project planning, which is a forward looking exercise concerned with new markets, new products and new facilities. Project planning is, therefore, to deal with a greater degree of uncertainty, and demands a high order of judgment on the part of strategist due to the risks involved.

Strategic planning refers to the formulation of a unified, comprehensive and integrated plan aimed at relating the strategic advantages of the firm to the challenges of the environment. It is ' concerned with appraising the environment in relation to the company, identifying the strategies to obtain sanction for one of the alternatives to be interpreted and communicated in an operationally useful manner. Thus, strategic planning provides the framework within which future activities of the company are expected to be carried out. Compared with project planning, the time span of discretion in strategic planning is much longer, the degree of uncertainty and corresponding risks involved are much greater, and judgment to be exercised is of more importance.

In asmuch as strategic planning detemines the future direction of a company, corporate planning is essentially based on strategic planning, and at the same time takes care of project planning and operational planning. Thus, corporate planning is described as a formal systematic managerial process, organised by responsibility, time and information, to ensure that operational planning, project planning and strategic planning are carried out regularly to enable top management to direct and control the future of the enterprise. It follows that corporate planning is not synonymous with long-range planning. Corporate planning is concerned with determination of objectives and developing means to achieve the objectives. It may encompass both short periods as well as long periods. The time span depends on how far ahead a company wants to forecast and to plan, which, in turn, depends upon the nature of business that the company wants to be in and commitment of resources required for it. For instance, in the modern heavy engineering industry, commitment of resources is generally required for a fairly long period-10, 15 or 20 years.

Thus corporate planning in an engineering enterprise will involve long-term considerations regarding market demand, technology and such other factors. It will have a short time horizon in the case of garment industry. Long-range planning, however, necessarily, connotes planning with a long-term horizon in view, generally five years or more. Corporate planning in capital-intensive industries is always associated with long-range planning. Besides, corporate planning is concerned with the exisiting products in existing markets as well as new products and new markets.

Strategic Planning and Operational Planning

When comprehensive corporate planning is divided into strategic and operational planning, the sphere of activities, is defined on the basis of their objectives and scope in the total management process.

From this point of view, the examples of strategic planning in an organisation may be: planned growth rate in sales, consideration of how much growth is to be achieved by internal development as opposed to mergers and acquisitions; planned diversification by technologies, types of products, customers and geographical areas; comparatively important planning activities in the areas of organising, staffing, finance, etc. which affect all major functions. As against strategic planning, operational planning can be defined as follows:

Operational planning is the process of deciding the most effective use of the resources already allocated and to develop a control mechanism to assure effective implementation of the actions so that organisational objectives are achieved.

Operational planning taken in this way may include: adjustment of production, marketing and financial capacity of the organisation to the expected level of operations, in both the short term and long term; increasing the effciency of operating activities through analysing past performance, budgeting future costs, developing control over costs and efficiency; programming the comprehensive and specific details of future short term operations. On the basis of the explanation of strategic and operational planning, following is the distinction between strategic planning & operational planning:

(1) The type of envirnoment between two types of planning is different. Strategic planning takes into account the external environment and tries to relate the organisation with it. It usually encampasses all the functional areas of the organisation and is effected within the existing and long term framework of economic, social, technical and political factors. Operational planning focusses on internal organisation environment so as to make the effective us given resources.

2. Strategic planning is usually conducted by top level management and other specified planning staff in the organisation. At this level people can take overall view of the organisation and have necessary capability to relate the organisation with the external environment. Operational planning is usually spread over a wide range within the organisation and is generally performed by operating

managers with the help of the subordinate staff. Since two planning groups are widely separated in the organisation, some incompatibility may exist between two types of planning. Therefore, there is need for integrating these two in order to have better planning effects.

3. Strategic planning guides the choice among the broad directions in which the organisation seeks to move and cope the general planned allocations of its managerial, financial physical resources over future specified period of time. Operational planning, on the other hand, focusses on the ways and means by which each of the individual functions may be programmted so that progress may be made towards the attainment of organisational objectives. In performing a function, operational planning puts questions:

(i) what objectives and conditions must be met ? Within the framework of these questions, operational plans are formulated. Usually the answers of operational planning tries to achieve the results and actions suggested by the strategic planning. (ii) why is the action required? (iii) what are the results of the action required? (iv) what will the action accomplish? (v) what action is to be taken?

4. Strategic planning precedes the operational planning since the later is primarily the implementation of the former. Since stratgic planning sets trends and direction for managerial actions, its use horizon is usually quite large say five years or so. Operational planning is heavily concerned with short term programmes implementing step by step progress towards basic organisational goals, organisational depth and fiancial resources. These restrictions on the organisation potential accomplishment are more prevalent in the short term the over a long term; therefore, strategic planning must recognise the limits of what operational planning can realistically be undertaken in given time periods. Thus strategic planning is restricted by the practical limitations under which operational planning operates.

ORGANISATIONAL OBJECTIVES

Organisational objectives seek to direct the efforts of all members of a team while personal goals are motives of people working in the team. Efficiency is high when the two types of objectives are mutually supportive or compatible. Organisational objectives are the goals established to guide the efforts of the company and each of its components. Objectives are variously referred to as purposes, goals, missions, or targets. The establishment of objectives is a very important step in planning. Planning can be effective only if objectives are carefully selected. A clear statement of purpose understood by one and all is the best guarantee of effective management. Objectives must be actionable, that is, meaningful to the manager who is to achieve them. Objectives or goals must be specific and capable of accomplishment. They must be identified in such a way that ultimate success or failure can be determined.

The above description reveals the following characteristics of Organisational Objectives:

(1) Every organisation has number of economic, social and human objectives rather than a single aim. As stated earlier, objectives are required in every area of business where the success and survival of the business is important. Every department or division has its own objectives in addition to the overall objectives of the organisation. Different objectives should be balanced with one another. A business firm has both general and specific objectives are narrow in scope *e.g.*, to reduce absenteeism. Organisational goals are sometimes divided into (a) maintenance goals, and (b) productivity goals. Maintenance goals are the expression of the desire to ensure the existence of the enterprise, while productivity goals as at improvements in performance.

2. Objectives are the ultimate ends or results towards which an organisation and its members strive at all times. All activities and resources of an enterprise are directed towards the achievement of common and specified objectives.

3. Objectives are the standing plans which recurringly guide action. They are the basis of other plans such as policies, procedures, programmes, etc.

Objectives are the concrete expressions of the purposes of an enterprises. Primary or major objectives provide the principal reasons for the establishment of the enterprise while collateral objectives supplement and contribute to the primary objectives. Organisational objectives are the basis of long range planning whereas departmental objectives provide the basis for short range planning. Different organisations have different objectives and there is no universal set of objectives. Objectives must, however, be practicable, consistent and clear cut. There must be proper coordination between major and derivative goals and between long range and short range objectives. Objectives should be specific, verifiable and well planned. There must be active participation of all concerned in the determination of objective.

4. Objectives are arranged in a hierarchy which is known as the 'Ends and Means Chain.' Objectives of a lower order act as the means for the achievement of higher level objectives. For instance, the organisational objectives are more basic than the departmental objectives.

5. Objectives may be long-term or short-term. Long-term. objectives refer to the objectives to be achieved over a long period of time while short-term objectives are to be achieved within a period of one to two years. Short-run objectives are steps towards long-term objectives.

Impact on Strategic Planning Programme

(a) Clear and specific objectives avoid conflicts and misunderstanding. They facilitate unified action and integration of efforts on the part of members of the organisation. When objectives are clearly defined and there is agreement on them, every individual tries to adjust his actions and this leads to voluntary coordination. Thus objectives serve as the important tool of management. They define excellence inorganisational performance. Without objectives, the manager possesses no tools for deciding whether performance is satisfactory or disappointing. By delimiting the course of the operations, objectives help to avoid misdirecting of the resources and to ensure maximum utilisation of the assets of the firm.

(b) Well-pefined objectives help in effective delegation and decentralisation of authority. By providing clear-cut guidelines for action, they avoid the need for detailed and specific guidance on the part of management. Knowledge of objectives helps to transform random behaviour into systematic efforts. Goals are vital links in planning process.

(c) As there exists an ends and means relationship between objectives, objectives make for consistent and unified planning. Objectives provide the common denominator for different types of plans. The entire process of management concerns itself with means to achieve objectives.

(d) Objectives serve as the standards with which actual performance can be evaluated. They are also helpful in fixing responsibility. In this way, objectives provide the basis for control. Performance can continually be evaluated in terms of how well the organisation is moving in the direction of its objectives.

(e) Objectives provide a sense of purpose. They imporve the motivation and morale of members of the organisation by making the job meaningful and worthwhile. They serve as guide-posts to action and efforts. Objectives are key to effective planning as plans have no meaning unless they are designed to achieve certain well defined objectives. By defining objectives, management establishes the image or character of the firm.

In the words of Ordway Tead, "it is difficult to overstress the notion of the purpose, aim, objective or goal of the organisation as fundamental to every view of or element in administration."

Planning can be a useful managerial function only if objectives are properly spelled out. Therefore, every enterprise should state its objectives precisely and clearly.

Operational Planning

Operational planning is lower-level planning and is based on sub-goals derived from organisational objectives. The focus is on managing the day-to-day affairs of the company. The primary responsibility for implementation of operational plans rests on the operating level of management; middle-level executives or line managers, who are guided by the senior management with regard to the formulation of strategies. In managing the day-to-day affairs, operating managers are guided by a set of policies, proceduress rules, forecasts, targets and budgets. In this manner, all operating managers, in different functional areas, implement their respective plans. Operational plans, therefore, are parts of the overall organisational plan and work in tandem with each other. Operating plans and operating managers are to be distinguished from operations plans (which relate to the production function) and operations managers (who look after the production activities).

Management by Objectives

Management by objectives, *per se,* is not a type of planning system; it is a systems approach to managing by emphasising the role of objectives. Operationally, it facilitates planning and the implementation and control of plans. The organisational objectives are divided into divisional or departmental objectives which are further subdivided into individual objectives. Such an interlocking system of objectives serves as the basis for managing, evaluation and control of performance. Thus management is concerned with setting of objectives, goals and targets which are a part of the planning function.

Project Planning

In a broader sense, project planning relates to planning for a clearly indentified programme or a set of tasks such as construction project. Within organisations, and in a narrow sense, project planning refers to planning done for a specific task like product development. The nature of each project is unique and planning is done for each project individually. The emphasis in project planning is on working within set time and resource constraints. The form of organisation used is a temporary structure known as matrix organisation. Project planning derives its goals from the organisational objectives. An organisational strategy, for implementation, may require many plans and programmes each programme includes several projects.

Short-tenn (Short range) Planning

Deciding about the planning period the number of years ahead for which planning is done-is an· important decision. There is no definite planning period on the basis of which plans could be classified as being of a short or long duration. It would depend, among other factors, on the uncertainty present in the future or the nature of products. For companies in the oil exploration business the planning period would be long-up to 20 years or more-while a fashion garments manufacturer may not plan for more than a year. A basis on which plans could be termed as short-or long-range is the commitment principle: "a period of time in the future necessary to foresee, as well as possible, the fulfilment of commitments involved in decisions made today." Ordinarily, plans for less than one year are termed as short-range and those for 3 to 5 years are long-range plans. Short-range planning involves making plans which are based on current data. These are the immediate goals to be achieved, present commitment of resources, minor changes in schedules, policies and requirements, and mid-term appraisals. Short-range plans operate within the framework of long-range plans. Sometimes, medium-range planning can also be undertaken which froms a linkage between the short and long-range plans.

Long-terms (or Long range) Planning

Long-range planning as the name indicates, deals with planning for a future period of time. The planning process involves a systematic indentitication of opportunities and threats so that managers may use the date to make current decisions in order to use the opportunities and avoid the threats. By consideration of the future developments, as manager can assess the futurity of current decisions the likely impact that a decision taken now is going to make in the future and make current decisions accordingly. In this manner, long-range planning deals with issues which are of the vital significance and have long-term impact. There are many other terms used to planning which is for a long term is of vital significance, and is concerned with the futurity of current decisions.

Contigency Planning

The contingency approach rests on the premise that there is he one best way to solve a problem, the right aproach depends on the situation. Envirnomental conditions on which much of long-term planning rests, change so rapidly that policy makers are often constrained in making tenable assumptions regarding future developments. Too much formal planning does not seem to work under such conditions. A realistic approach to contain these problems, is to adopt contingency planning. This involves taking action in incremental steps, reassessing strategies at each stage and reformulating plans in order to reach a predetermined goal. The planning has to be done repetitively making contingency planning an iterative process.

For example, a company manufacturing refrigerators faces competition in the market as a result of which it modernises its operations. In the next stage, it raises capacity levels to take advantages of economics of scale. Further, in order to offset seasonal fluctuations, it starts making watches and, thus, diversities into a new area. The three steps of modernisation, expansion and diversification, show that the company has reviewed its strategies at each stage and tries to ensure survival and profitability by adopting contingency planning. Has the conditions been different at any of the three stages, the company would have adopted a different approach. Such an approach would have been contingent on that situation.

Strategic Planning

Strategic planning is a process which, through an examination of external and internal factors for an organisation, results in a set of mission, purpose, objectives, policies, plans and programmes for implementation. In this manner, strategic planning results in action designed to implement a strategy. A view of strategic planning is that the objectives and goals, and the strategies designed to achieve them, give rise to two types of plans. These are the operating and strategic plans. The operating plans are implemented by the different units in an organisation while strategic plans are implemented through projects. Strategic planning is considered a part of wider system of managing through strategy, *i.e.* strategic management.

Comprehensive or Systematic or Corporate Planning

Corporate planning is a term to denote a formal, comprehensive, and systematic appraisal of environmental and internal factors in order to evolve strategies to achieve organisational objectives. It is formal as it requires formulation of plans, strategies, and policies on the basis of documents and figures. It is comprehensive as it deals with all types of plans: short and long-range, corporate, divisional and functional and strategic and operational plans. It is systematic as it covers the whole planning process in a logical and sequential manner. Due to its nature, corporate planning is also known as comprehensive corporate planning, comprehensive planning, comprehensive planning or systematic planning.

In practice, a team of corporate planners assists the senior managers in determining objectives and goals to be achieved, strengths and weaknesses of the company, the opportunities and threats operating in the environment, and the strategies and action plans to be adopted. The corporate planners are also involved in continuous monitoring of the implementation process of plans and the process taking place. On the basis of such an evaluation, the strategies and action plans are reviewed and reformulated, if necessary.

Corporate planning is a term often used synonymously with long-range planning and strategic planning. It is also a term rarely found in American, literature pertaining to business policy. But otheres including India books, often use the term 'corporate planning'. Some of the earlier books published in the area of business policy in India carried the title of Corporate Planning.

The term 'corporate planning' is also used extensively in management journals, popular business magazines, and in industry. Management courses in the area of business policy offered by institutions and Universities in India are also known as corporate planning courses. Notwithstanding the popular use of the term 'corporate planning', normally, it is taken to be synonymous with long-range planning and strategic planning.

Problem of Semantics in Terminology: Planning Terms

As in Section, we deal with the problem of semantics in terminology related to various planning terms that have been used above. For this purpose, we take up four combinations of terms as examples.

(1) Long-range Planning-corporate Planning-strategic Planning. These three terms, in groups of two each at one time, have been considered above. Much of what has been stated is also valid for these three terms jointly. Individually, these terms do mean different things to different people. Historically, they have emerged at different times. Each of these terms has come to signify planning systems that have been invented in response a unique set of envirnomental factors. With regard to the literature in the area of business policy, writers have extolled the virtues of one planning system while treating the others as secondary. But the differnces between them, as of today, are at best, academic. Practitioners do not view them differently, many authors also adopt an approach of using them interchangeably. A reasonable approach, in our opinion, would be to consider the nature of planning involved. If the planning is done at a senior level of management, is sufficiently long-range is valid for the company as a whole, and is of vital pervasive or continuing importance, it can either be called long-range, corporate or strategic planning. The basic thrust in such planning has to be on the process of indentification of opportunities and threats in the environment and their matching with the strengths and weaknesses of the company in order to formulate strategies to achieve the objectives, purpose and mission of the organisation.

(2) Long-range Planning-strategic Planning. Ansoff differentiates long range planning ("Where future is expected to be predictable through extrapolation of the historical growth") and strategic planning (" ...future is not necessarily expected to be an improvement over the past nor is assumed to be extrapolable") Steiner, Miner and Gray do not differentiate long-range (also corporate) planning and strategic planning stating that "strategic planning is the pharse most widely used today." Sometimes, strategic planning is considered an emerging term for corporate planning, which itself is thought to be a successor to long-range planning. For all practical purposes, however, both the terms are considered to be synonymous.

(3) Long-range Planning-corporate Planning. Some authors, specially the earlier ones, differentiate between these two terms. Argenti is of the opinion that not all long-range plans are corporate all corporate plans are necessarily long-range. Ansoff equates both and says that long-range planning is "sometimes called corporate planing." Sometimes, corporate planning is taken as planning for the whole company as contrasted with functional plans. Others do not consider corporate plans as simple aggregates of functional plans. Occasionally, corporate planning is thought to be a combination of long and short-range plans. However, the most accepted approach presently is to consider both long-range planning and corporate planning as synonymous for all practical purposes.

(4) Corporate Planning-strategic Planning. These terms are also mostly taken as being synonymous. But there is a different view. "Although corporate planning and strategic planning are closely linked", says Argenti, "they are not synonymous either". Corporate planning can be divided into two parts, according to Agrenti. The first relates to deciding the corporate objectives and the second to the determination of corporate strategies. So, "strategic planning is the second part of corporate planning". The present trend as exemplified to consider both these terms, as well as long-range planning to be synonymous for all practical purposes.

(5) From Strategic Planning to Strategic Management. While strategic planning helps to resolve the problem of strategy formulation on the basis of mission and objective-setting and the analysis of environmental and internal factors, it falls short of taking into account a few relevant aspects. Asnoff *et al.* deal with these shortcomings in terms of three variables. First with regard to managerial problems, strategtc planning considers the external linkages with the environment "under a basic' assumption that the internal configuration will remain essentially unchanged". Second, dealing with process of resolving managerial problems, it covers only problem-solving (or planning) while assuming that implementation and control will follow. Thirdly, the variables included in strategic planning analysis are exclusively "techological-economic informational while soical and political dynamics both within and outside the organisation are assumed to be irrelevant and unaffected".

The sub-variables, which have been excluded from consideration, have a major impact on resolving strategic problems. For instance, it is essential to consider the impact that formulation of strategy, and changes in it, have on the organisation. Again, the solution of managerial problems can only be done through a comprehensive approach that not only considers formuation but also implementation and control of strategy. Factors like psychosociological and political dimensions of policy-making are essential for diagnosing the myriad of problems faced by managers.

Strategic management, a newer and broader concept of managing organisation strategically, takes into account all the aspects of managerial.

LIMITATIONS OR STRATEGIC PLANNING

Strategic Planning in management is essential but there are practical limitations to its use. The reasons why people fail in strategic planning emphasise the practical difficulties encountered in planning. A number of limits within which planning has to operate make this undertaking difficult. Following are the limitations:

(1) Problems of Change. The above factor works more as limiting factor in the light of changes in future conditions. In a complex and rapidly changing environnment, the succession of new problems is often magnified by implications that make planning most difficult. The problem of change is more complex in long-range planning. Present conditions tend to weigh heavily in planning, and by overshadowing future needs, may sometimes results in error of judgment. Such factors as changing technology, consumer tastes and desires, business conditions, and many others change rapidly and often unpredictably. In such conditions, planning activities taken in one period may not be relevant for another period because the conditions in two periods are quite different.

(2) Failure of Poeple. There are many reasons why people fail in planning, both at the fomulation level as well as implementation level. Some of the major failures are lack of commitment to planning, failure to develop sound strategies, lack of clear and meaningful objectives, tendency to overlook planning premises, failure to see the scope of the plan, failure to see planning as a rational approach, excessive reliance on the past experience, failure to use the principles of limiting factors, lack of top management support, lack of delegation of authority, lack of adequate control techniques, and resistance to change. These factors are responsible for either inadequate planning or wrong planning in the organisations concerned.

(3) Lack of Accurate Information. The first basic limitation of strategic planning is the lack of accurate information and facts relating to future. Planning concerns future activity and its quality will'be determined by the quality of forecast of future events. As no manager can predict completely and accurately the events of future, the planning may pose problems in operation. This problem is futher, increased by lack of formulating accurate premises. Many times, managers may not be aware about the various conditons within which they have to formulate their planning activities.

(4) Inflexibilities. Managers while going through the strategic planning process have to work in a set of given variables. These variables may be more in terms of organisational or external. These often provide considerably less flexibility in planning action.

(A) Internal. Major internal inflexibilities that may limit planning are related to human psychology. Organisatonal policies and procedures, and long-term capital investment. The first internal inflexibility is in the form of human psychology in that most of the people have regard for the present rather than for future. The present is not only more certain than future, it is also more desirable, and more real. Thus, resistance to change is a basic factor which works against planning because planning often depends on the changes.

People may have feelings that if planning is soft-pedalled, the changes and the possible danger of future will be minimised. For them, planning tends to accelerate change and unrest.

Second type of internal inflexibility emerges because of organisationnal policies and procedures. Once these are established, they are difficult to change. Though these policies, procedures, and rules are meant to facilitate managerial functions by providing guidelines, they often are too numerous and exacting that they leave very little scope for managerial intiative and flexibility. Since managers have to plan for future which is not static but changing, they often find themselves in great constraints. Such problems are more common in bureaucratic organisations where rules and procedures are the matters of prime concerns.

Third type of internal inflexibility comes because of long-term capital investment. Long-term planning is not a process of making future decisions, but a means of reflecting the future in todays decisions. If the organisation has taken a long-term investment, it is committed by that and future actions have to be taken in the light of the investment. Thus managerial planning is limited to that extent.

(B) External. Beside the internal inflexibilities, managers are contronted with many external inflexibilities and they do not have control over these. These factors may be social technological legal labour union, geographical and economic. The managers have to furmulate their plans keeping in view the demand of these factors. Thus their scope of action is limited making planning ineffective in many cases.

(5) Time and Cost. While going through the strategic planning process, managers should also take into account both time and cost factors. The various steps of planning may go as for as possible because there is no limit of precision in planning tools. But planning suffers because of time and cost factors. Time is a limiting factor for every manager in the organisation on, and if they are busy in preparing elaborate reports and instructions beyond certain level, they are risking their effectiveness. Excessive time spent on securing information and trying to fit all of it into a compact plans is dysfunctional in the organisation.

(6) Rigidity. Often people feel that planning provides rigidity in managerial action. Many types of internal inflexibilities, discussed above, may be results of planning itself. The planning stifles employee intiative and forces managers into rigid or straitjacket mode of excecuting their work. In fact, rigidity may make managerial work more dificult than it need be. This may result in it delay in work performance, lack of intiative, and lack of adjustment with changing environment. Many people feel that planning is limited in value because best results can be obtamed by a muddling through types of operation in which each situation is tackled when and if it appears pertinent to the immediate problem. Though this factor of rigidity of planning is limiting factor, but without planning , it is really difficult to operate particularly in large organisations.

The planning also involves cost on the part of the organisation. The various factors analysed above contribute to the limitations of strategic planing, either making, planing ineffective or making lesser degree of planned work.

Important Factors for Making Strategic Planning Effective

It is not sufficient to say that managers must take actions to make strategic planning effective, but they must be clear as to what actions can be taken in this direction. Following factors are important for making planning effective.

(1) An Open Systems Approach. The problems of planning should be dealt through open systems approach. It suggests that managers must take into account interactions with their total environment in every respect of planning. Open systems approach makes it necessary on the part of the managers that they take into account the environmental variable such as, technological, social, cultural, legal, political, and economic. Further, they must also take into account the internal interaction pattern that is, how their planning process is affecting others and is affected by others. When managers take all these factors into account is affected by others. When managers take all these factors into account, they are in better positions to plan and execute their actions.

(2) Participation in Planning. As discussed above, planning progress should be a joint one. The best planning is likely to be done when managers are given an opportunity to contribute to plans affecting the area over which they have authority. Participation in planning affecting managers areas of authority at any level through their being informed contributing suggestions and being consulted, leads to good planning, commitment, loyalty, and managerial effectiveness.

The various methods of participation in planning process may be followed in the organisations depending upon their requirements and understanding of the people.

(3) Integration of Long-term and Short-term Plans. Managers often focus their attention only on very short-term plans, even if they plan. As discussed earlier, a good planning process involves integration of long-term and short-term plans. A short-term plan contributes towards the achievement of the long-term plan. Thus, if a manager is planning for very short period, he must take into account his long-term plans also. He must constantly watch and review that his short-term plans contribute to his long-term plans. If this is not the situation, he must modify his course of action which may include modification in both long-term and short-term plans.

(4) Communication of Planning. Many planning efforts fail because managers do not adequately emphasise the role of communicating various planning elements, such as, goals, strategies, policies, and planning premises. If these are communicated clearly, adequately, and timely, the managers are motivated and initiated to take planning process. Which may be necessary for them. When a manager understands the various aspects of planning, he is in a better position to foresee his future course of action and may develop a habit of planning every course of future action.

(5) Initiative. Planning to be effective must have the initiative and support of top level management. It is the top level which is responsible for success or failure of any organisational process, and planning is no exception. The basic objecitives which are set at the top level must be two-way process which involves people at other levels also. Further, when top management rigorously reviews subordinates programmes, it naturally stimulates planning interest throughout the organisation. The planning action by top management does not suggest in everything win come from the top and subordinates will do nothing, rather the planning process should be a joint one.

(6) Establishing a Climate. The managers should try to establish a climate where every person in the organisation takes planning action. Every superior managers should remove obstacles. to planning and present facilities for planning. This can be done by setting clear goals, establishing and publishing applicable significant planning premises, involving all managers in planning process, reviewing subordinate plans and their performance, and assuring appropriate staff assistance and information at all levels of management.

INADEQUATE PLANNING IN INDIA

There are many factors which affect the corporate planning and are not quite conducive to Indian organisations. The need for an extent of corporate planning within any economy is governed basically by the following factors:

(a) Scarcity of resources,

(b) Government policy and control,

(c) Competition facing the firm, and

(d) Size of the firm.

There is substantial interdependence among these factors and the intensity of impact of each one of the these factors may vary from country to country from firm to firm within the same country, or from time to time within the same organisation. A study related to the cross-cultural management philosophy, practices and effectiveness with particular reference to India have suggested the following propositions:

All other factors being the same, the higher a firm's score on the management philosophy (*i.e.*, attitudes toward various components of society internal and external to the firm) index, the greater will be its concern for long-range planning.

The greater the degree of competition the greater will be the need for long-range planning by the individual company.

The greater the degree of economic and political instability, the lesser the likelihood that private industrial enterprises will undertake systematic long-range planning.

The greater the degree of government control over prices and the availiability of raw materials, the lesser the likelihood that the firm will undertake systematic long range planning.

The greater the degree of governemental hostility toward the business community, the lesset the likelihood that a firm will undertake systematic long-range planning.

The implication of the above propositions is given usually low score on management philosophy among Indian organisations : these constraints are likely to be stronger enough to subdue the passion for long-range planning, apart from management philosophy. Following. characteristics of Indian environment work against formulation of the plans by Indian organisations:

(1) As regards the size of the organisation, the Monopolies and RestrictiveTrade Practices Act, 1969, sets constraints on expansion and diversification strategy through the limits on assets size (Rs. 20 crores) and market share (33.3 per cent). Thus area of expansion and diversification - most important area of LRP for larger organisations— is defined by Government regulations. Further constraints are out on organisations, with foreign-majority equity holding and public sector organisations, though there is a basic difference. The former organisations' area of business is determined by Government, thus narrowing the scope of discretionary planning. In the case of the

latter, business goals in terms of areas of activity are pretty clear and stable.

(2) Lack of resources in general also creates barriers in formulation and implementation of plans. There is a competition for claims for resources—specially materials, infrastructural facilities, such as, power transport finance, managerial manpower. Since many of these resources are canaiised and controlled through Government agencies, there is no competition in the supply resources. It verges more on monopoly—rationing supplies to a large number of competing organisations. Many of the organisations view that constraining forces effective plan implementation are the Government policy, licensing policy, delay in procurement of machinery and equipment, erratic supply of raw materials, shortcomings in transport and communication facilities, and delay in implementation of projects in other sectors.

(3) There is not enough degree of competition among sellers because of sellers' market conditions. Though in some consumer goods, the conditons of the market have changed, there is high rate of returns. Thus for most organisations, a fair amount of rate of return is assured. The market is further accentuated by growing population and market size, fairly stable consumer tastes, progressive derming of areas of business by Government in which organisations can go. As such many organisations do not see any need for systematic planning. This is supported by non-existence of separate planning division in most of the organisations.

Thus either because of lack of appreciation of need for planning or because of prevailing conditions working against effective formulation and implementation of plans, some organisations do not make attempts to look beyond a year and others accept the conditions as constraints in their attempt at planning. The factors—degree of competence, ownership professional training of management, and perception of Government attitude towards the companies may account to some extent for the difference in attitudes.

❐

9

Process of Control

CONTROL is any process that guides activity towards some predetermined goals. Thus control can be applied in any field such as price control, distribution control, pollution control, etc. However, control as an element of management process can be defined as the process of analysing whether actions are being taken as planned and taking corrective actions to make these to conform to planning. Thus control process tries to find out deviations between planned performance and actual performance and to suggest corrective actions wherever these are needed. For example, Terry has defined control as follows:

"Controlling is determining what is being accomplished, that is evaluating the performance and, if necessary, applying corrected measures so that the performance takes place according to plan."

Based on the definition of control, its following features can be identified:

1. Control is a Continuous Process. Through managerial control enables the manager to exercise control at the point of action, it follows a definite pattern and time-table, month after month and year after year on a continuous basis.

2. Control is Forward Looking because One can Control Future Happenings and not the Past. However, on control process always the past performance is measured because no one can measure the outcome of a happening which has not occurred. In the light of these measurements, managers suggest corrective actions for future period.

3. Control is both can Executive Process and, from the Point of View of the Organisations of the System a Result. As an executive process, each manager has to perform control function in the organisation. It is true that according to the level of a manager in the organisation, the nature, scope, and limit of his control function may be different as compared to a manager at other level. The word control is also preceded by an adjective to designate a control problem, such as, quality control, inventory control, production control, or even administrative control. In fact, it is administrative control which constitutes the most comprehensive control concept. All other types of control may be subsumed under it.

4. A Control System is a Coordinated-Integrated System. This emphasises that, although data collected for one purpose may differ from those with another purpose, these data should be reconciled with one another. In a sense, control system is a single system, but it is more accurate to think of it as a set of interlocking sub-systems.

The last and the most important function of management is to control. If the function of control is not taken seriously and sincerely in the enterprise, the enterprise cannot think of achieving its pre-determined objectives, howsoever, the best available factors of production may be. Control is the activity through which the efforts are made to ensure that all the activities of the enterprise may be carried on according to the pre-determined plans, programmes and procedures. If anything is not going in accordance with the pre-determined rules and procedures, the efforts are made to diagnose the reasons and to remove them. The term Managerial Control has been defined by some eminent authors as follows:

Koontz and O' Donnell, "The managerial function of Control is the measurement and correction of the performance of subordinates in oder to make sure that enterprise's objectives and the plan devised to attain them are accomplished."

Henry Fayol, "Control consists in verifying whether everything occurs in conformity with the plans adopted, the instructions issued and principls established. It has the object to point out the weaknesses and errors in order to rectify them and prevent their recurrence."

Mary Cushining Niles, "Control, thus viewed is an aspect and projection of planning, whereas planning sets the course. Control observes deviations from the course and initiates action to return to the chosen courses or to an appropriately changed one"

On the basis of analytical study of above definitions, it may be concluded that the managerial control is a process through which the performance of subordinates is evaluated to see whether the activities of the enterprise are going on in the required manner or not. Whether the employees of the enterprise are doing their jobs according to the orders and directions issued to them or not. If anything is found wrong, remedial measures are taken for that so that the activities of the enterprise may go on in the right way and in the right direction in future.

Objectives of Managerial Control

Prof. Davis and Statson have described the following objectives of managerial control.

1. To find out the time of completion of a job, the category of the job and the final cost of the job.
2. To find out the time consumed in a certain amount for the work.
3. To find to available resources and facilities for the performance of different works.
4. To find out whether the desired results have been achieved of the desired quality in the standard time or not.
5. To find out how can these problems be overcome and what steps are being taken for the same.
6. To ensure that the problems and hinderances may not repeat.
7. If there is any delay or any change or hinderance in the performance of work to find out the reasons for the same.

In brief, the main object of managerial control is to get the work done by a manager from his subordinates according to predetermined standards. If any difficulty or problem arises in the performance of work, best efforts are made to solve the problems so that the work may go on in the required manner and the predetermined objectives of the enterprise may be achieved easily.

Nature and Characteristics of Managerial Control

The nature and characteristics of managerial control may be described as under:

1. Last Process. Managerial control is the last process of management because the work of control starts after planning, organisation, direction, co-ordination and motivation.

2. Essential at Every Level of Management. Management is not a specific function to be performed at any specific level of management. It is required at every level of management for all the activities and in all the departments.

3. Dynamic Process. Control is a dynamic process of management because in this process, necessary changes are made keeping in view the changed circumstances of the enterprise.

4. Continuous Process. Control is the continuous process of management. It continues so long as the production continues in the enterprise.

5. Control on Future Events. In the process of control, all the best efforts are made to check the possible losses in future. In fact, managerial control is a process of directing the activities of the enterprise for future on the basis of the past experiences.

6. Attainment of Goals. The main object of control is to ensure the proper functioning of the enterprise according to predecided rules, policies, plans, procedures and programmes. It aims at the attainment of pre-decided objectives of the enterprise.

7. Based on Scientific Principles and Statistical Factors. The process of control is based upon scientific principles and statistical factors. The process of control is not based upon personal assumptions and emotions.

Area or Span of Managerial Control

The span of managerial may be described as under:

1. Control Over Organisation. The process of control maintains control over the organisation of the enterprise. For this purpose, an organisation chart, and an organisation scale is maintained in the enterprise describing the organisational structure of the enterprise in detail.

2. Control Over Policies. The success of an enterprise largely depends upon its policies. Therefore, the process of control, controls the policies of the enterprise.

3. Control over Capital Expenditure. It is very necessary to control the capital expenditure of an enterprise. For this purpose a committee is established in the enterprise which is held responsible for preparing a capital budget and evaluating alternative capitals. This committee keeps a complete control over capital expenditure of the enterprise.

4. Control Over Personnel. The success of an enterprise depends upon its personnel. If the workers and employees of the enterprise do not work according to the policies, plans and programmes of the enterprise, the enterprise cannot achieve its pre-determined objectives. Therefore, it becomes imperative to have a control over the personnels of the enterprise. This function is performed by the personnel manager.

5. Control Over Costs. The real success of an enterprise is to make the maximum profit and to render the maximum service to the society. This can be possible only if the cost of production of the enterprise are properly controlled. For this, the standard costs are determined for different products. These standard cost are compared with the actual costs of production and all the efforts are made to control and check unfavourable variances.

6. Control Over Wages and Salaries. It became, very necessary in an enterprise to control the wages and salaries. The process of job evaluation is adopted in the enterprise to control its wages and salaries. On the basis of job evaluation, different rates of wages and salaries for different employees are determined.

7. Control Over Research and Development. The department of research and development must be properly controlled in an enterprise for the growth and development of the enterprise. Separate budgets are prepared for research and development and every project of research is thoroughly analysed discussed and evaluated.

8. Control Over Production. Both the quantity and quality must be under the control of the Chief Engineer of the enterprise. The products must be of the good quality so that there may meet the demands of the competitive market.

9. Control Over Manpower. It is very important in an enterprise to control its manpower. The manpower of an enterprise must be limited and in required number. If the manpower in an enterprise is more or less than its requirements, it may prove harmful for the enterprise.

10. Overall Control. A master plan is prepared for the overall control in an enterprise. This master plan contains all sub-plans for all the departments. Budgetarys control system is adopted to have a complete control over the activities of the enterprise.

Essential Elements of Managerial Control

The attainment of objects and targets by an enterprise depends to a large extent upon its process of control. The process of control must be very effective so that employees of the enterprise may work according to pre-decided plans, policies and programmes and the enterprise may achieve its pre-determined objectives. There are certain principles which must be followed to make the process of control effective. Essential elements of the process of control may be described as under:

1. The process of control must be according to the organisational structure of the enterprise.
2. The process of control must be according to the needs and objects of the enterprise.
3. The process of control must be such which may disclose the variances of an earlier stage so that the earliest steps may be taken to overcome the variances and to protect the enterprise from losses.
4. The system of control must be flexible so that necessary changes may be made in it according to the need of the time.
5. The process of control must be clear and easy to understand so that it may be followed by the employees of the enterprise fully and clearly.
6. Rights, duties and responsibilities of every department must be clearly defined.
7. Special emphasis must be paid on adopting the corrective measures in the enterprise.
8. The process of control must be based on method impartial.
9. The process of control must be economical. It follows that the benefits of the process of control must be more than its costs.
10. Control must be a continuous process of an enterprise and not a specific function.

STEPS IN CONTROL PROCESS

The systems, processes and techniques of control are same whatever the area of their application may be. As pointed out earlier, control is reciprocally related with planning. It is performed in the contexts of planning and aids planning in two ways; it draws attention to situations where new planning is needed; and it provides some of the data upon which plans can be based. Apart form reciprocal relationships, it has circular relationship with planning as explained by Fig. The figure identifies the various steps in control process which are necessary for its relationship to planning. These steps may broadly be classified into four parts:

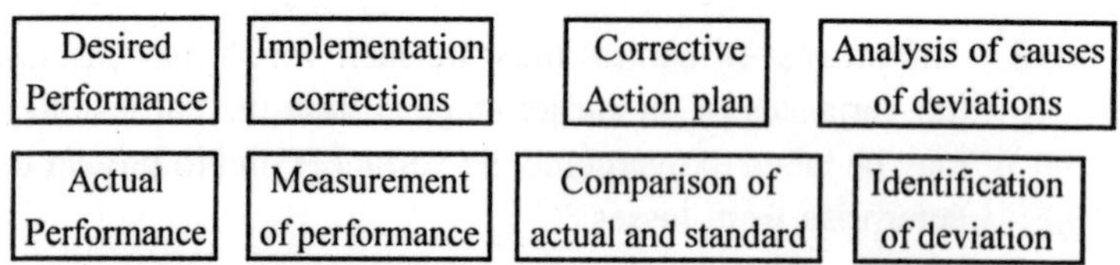

Fig. Management control process.

1. Establishment of Control Standards. Every function in the organisations begins with plans which are goals, objectives, or targets to be achieved. In the light of these, standards are established which are criteria against which actual results are measured. For setting standards for control purposes, it is important to identify clearly and precisely the results which are desired. Precision in the statement of these standards is important. In many areas, great precision is possible. However, in some areas, standards are less precise. Standards may be precise if they are set in quantities-physical, such as volume of products, man-hour or monetary, such as costs, revenues, investment. They may also be in other qualitative terms which measure performance.

Control standards are most effective when they are related to the performance of a specific individual, because a particular individual can be made responsible for specific results. However, sometimes accountability for a desired result is not so simply assigned, for example, the decision regarding investment in inventory is affected by purchase, rate of production, and sales. In such a situation, where

	Upper Limit
Acceptable range	Performance Data
	Lover Limit
	Time or Quality

Fig. Control Range

no one person is accountable for the levels of inventories, standards may be set for each step that is being performed by a man.

2. Measurement of Performance. The second major step in control process is the measurement of performance. The step involves measuring the performance in respect of a work in terms of control standards. The presence of standards implies a corresponding ability to observe and comprehend the nature of existing conditions and to ascertain the degree of control being achieved.

The measurement of performance against standards should be on a future basis, so that deviations may be detected in advance of their actual occurrence and avoided by appropriate actions. Appraisal of actual or expected performance becomes an easy task, if standards are properly determined and methods of measuring performance which can be expressed in physical and monetary terms, such as production units, sales volume, profits, etc. can be easily and precisely measurable, The performance which is qualitative and intangible, such as human relations, employee morale, etc. cannot be measured precisely. For such purposes, techniques like psychological tests and opinion surveys may be applied. Such techniques draw heavily upon intuitive judgment and experience, and these tools are far trom exact.

3. Comparing Actual and Standard Performance. The third major step in control process is the comparison of actual and standard performance. It involves two steps. *(i)* finding out the extent of deviations, and *(ii)* identifying the causes of such deviations. When adequate standards are developed and actual performance is measured accurately, any variation will be clearly revealed. Management may have information relating to work performance, data, charts, graphs and written reports, besides personal observation to keep itself informed about performance in different segments of the organisation. Such performance is compared with the standard one to find out whether the various segments and individuals of the organisation are progressing in the right direction.

When the deviation between standard and actual performance is beyond the prescribed limit, an analysis is made of the causes of such deviations. For controlling and planning purposes, ascertaining the causes of variations along with computation of variations is important because such analysis helps management in taking up proper control action. The analysis will pinpoint the causes which are controllable by the person responsible. In such a case, person concerned will take necessary corrective action. However, if the variation is caused by uncontrollable factors, the person concerned cannot be held responsible and he cannot take any action.

Measurement of performance, analysis of deviations and their causes may be of no use unless these are communicated to the person who can taken corrective action. Scuh communication is presented generally in the form of a report showing performance standard, actual performance, deviations between those two tolerance limits, and causes for deviations. As soon as possible, reports containing control information should be sent to the person whose performance is being measured and controlled.

4. Correction of Deviations. This is the last step in the control process which requires that actions should be taken to maintain the desired degree of control in the system or operation. An organisation is not a self-regulating system such as thermostat which operates in a state of equilibrium put there by engineering design. In a business organisation this type of automatic control can not be established because the state of affairs that exists is the result of so many factors in the total environment. Thus, some additional actions are required to maintain the control. Such control action may be *(i)* review of plans and goals and changes therein on the basis of such review; *(ii)* change in the assignment of tasks; *(iii)* change in existing techniques of direction, *(iv)* changes in organisation structure; provision for new facilities, etc.

In fact, correction of deviation is the step in management control process which may involve either all or some of the managerial functions. Due to this, many persons hold the view that correcting deviations is not a step in the control process. It is the stage where other managerial functions are performed.

Essentials of Effective Control System

Control is necessary in every organisations to ensure that everything is going properly. Every manager, therefore, should have an effective and adequate control system to assist him in making sure that events conform to plans. However, control does not work automatically, but it requires certain design. While the basic principles involved in designing a control system in organisations may be universal, the actual system in an organisation requires some specific design. In this tailoring of control system, there are certain requirements which should be kept in mind.

1. Promptness in Reporting Deviations. The success of a thermostat lies in the fact that it points the deviation promptly and takes corrective actions immediately. Similarly, an ideal control system detects deviations promptly and informs the manager concerned to take timely actions. This is done through designing good appraisal and information systems.

2. Forward Looking Control should be Forward Looking. Though many of the controls are instantaneous, they must focus attention as to how future actions can be conformed with plans. In fact the control system should be such that it provides aid in planning process. This is done in two ways: it draws situations where new planning is needed, and it provides some of the data upon which plans can be based.

3. Reflecting Organisational Needs. All control systems and techniques should reflect the jobs they are to perform. There may be several control techniques which have general applicability, such as, budgeting, costing, etc. However, it should not be assumed that these may be utili sed in all situations. The managers should choose an appropriate tool for control which helps him in controlling actions according to plans.

4. Objectives. The control should be objective, definite, and determinable in a clear and positive way. The standards of measurement should be quantified as far as possible. If they are not quantifiable, such as, training effectiveness, etc. they must be determinable and verifiable. If the performance standard and and measurement is not easily determinable, many subjective elements enter into the process which catch the controller and controlled on wrong footing.

5. Simple. Control system must be simple and understandable so that all managers can use it effectively. Control techniques which are complicated such as complex mathematical formulae, charts, graphs, advanced statistical methods and others techniques fail to communicate the meaning of their control data to the managers who use them. Effective control requires consistency with the positions. operational responsibility, ability to understand, and needs of the individuals concerned.

6. Flexible. Control system should be flexible so that it remain workable in the case of changed plans, unforseen circumstances, or outright failures. As Geotz has remarked, "A control system should report such failures and should contain sufficient elements of flexibility to maintain managerial control of operations despite such failures." Much flexibility in control can be provided by having alternative plans for various probable situations. In fact, flexible control is normally achieved through flexible plans.

7. Pointing out Exceptions at Critical Points. Control should point exception at critical points and suggest whether action is to be taken for deviations or not. Some deviations in the organisations have no impact while others, though very little in quanty, may have great significance. Thus, control system should provide information for critical point control and control on exception. The critical point control stesses that effective control requires attention to those factors critical to appraising performance against an individual plan. The control on exception requires that manager should take corrective action when there is exception a deviation. There more a manager concentrates his control efforts on exceptions, the more efficient will be the results of his control.

8. Economical. Control should be economical and must be worth its costs. Economy is relative, since the benefits vary with the importance of the activity, the size of the operation, the expense that might be incurred in the absence of control, and the contribution the control system can make. The economy of a control system will depend a great deal on the manager's selecting for control only critical factors in areas important to him. If tailored to the job and the size of the enterprise, control will be economical. A large-sized organisation can afford highly complicated techniques, sophisticated tools of control and more elaborate system of control, but a small-sized organisation cannot afford these because of the cost factor.

9. Reflecting Organisational Pattern. The control should reflect organisational pattern by focusing attention on positions in organisation structure through which deviations are corrected. Organisation structure, a principle vehicle for coordinating the work of people, is also a major means of maintaining control. Thus, in every area of control, it is not enough to know that things are going wrong unless it is known wherein the organisation structure the deviations are occurring. This enables managers to mix up the responsibility and to take corrective actions.

10. Motivating. Control system should motivate both controller and controlled. While the planning and control are necessary for economical operations, researches in human relations show that planning and control are, more often than not, antagonistic to good human relations. Sometimes, they may even tend to deprive the people in the organisations one of man's basic needs a sense of powerful and worthwhile accomplishment. The design of control system should be such that aims at motivating people by fulfilling their needs.

Principles of Effective Control System

The control process is not automatic. It is deliberate. An effective control system should have the following principles:

1. Controls must be Understandable. The individuals must understand what the control system is attempting to do. Sophisticated control tools are increasingly used now-a-days in the system and the managers must have a thorough knowledge of these before operating. They must first understand the usefulness of the control advices before they use them. It requires proper training and employment of competent people in the execution of control system. Without proper understanding if managers use the recently innovated control devices it would be catastrophic to the organization and have adverse consequences. So understanding and proper knowledge of devices are the foremost important essentials in the control system.

2. Controls must be Economical. Control should be worth its costs. This requirement is deceptively simple. It is because a manager may have a difficulty in finding out what is 'worth' or what are the cost involved in it. As a matter of fact, economy is a relative concept because costs and benefits vary for different operations. Control system however becomes economical if appropriately tailored to the job/task, and the size of organization. A big organization may afford sophisticated and high-cost techniques of control in its system whereas a small organissation may not afford that. The important limiting factor in control system, therefore, is cost.

3. Controls must be Flexible. Flexibility is another essential thing in the wake of rapidly changing and widely fluctuating economic and organizational environments. Standards and plans on which controls are based frequently need modification or revision when underlying circumstances change. Flexibility in control is generally achieved through flexible budgets. For example, in the case of economic prosperity a particular type of budget is suited to the organization, whereas in the context of economic depression such budget is unsuitable and an altogether different budget may be called for. If the organization rigidly follows the budget that suits prosperity, it cannot operate with it under depression and ultimately organization will be doomed to failure. flexibility makes control workable in the face of changes plans, unforseen circumstances or outright failures.

4. Controls must be Objective. The effective control system calls for objective, accurate, suitable and definite standards or plans. If control are subjective then a manager's or subordinate's personality may influence judgments and hence there may be any element of bias in decisions leading to ineffective performance. No doubt, management of things in an organization, contain many subjective elements but for effective performance, controls must be objective and clearly quantifiable and verifiable:

5. Control System should Provide Useful, Understandable Information. Information that is valuable to some individuals may be totally useless for others. An effective control system provides information to the right people who can use them in correcting deviations and fostering growth. Further, some people like information in complex tables of data or voluminous computer printouts, some others like chartwise presentation. Methematicians and statisticians like the information in the mathematical form. An effective control system must have the characteristics of supplying the information in the required form for the purpose of analysis. It will be appreciared by the members in the organization, because people get the information they need in the form they will understand and make proper use of it.

6. Control should Recognize the Importance of the Time Element. Timeliness is one very important factor that cannot be ignored in controlling. Effective control system attaches great importance to the time element. Controls should quickly report deviations. Appropriate actions should be taken without much loss of time, or delay. Time is precious in some matters like cash management, inventories etc. Wrong decision taken in right time is fare better than right decision taken too late. The loss will be much more if delay is made in taking correctrve action.

7. Controls should be Selective. For every organization there are certain key determinants of efficiency and effectiveness. An effective control system considers management be exception as an important concept to be practised in reality. Also management should concentrate on certain control points which are key to organization's success. It is, in fact, the secret of success of an organization. It should be pointed that these key points differ in different organizations and hence control system will also be different and must be tailored to the situations existing. Sometimes it so happens that managers and employees may spend much of their time trying to control activities that are relatively unimportant to organization's success while possibly ignoring, neglecting or paying inadequate attention to the key point. It is the secret (reason) of failure sometimes.

8. Control should be Forward-Looking. It is a misconception that control is a post-mortem of events or thing. An effective control system is always aiming at future. Control aids in further planning. It is rightly said that the starting point of planning is control. Control through feedback provides a framework within which planning on new lines can be undertaken. Control system must also have a feedforward subsystem that helps in correct and accurate planning. Planning is looking ahead and control is looking back! is an outdated concept nowadays. In fact, control always looks forward, of course, through planning. To say it in simple words, planning and controls are inseparable twins. We do not know where one starts and where one ends. We do not know where one ends and other starts.

9. Control should Lead to Corrective Action. Merely discovering deviations in the performance of operations is not enough, an effective control system must lead to appropriate and corrective action. The system must also disclose the key areas of concentration where are the problem areas,. who are responsible for that etc. Management control system must also provide various alternative courses of action for different problems. Control system must also suggest the ways of improving the performance, evaluating and implementing these suggestions is then the task of management.

10. Controls should Reflect the Organization Structure and Needs. Effective control system is that which reflects the organizational structure, positions and needs and plans. Organization structure clarifies the roles of people in organization and control system reflects as to who is responsible for what, execution of plans and for any deviations from them. Control system must be such that it is best suited to the organization structure. There may be several control techniques having different applications, for example, cost accounting, cost control, budgetary control, PERT,CPM etc. Management must rightfully apply these techniques depending on the structure, positions and needs in the organization. Control system will be said to be effective only when appropriate techniques of controlling are applied in right situations. In appropriate use of techniqes render the system ineffective and as such detrimental to the growth of an organization.

❐

10

Industrial Growth and Policy

At the time of independence, India was industrially and economically backward. In 1951-52, the share of agriculture was 56.5 per cent of GDP while the share of industry was just 13.3 per cent. Due to the programme of industrialisation, the share of industrial sector has gone up to 25.0 per cent in 2000-01. The industrial sector has become well diversified. The structure of industrial growth in India during the five decades of planning can be more easily examined and analysed under two broad heads *viz.*, *(I)* Industrial growth and *(II)* Pattern of industrialisation.

I. INDUSTRIAL GROWTH

India's industrial growth can be looked from three different aspects:

(i) Growth rate in industrial output.

(ii) Industry's contribution to employment.

(iii) Industry's contribution in national income.

(i) Growth Rate in Industrial Output. The compound rate of growth was quite impressive during the first three plans. The industrial growth rate in first plan was 5.7 per cent and it rose to 7.2 per cent in second plan and further to 9.0 per cent in third plan. During the eleven year period (1996 to 1976) growth rate declined to 4.1 per cent per annum. The position did not improve even after.

Industrial Growth Rate

Period	*Annual growth Rate (per cent)*	*Period*	*Annual Growth Rate (per cent)*
1951-1956	5.7	1985-90	8.5
1956-1961	7.2	1990-91	9.0
1961-1966	9.0	1991-92	0.8
1966-1976	4.1	1992-94	0
1976-1980	3.8	1994-97	8.6
1980-1985	6.4	1997-2002	4.9

1975-76 as the annual rate of industrial growth during the four period (1976-80) remained very low *i.e.* 3.3 per cent per annum. During sixth plan *i.e.* 1980-85 the industrial activities picked up and achieved the growth rate of 6.4 per cent per annum. The industrial growth rate during 1985-90 (Seventh plan) was satisfactory *i.e.* 8.5 per cent per annum. Industrial sector requested a robust growth of 9.0 per cent in 1990-91. However, industries suffered a serious set-back in 1991-92 and production declined by 0.8 per cent. In the following year there was near stagnation. The industrial recovery started in 1993-94 and in two four period from 1993-94 to 1996-97 the industrial production increased at the annual rate of 8.6 per cent which is quite encouraging. But the indstrial growth declined again during the Ninth Five Year Plan (1997-2002) and it has been 4.9 per cent per annum. In the terminal year of this plan the rate of industrial growth registered a further decline and was low as 2.7 per cent.

(ii) ***Industry's Contribution to Employment.*** The contri-bution of industrial sector in providing employment is not encouraging. During 1951 to 1969, factory production rose at an annual compound rate of 7 per cent per annum,

while employment rose at less than 3 per cent per annum. Recent estimates of employment elasticity with reference to the growth of manufacturing sectors shows that employment elasticity India is falling. The employment elasticity in manufacturing sector during 1972-73 to 1977-78 was 1.0 and it declined to 0.67 in 1977-78 to 1983 and further to 0.33 during 1983 to 1993-94.

If we look at the absolute number of workers employed in manufacturing sector, we find that it has increased from 34.03 million in 1983 to 42.50 million in 1933-94 and further to 48.01 million in 1999-2000. In absolute terms it looks quite impressive however in per centage terms, the importance of manufacturing as a provider of employment has not changed significantly. The per centage of workers employed in manufacturing sector has marginally increased from 11.3 per cent during 1983 to 1993-94 to 12.1 per cent in 1999-2000.

(iii) Industry's Contribution to National Income. During the first three plans, similar trends relating to the distribution of NDP by different sectors were aslo observed in India. The share of the secondary sector to the NDP went up from a meager 13.3 per cent in 1950-51 to about 17.0 per cent in 1960-61; correspondingly, the share of the primary sector declined from 59.2 per cent in 1950-51 to 50.1 per cent in 1960-61. The fact that during this period, the national income has recorded a sizable increase would prove the fact that industrial production was increasing at a faster rate than agricultural production. In the subsequent decade, however, this trend could not be maintined but the share of the scondary sector, was still rising and it reached at 19.7 per cent in 1970-71. Over the seventies no change worth mentioning occurred in the structure of national output, except during 1967-77 when industrial production had shown a remarkable recovery. Eighties, however, brought a welcome change, as borne out by the recent CSO data.

Based on the 1980-81 prices (the new base year now being used by the CSO), industry share in NDP which is reported as 23.3 per cent in 1981-82 went up to 25.9 per cent in 1991-92. However, during the 1990s the share of industrial sector declined and it was just 21.7 per cent in 1999-2000. But during the year 2000-01, it has increased to 23.0 per cent.

II. PATTERN OF INDUSTRIALISATION

The second important aspect of industrial growth relates to the pattern of industrialisation that has been followed since Independence. The pattern of industrialisation can be studied under two heads: *(a)* Functional Pattern of Industries, and *(b)* Ownership Pattern of Industries.

A. Functional Pattern of Industries

The pattern of industrialisation can be studies with the help of the following three criteria.

(i) compound rates of growth in different industries;

(ii) change in weights assigned to different industries;

(iii) contribution to the value-added.

(i) Compound Rate of Growth in Different Industries. Four distinct phases relating to the compond rates of growth in different industries can be observed, *viz.* *(a)* the first phase till mid-sixties, *(b)* the second phase of 1965-80, *(c)* the third phase of 1981-91, and *(d)* the fourth phase since 1991-92 onwards. In the earlier phase, the rate of growth of industries, in general, had picked up very fast. A major contribution in this direction was made by the basic and capital goods industries. The annual rate of growth in basic industries had gone up from 4.7% during 1051-55, to 10% during 1955-60: similarly, the annual rate of growth in capital goods industries had gone up from 9.8% during 1951-55 to 13.3% during 1955-60, and further to 19.6 during 1960-65. On the contrary, consumer goods industries recorded only a marginal growth. The annual rate of growth in these industries was only 4.8 during 1955-55 which came down to 4.4% during 1955-60, and recorded a little improvement to go up 4.9% during 1960-65. In short, the pattern of industrilisation that evolved during the first fifteen years had shown two features: one, a rapid growth of basic and capital goods industries, and two, a slow growth of consumer good industries. This pattern was in consonance with the strategy of growth evoloved during the Second Plan and followed during the subsequent Plan.

In the next phase, beginning with the mid-sixties the rate of industrial growth, as already seen, began to trigger off. The growth of basic and capital goods industries has been slower than in the past and also slower than even the meagre average growth in industrial output; where growth has been moderately high, a majority of the industries belonged either directly or indirectly to elite-oriented consumption goods' sector, like consumer durables. In the third phase, as would be seen from table below, basic goods industries picked up fast and their rate of growth accelarated between the Fifth and Sixth Plan periods, intermediate goods industries and consumer goods industries slowed down. In the first half of the Seveth Plan it was the capital goods industries sector that recorded the stupendous growth as also the basic goods industries. Intermediate goods and consumer goods industries picked up well during the First year of the Plan, but subsequently lost momentum. Over all, the growth momentum in the industrial sector during these two plans, as also during the first three years of the Seventh Plan, was maintained largely by growth in basic goods industries.

The table reveals that the industrial growth rate during 1980-81 to 1991-92 (Sixth and Seventh Plan) was 7.8 per cent and it reduced to 6.6 per cent during 1992-93 to 2000-01 (post-reform decade). This poor performance is basically due to a steep fall in the rate of growth of capital goods sector. On the other hand, the intermediate goods sector and consumers goods sector put up a better performance during 1992-93 to 2000-01. The main causes for poor performance of industrial sector are exposure to external competition, slowdown in investment, the infrastuctual constraints, lack of funds for expansion, sluggish growth in exports, anomalies in tariff structure and contraction in consumer demand.

(ii) Changes in Weighs Assigned to Different Industries. The pattern of industrialisation can also be studied with the help of changes in weight assigned to different industries. These weights are generally expressed in proportion to their share in value added in the organised manufacturing sector. The weight of capital goods industries expanded from 4.21 per centages points in 1956 to 11.76 per centage points in 1960 and further to 18.66% in 1965; subsequently, the weight of consumer goods industries declined from 48.37 in 1956 to 37.25 in 1960, and further to 30.89 in 1965. It, however, increased to 31.03 in 1970. During the seventies, the weight of basic and capital goods industries kept on falling down, while that of consumer goods industries moved up.

(iii) Contribution to the Value Added. The industrial sector growth rate in post-reform decade has declined in comparison to the pre-reform decade. Similarly the compound annual rate of growth of manufacturing sector during the 1990-91 to 1998-99 has also fell in comparison to pre-reform decade.

The rate of growth of growth value added in industry during pre-reform period was highest *i.e.* more than 7.0 per cent per annum. But the gross value added in industry during the eight year period of 1990s (1990-91 to 1998-99) was just 5.91 per cent per annum. It was lowest. This shows that economic reforms and 'opening up' of the inudstrial economy in 1990s did not accelerate industrial growth as expected but slowed it down. Moreover, as the above table shows the growth record during the reforms of 1990s has been worse than the during 1980s.

B. Ownership Pattern of Industries

On the basis of the type of ownership, the industrial units can be divided into the following categories: *(i)* public sector, *(ii)* joint sector and *(iii)* private sector. Table presents information on the structure of Indian industrial sector by type of ownership for the year 1996-97.

This table reveals the following factors regarding the structure of Indian industries by type of ownership:

1. The total number of factories in 1996-97 was 1,34,556 of which as many as 1,22,772 (*i.e.* 91.2 per cent) were in the private sector. Only 8,825 units (6.6 per cent) were in the public sector.

2. Of the total fixed capital of Rs. 3,84,560 crore in the industrial sector in 1996-97, as much as Rs. 1,42,156 crore (*i.e.* 36.9 per cent) was in the public sector. The share of the private sector was Rs. 2,12,920 crore (*i.e.* 55.4 per cent). Thus with only 6.6 per cent of the factories, the public sector had 36.9 per cent of fixed capital. This shows that the public sector units are much more capital intensive as compared with the private sector units.

3. Out of the gross output of Rs. 6,92,520 crore, the private sector units contributed Rs. 4,81,218 crore (or 69.5 per cent). As against this, the public sector units contributed Rs. 1,51,174 crore of gross output which is 21.8 per cent of the total.

4. Total employment in the industrial sector was 9,707 thousand in 1996-97. Of this, 71.0 per cent were employed in the private sector and 23.5 per cent in the public sector.

5. The Industrial Policy Enquiry Committee which was constituted by the Government of India in July 1967 under the chairmanship of Dr. Subimal Dutt had strongly recommended the setting up of the joint sector. However, the concept proved to be a still born child. As is clear from table only 2.2 per cent indusrial units were in the joint sector in 1996-97 and they possessed only 7.6 per cent of fixed capital and provided employment to only 5.5 per cent industrial labour. Their share in gross output was 8.7 per cent and in value added, 8.0 per cent in 1996-97.

6. The total value added in the industrial sector in 1996-97 was Rs. 1,43,076 crore. Of this, private sector contributed

Rs. 94,664 crore (66.2 per cent) and the public sector contributed Rs. 36,915 crore (25.8 per cent).

Features of Industrial Growth

Some distinguishing, but disturbing, features of the industrial development process in India can be indentified as follows:

Firstly, along with external financial assistance, technological dependence on MNCs increased. The old private foreign capital, which had operated in the colonial period, worked mainly through branches in India or through managing agency house. It was organised in pools which were small by the standard of metropolitan countries and operated in areas like trade, finance and export oriented activites. A goods part of this capital either left the country in the wake of independence or clung on in a stagnant or precarious state. The new private foreign capital which entered particularly during the Second and Third Plans went into technologically intensive areas and produced mainly for the domestic market which was cordoned off by high protective barriers.

Secondly, industrial growth was accompanied by a considerable increase in the country's indebtedness. The share of foreign aid, as a proportion of gross investment, of Plan outlay and of national income increased dramatically during the decade 1955-65. The entire industrialisation drive, however, impressive, was indeed far from being financially self-reliant.

Thirdly, industrialisation in India had virtually a negligible impact on either unemployment or the sectoral distribution of the work-force. The employment-creating capacity of industrialisation was not enough either to make a dent in the backlog of urban unemployment which also experienced a natural growth over time or to absorb immigrants from rural areas. The economic stagnation since the mid-sixties worsened the unemployment situation.

Fourthly, inudstrial growth in India has been accompanied by a virtual stagnation in real wages. This is not to say that with changing industrial composition and the creation of many more skilled job, opportunities have not been opened up or utilised but the picture of stagnation remains roughly valid for any particular category of workers, especially unskilled workers.

Fifthly, although the share of agro-based industries has dclined over the years the impact of agricultural growth on industrial growth does not seem to have weakened. This is borne out by the fact that as Prof. K.N. Raj has noted the fluctuations in indusrial production are preceded by fluctuation in agricultural production.

Finally, few of the industrial groups appear to have been interested in providing for systematic reasearch. In this respect, the Indian experience has been contrary to the Japanese and this lacuna, to be traced historically perhaps to the dominance of trading and money lending communities in industrial entrepreneurship in India and an explicit state policy for import-substitution in an attentuated from through the planning period for different reasons arising primarily from the operation of industrial and trade policies.

Problems of Industrial Growth

(i) Growth of Big Industrial Houses. Despite the various policy measures taken by the Government such as the MRTP Act and the licensing policy, the share of the large industrial house in the total assests of the private corporate sector has increased. According to Prof. S.K. Goyal, "during the period 1964 and 1976, the number of Big Houses in India rose from 33 to 75; and the number of large independent undertakings increased from 8 to 26. The combined assets of the big houses and the large independent undertakings expanding from Rs. 2,412.04 crore to Rs. 8,955.70 crore in 1979, *i.e.*, an increase of 271.3% in 13 years". And, similarly, a recent study by the Economics Times Research Bureau has brought out that as on March 31, 1990, the 20 large industrial houses had assets worth Rs. 33, 919 crore constituting 68.9 per cent of the assets of 78 large industrial houses. The top 10 houses, have total assets worth Rs. 1,53,091 crore in the year 1998-99. The largest house in terms of assets and not sales in Tata. This industrial house had assets worth Rs. 47,446 were in 1998-99. This shows that large indusrial houses worth most in the post liberalisation phase.

(ii) Increase in Regional Imbalances. Another unfavourable aspect of the industrial science is the imbalance that exists in the industrial development of different regions. Massive investment in the Central sector projects in the expectation that this would have a wide ranging 'ripple effect' in stimulating small and ancillary industries have not succeed in many states such as Bihar, Orissa and Madhya Pradesh. The natural tendency of enterpreneurs to go where the infrastructure is strong, markets are close and various services are readily available cannot be ignored.

(iii) Higher Cost of Industrial Product. Another weakness of the industrial scene is the high cost of some of its products as compared to international prices. *(a)* This has partly arisen out of the absence of healthy competition, a situation which industrial licensing tends to foster. High tarriff barriers and tight controls on imports have tended to shield these units from international competition and projected them from the consequences of the relatively low rate of inflation in India as compared to other countries. Non-competitiveness, in general, has resulted in the slowing down of growth through a pervasive waste in the utilisation of scarce capital resources or a parts of the economy. Dealing with it is, therefore, important not only for the export effort but more fundamentally to bring about an acceleration in the rate of economic growth in the country. *(b)* High costs have sometimes been a direct outcome of the Government's licensing policy. Where the demand was large enough to sustain only one plant of an economic size, several plants with suboptimal capacity were licensed in the name of diffusing ownership and preventing monopolies. *(c)* In the policy of import substitution also insufficient attention has been paid to costs and a few industries have been set up whose cost of production is not low according to international standards. While this may be necessary in certain strategic areas, it was not essential in many other.

(iv) Industry's Dependence on the Government. A consequences of a regime of government-imposed constraints has been that the industry has become heavily dependent upon the government. Hence the contradictory demands that the government should reduce this tax or duty (to protect an importer), raise that duty (to protect a local manufacturer), make imports easier or more difficult, allow the expansion of capacity (to achieve economies of scale) or prevent new capacity from coming up (to protect existing producers), etc. If an individual unit or an industry faces a problem and a simple, adaptive answer is elusive, the tendency is to run to the government for help without making a thorough search for self-relient solution. This habit has become widespread and even those without fewer controls often fall a prey to the soft option of appealing to the government for an instant solution usually with a penalty to offers or to the economy as a whole.

(v) Sickness in Industry. The incidence of sickness in large and medium-scale industries has increased in recent year; and in the case of some of the traditional industries like cotton textiles, jute textiles and sugar, the economic viability of a large number of units has been seriously eroded. The phenomenon of industrial sickness not only tends to aggravate the problem of unemployment, but also renders infructuous capital investment any generally creates an adverse climate for further industrial growth. While in advanced countries, where there are adequate social security benefits, this is accepted as a normal features of the industrial scene, such sickness has much more serious economic consequences in a country where unemployment is a major problem and resources are scarce.

(vi) Growing Dependence of the Organised Private Sector on Financial Institutions. The growing capital-intensive nature of industry and relatively high corporate tax rates have increased the dependence of the organised private sector on financial institutions. This has meant that the role of financial institutions in financing new ventures has grown substantially. Increasingly, therefore, the agencies which determine the pattern and structure of industrial growth are the term lending institutions rather than the Industrial Licensing Committee which at best can play a negative role. Since this is not the purpose for which these institutions were set up, some new mechanism would have to be devised to ensure that the flow of funds from financial institutions is in accordance with national priorities.

(vii) Lack of Proper Employment Planning. Perhaps the most serious lacuna in our industrial planning has been the lack of attention paid to the employment implications in choosing technologies. The main victim of this policy has been the cottage sector where the growth of industries like textiles, oil crushing, shop making, matches, leather and leather goods has been stifled. Another area in which industrial development could have been directed better both from the point of view of cost reduction and employment generation is the development of ancillaries particularly by way of off-loading existing low technology activities to the small-scale and ancillary industry. While there have been areas and industries which have done well in this field, the rate of growth of ancillaries suggests that inadequate attention has been paid to this problem.

(viii) Underutilisation of Industrial Capacity. Another major problem of industrial development in India has been the underutilisation of industrial capacity. Some of the important industries have been reporting utilisation rates of only 50 to 60 per cent. Underutilisation poses serious problems to the process of growth. All out efforts have to be made to create conditions conductive to optimm utilisation of capacity.

(x) Poor Productivity Performance. Dr. Hollis Chenery in a recent study covering 40 countries has found India at the bottom of the list in terms of productivity growth. Productivity growth has been a major contributing factor, in the economic growth of many industrial countries. Productivity can be measured either in the form of a partial productivity like labour productivity, capital productivity and material productivity, or as total factor productivity (TFP). Labour productivity can be defined as the output per unit of labour.

Other partial productivities are also similarly defined. TFP is defined as the ratio between real product or output and real factor input (a weighted sum of the different inputs). TFP is a better measure of productivity as it relates output to all the conventional inputs simultaneously.

INDUSTRIAL POLICY

At the time of independence, there was no well coordinated industrial policy of India. The Government of India along with investors and entrepreneurs felt the need of a well coordinated industrial policy because rapid growth of industries was almost impossible in the absence of such an industrial policy. Consequently within less than one year after independent the Government of India announced the Industrial policy Resolution on 6th April 1948.

INDUSTRIAL POLICY RESOLUTION 1948

The Government of India evolved its first new Industrial policy after independence which envisaged a mixed economy with overall responsibility of the government to secure planned development of industries and their regulation. The government also acknowledged the valuable role of the private entreprise properly directed and regulated. The main features of this industrial are the following:

(i) Acceptance of the importance of both private and public sectors.

(ii) **Division of the Industrial Sector.** The Resolution divided industries in four categories namely—*(a)* industries where state has the monopoly (3 industries); *(b)* mixed sector (6 industries); (c) the field of government control (18 industries); and (d) the field of private enterprise (all other industries not included in the above three categories.

(iii) Role of small and cottage industries.

(iv) Other important features (less importance to foreign investment, harmonious relations between management and labour force).

Indian capitalists were satisfied with the Industiral Policy Resolution of 1948 since the role assigned to the public sector in that policy was, on the whole, acceptable to them. However, there were certain weakness and gaps in the 1948 policy and it was subjected to a number of criticisms.

INDUSTRIAL POLICY RESOLUTION OF 1956

In 1956 came the second Industrial policy Resolution of the Government of India which sought to start an era of stabilisation against the background of the declared goal of a socialist pattern of society.

The 1956 Resolution laid down the following objectives for the industrial policy: *(i)* to accelerate the rate of growth and to speed up industrialization; *(ii)* to develop heavy industries and machine making industries; *(iii)* to expand public sector; *(iv)* to reduce disparities in income and wealth; *(v)* to build up a large and growing cooperative sector; and *(vi)* to prevent monopolies and the concentration of wealth and income in the hands of a small number of individuals. The main features of this Resolutions are the following:

1. **Division of the Industrial Sector.** As against four categories in the 1948 Resolution, the 1956 Resolution divided industries into the following three categories:

   (a) Monopoly of the State. In the first category, those industries were included whose future development would be the exclusive responsibility of the State. Seventeen industries were included in this category and were listed in Schedule A. Ofthese, four industries—arms and amunition, atomic energy, railways and air transport, were to be governement monopolies. In the remaining 13 ir dustries, all new units were to be established by the State. However, existing units in the private sector were allowed to subsist and expand.

   (b) Industries Left for Private Sector. All industries not listed in schedules 'A' or 'B' were included in the third category. The main role of the state in this category was to provide facilities to the private sector to develop itself.

(c) ***Mixed Sector of Public and Private Enterprise.*** In this section 12 industries listed in Schedule B (appended to the Resolution) were included. In these industries, State would increasingly establish new units and increase its participation but would not deny the private sector opportunities to set up units or expand existing units.

2. **Assistance and Control of Private Sector.** According to the 1956 Resolution, the government could assist expansion and development of private sector through participation in its risk capital and share capital and by providing other types of services, fiscal incentive etc. However, the private sector was also to fit into the "framework of the economic and social policy of the State". Thus, the private sector was to remain subject to various government regulations and controls. Such regulation and control was to be exercised by the government through the Industries (Development and Regulation) Act, 1951, and other related legislations.

3. **Importance of Small-scale and Cottage Industries.** The 1956 Resolution recognized the importance of small-scale and cottage industries just as the 1948 Resolution had done. Such industries could create large scale employment opportunities, ensure a more equitable distribution of income and wealth, and help in effective mobilization of human and physical capital. Assistance to this sector was to be provided either through direct means or through indirect means.

4. **Mutual Dependence of Public and Private Sectors.** The only four industries in which private sector was not allowed to function were arms and ammunition, atomic energy, railway and air transport. In all other industries either to private sector was allowed to operate freely or its help could be obtained if the government deemed fit.

Accordingly, the 1956 Resolution emphasized not only the mutual coexistence of private and public sectors but also provided for their mutual cooperation and help.

5. **Technical and Managerial Personnel.** Shortage of technical and managerial personnel to carry out the programmes of industrial development in the economy has been accepted and emphasized by the government right from the beginning of the planning era. According, the 1956 Resolution advocated the establishment of proper technical and managerial cadres through the organisation of apprenticeship schemes of training on a large scale, establishment of technical institutions, etc.

6. **Reduction of Regional Inequalities.** The 1956 Resolution called for reduction in regional imbalances and inequalities. For this purpose it was advocated that transport facilities, power and other facilities should be provided in the backward regions. Stress on balanced development of agriculture and industry in each region was also laid.

An Appraisal of the Industrial Policy of 1956. The industrial policy of 1956 contemplated a mixed or controlled economy in which public and private enterprises work hand in hand so as to make the development plan a success. The industrial policy of 1956 has been appreciated for bringing about an excellent synchronisation between government's industrial policy and industrial development programmes included in the plan. The 1956 industrial Policy was a positive Policy improvement over the 1948 industrial policy since it was broader and more liberal. The 1956 industrial policy has held good till today even though some changes have been made in it in the last few years.

INDUSTRIAL POLICY RESOLUTION OF 1980

The 1980 industrial policy is based on 1956 Industrial policy. As a matter of fact it is a supplement to it. The new Industrial production through optimum utilisation of the installed capacity and expansion of industries. The policy emphasises on rapid and Balanced industrialisation of the country with a view to benefitting the common man by increasing availability of goods at reasonable prices, larger employment and higher per capita income. The new policy aims at the revival of the economy by solving the problems of shortages of major industrial inputs like energy, transport and coal. This industrial policy has been formulated to achieve these objectives-modernisation, expansion and development to backward areas or regions.

The 1980 industrial policy also emphasise the need to make available the benefits of industrialisation to all the sectors of the society by extending preferential treatment to agro-based industries, by promoting the development of small, medium, and large enterprises, by promoting the dispersal of industries in backward rural and urban areas and protecting consumers against high prices and bad quality of goods.

Chief Objectives and Features. The 1980 industrial policy envisages the following objectives:

(i) Maximum use of the existing production capacity;

(ii) to obtain the highest level of production;

(iii) to remove regional imbalance by giving priority to development of industrially backward areas;

(iv) to give priority to agro based industries and there by strengthen the agricultural base;

(v) to accelerate the development of export oriented and import substitution industries;

(vi) to create more employment opportunities;

(vii) to encourage economic federation through coordinate development of small medium and large enterprises;

(viii) to protect consumers against high prices and bad quality goods.

Growth of Cottage, Village and Small Industries. The limits of Industries were enhanced as follows:

(i) tiny units-from one lakh rupees to two lakh rupees.

(ii) ancillary units-from fifteen lakh rupees to 25 lakh rupees.

(iii) small scale units-from ten lakh rupees to twenty lakh rupees.

Sectors where efficient production can be secured on a small scale would continue to be reserved for future expansion only by the small scale units.

3. Public Sector. The policy statement reiterates that public confidence in the public sector would be restored and the public sector would continue to occupy a vital position in the country's economic structure.

4. Private Sector. The private sector industries would also be allowed to develop in accordance with the objectives and targets of national plans and policies. However, the government would not allow monopolistic tendencies to grow in the private sector units.

5. Export Production. This industrial policy statement also emphasises on increasing export production. To achieve this end 100 per cent export oriented units would be set up the existing units would be expanded exclusively for purpose of export.

6. Removal of Regional Imbalances. To achieve this end the policy encourages the establishment of new industrial units in industrially backward areas. Further, for securing greater regional balance the policy emphasises the dispersal of those industries in which economics of scale are not important. This would be economically and socially desirable. Special concession and government aids would be made available in industrially backward areas.

7. Sick Units. The industrial policy statement reiterates that strict action would be taken against those industrial units which are sick by their own mismanagement and financial misappropriation. Government would determine such sick units which are found in critical condition. The government would make effort to revive such sick units by encouraging them to merge into healthy units who are in a position to revive them.

8. Technological Self Reliance. The industrial policy statement lay adequate stress on keeping the technology in use up to date. To achieve this end import of technology particularly for export oriented and key industries may be liberalised.

NEW INDUSTRIAL POLICY 1991

The Congress (I) Government led by Mr. Narasimha Rao has announced the new industrial policy on July 24, 1991. The main aim of the new industrial policy is to unshackle the Indian industrial economy from the cobwebs of unnecessary bureaucratic control, to introduce liberalisation with a view of integrate the Indian economy with the world economy, to remove restrictions on direct foreign investment as also to free the domestic entrepreneur from the restrictions of MRTP Act. All these reforms of industrial policy have led the government to take a series of initiatives in respect of policies in the following areas:

1. Industrial Licensing. In the sphere of industrial licensing, the role of the government was to be changed from that of only exercising control to one of providing help and guidance by making essential procedures fully transparent and by eliminating delays. This calls for bold and imaginative decisions designed to remove restraints on capacity creation, which at the same time, ensure that over-riding national interests are not jeopardised. The industrial licensing will henceforth be abolished for all industries, except those specified, irrespective of levels of investment. These specified industries will continue to be subject to compulsory licensing for reasons related to security and strategic concerns, social reasons, problems related to safety and overriding environmental issues, manufacture of products of hazardous nature and arcticles of elitist consumption.

2. Foreign Investment. In order to invite foreign investment in high priority industries, requiring large investment and advanced technology, it has been decided to provide approval for direct foreign investment upto 51 per cent foreign equity in such industries. For the promotion of exports of Indian products in world markets, the government will encourage foreign trading companies to assist Indian exporters in export activities. Besides this, the government will appoint a special board to negotiate with such firms so that purposive negotiations can be carried out with such large firms which provide the avenues for large investment in the development of industries and technology in the national interest.

3. Public Sector Policy. Public enterprises have shown a very low rate to return on the capital invested. This has inhibited their ability to regenerate themselves in terms of new investments as well as in technology development. The result is that many of the public enterprises have become a burden rather than being an asset to the Government. The original concept of the public sector has also undergone considerable dilution. The most striking example is the take over of sick units from the private sector. The category of public sector units accounts for almost one-third of the total losses of central public enterprises. Another category of public enterprises, which does not fit into the original idea of the public sector being at the commanding heights of the economy, is the plethora of public enterprises which are in the consumer goods and services sectors.

It is time therefore that the Government adopt a new approach to public enterprises. Units which may be faltering at present but are potentially viable must be restructured and given a new lease of life. The priority areas for growth of public enterprises in the future will be the following:

(a) Essential infrastructure goods and services.

(b) Exploration and exploitation of oil and mineral resources.

(c) Technology development and building of manufacturing capabilities in areas which are crucial in the long term development of the economy and where private sector invesment is inadequate.

(d) Manufacture of products where strategic considerations predominate such as defence equipment.

Government will strengthen those public enterprises which fall in the reserved areas of operation or are in high priority areas or are generating good or reasonable profits. Such enterprises will be provided a much greater degree of management autonomy through the system of memoranda of understanding. Competition will also be induced in these areas by inviting private sector participation. In the case of selected enterprises, part of Government holdings in the equity share capital of these enterprises will be disinvested in order to provide further market discipline to the performance of public enterprises. There are a large number of chronically sick public enterprises incurring heavy losses, operating a competitive market and serve little or not public purpose. These need to be attended to.

4. Industrial Location Policy Liberalilsed. In a departure from the earlier locational policy for industries, the new industrial policy stated that in locations other than cities of more than 1 million population, there will be no requirement of obtaining industrial approvals from the Centre, except for industries subject to compulsory licensing. In cities with a population of more than 1 million, industries other than those of a non-polluting nautre, were required to be located outside 25 kms of the priphery. Major amendments in the industrial location policy were effected during 1997-98. Now notified industries of a non-polluting nature such as electronics, computer softwer and printing, may be located within 25 kms of the periphery of cities with more than 1 million population. Other industries are permitted only if they are located in designated industrial areas set up prior to July 25, 1991. Zoning and Land Use Regulation as well as Environment Legislation continue to regulate industrial locations.

5. Foreign Technology. With a view to injecting the desired level of technological dynamism in Indian industry, government will provide automatic approval for technology agreements related to high priority industries within specified parameters.

Similar facilities will be available for other industries as well if such agreements do not require the expenditure of free foriegn exchange. Indian companies will be free to negotiate the terms of technology transfer with their foreign conterparts according to their own commerical jüdgement.

6. Monoplies and Restrictive Trade Practices Act (MRTP) Act. With the growing complexity of industrial structure and the need for achieving economies of scale for ensuring higher productivity and competitive advantage in the international market, the interference of the Government through the MRTP Act in investment decision of large companies has become deleterious in its effects on Indian industrial growth. The pre-entry scrutiny of investment decisions by so-called MRTP companies will no longer be required. Instead, emphasis will be on controlling and regulating monopolistic, restrictive and unfair trade practices rather than making it necessary for the monopoly houses to obtain prior approval of Central Government for expansion, establishment of new undertakings, mergers, amalgamation and takeover and appointment of certain directors. The trust policy will be more on controlling unfair or restrictive business practices.

7. Abolition of Phased Manufacturing Programmes for New Projects. To force the pace of indigenisation in manufacturing, Phased Manufacturing Programmes have been in force in a number of engineering and electronic industries. The new industrial policy has abolished such programmes in future as the government feels that due to substantial reforms made in the trade policy and the devaluation of the rupee, there is no longer any need for enforcing the local content requirements on a case-by-case, administrative basis. Various incentives that are currently available to manufacturing units with existing Phased Manufacturing Programmes will continue.

8. Removal of Mandatory Convertibility Clause. A lare part of industrial investment in India is financed by loans from banks and financial institutions. These institutions have followed a mandatory practice of including a convertibility clause in their loans into equity if felt necessary by their management. Although this option has not generally been exercised, it has often been interpreted as an unwarranted threat to private firms of takeover by financial institutions. The new industrial policy has provided that henceforth financial institutions will not impose this mandatory convertibility clause.

❑

11

Role of Managers

In any, enterprise the manager has obligations towards:

1. Those who have appointed him.

2. Those whom he manages.

3. The general community.

To the first he owes a service commensurate with the authority invested in him. Such service does not extend to the approval of institutions and theories which may be contrary to moral principles. Management is not an isolated activity of human life and a law unto itself, but is subject to the same moral code which governs all other activities. The pursuit of an objective for its own sake should not be the dominating factor; such thinking leads ultimately to conflict with the other social groups. In business or industry it is the responsibility of managers to give the best possible service to their employers within the limits imposed by obligations to other groups which must also serve.

The individual worker's activities must be directed so that his personal task makes a real contribution to the total effort, and it must be recognized as such. Moreover, as the worker is concerned with his own dignity and status, his work must be directed so that it demands some measure of responsibility and initiative. One of the earliest managers to recognize this, obligation to his workers was Robert Owen (1771-1858) who has been described as "the pioneer of personnel management." As manager of a group of textile mills in New Lanark in Scotland he set out to improve the factory and domestic conditions of his employees. At the same time Owen addressed himself to social reform in the community of which the factory was the centre. The first syllable of management is man. Human labour is not a bit of merchandise, it is the effort of a human being. To the community, the manager owes the responsibility for providing goods or services at a reasonable cost. To this end there devolves on him the responsibility for ensuring the maximum utilization of the productive potential of the undertaking, and the allocation of these resources in a way best calculated to maintain a proper balance among the varied needs of consumers.

In accepting these responsibilities a manager must realize the need for a constant awareness of, and sensibility to the almost imperceptible changes in the industrial and social panorama, a readiness to review, and re-evaluate accepted ideas, practices, habits and customs to meet the demands of a changing world. We are perhaps too much inclined to regard the Industrial Revolution as an historical event of the past, whereas it was simply the beginning of a continuous industrial and social revolution of which we are still in the midst; our chief problem is one of adjustment and adaptation.

It is a mistake to concentrate on changes in technological procedures and to overlook the need to match such changes with corresponding adaptations in the pattern of social life. Perhaps at the root of this problem lies the question of the status of the individual.

In what does status consist? In the Middle Ages the answer would have been easy. Society, based on a rural economy, with a feudal system based on land tenure, had what seemed natural and inevitable lines of demarcation. The villein, the freeholder, the squire, the overlord, each had his place, and was conscious of the duties and responsibilities it involved. With the disintegration of that system, the spread of industry and commerce, the rise of a wealthy merchant class, the change from a rural to an urban civilization, the clear-cut distinctions of status became increasingly blurred. As the villein, the freeholder, the yeoman became the factory operative, as the squire became the commercial magnate, and the overlord the "captain of industry," status came increasingly to depend upon wealth, no longer synonymous with land; the distinction between the working, middle and upper classes was largely one of economic circumstance. With wealth came the opportunity to enjoy the physical amenities, the education, the culture, once the hall-mark of birth and gentle breeding. The power to maintain and increase that wealth was largely dependent upon the maintenance of a substantial monopoly of political power in the hands of the landed proprietors and the merchant and manufacturing classes. This joint monopoly was challenged when industrial workers, followed by others, learned to organize and to seek the amelioration of economic and social conditions through the ballot box. Equality of political status was achieved. Such equality in political power has, however, brought into sharper focus the inequalities in economic status. Legislation has reduced those inequalities, but whether we are on the road to economic egalitarianism is an interesting speculation.

There is, however, another aspect of status—what one may call the philosophic view. On this view man is a unique pheno menon in nature; he is born not only with a body to nourish arid a mind to cultivate, but also with a soul to save. By virtue of his human nature and divinely ordained destiny he is, literally, lord of creation. To fulfil that nature and achieve that end he is en lowed with certain natural rights, and subject to certain correlative duties. These rights are innate and inalienable, independent of colour and climate, independent also of economic circumstance. Such rights may be said not only to mark but to constitute his status. Status is not bestowed, achieved or conceded, but inborn. On this view, what are commonly regarded as the marks of status are merely accidents; status is neither humble nor exalted, when all are equally exalted. That is what we mean by human rights and the dignity of man. Few, probably, would deny the validity of the theoretical argument: the practical application is not yet universal. The abolition of slavery was comparatively recent; the idea of the "lesser breeds" and the victims of the colour bar are still withus. Nevertheless, it seems that many recent developments social, political and economic—indicate a tacit acceptance of this view.

Against this background the nature and status of the individuals of whom society is composed we may proceed to consider the question of social purpose. It may be advisable to make a distinction here between social purpose in industry and the social purpose of industry. While the latter is not directly relevant to our subject, it is sufficiently closely related to merit attention. In the Middle Ages the social purpose of industry seemed self-evident. Man lived in small communities. trade, commerce and industry were localized; manufactured goods were the product of the craftsman, supplying a local and primary need. Standards of quality were enforced by the guilds; moral laws had not yet been replaced by economic laws.

With the disintegration of that order and way of living, and the relegation of that philosophy to the schools to be followed in time by a phenomenal expansion in industrial productivity, there gradually grew the idea that as capital was acquired by hard work, saving, labour and abstinence, material prosperity was a sign of the divine approbation; those who did not enjoy it probably did not deserve to. The economist advocates of laissez-faire helped to complete a system by which wealth was amassed at the cost for many of most things that make life worth living. We are only gradually being compelled to re-discover some of the old truths, to realize that even commerce and industry can be firmly grounded only on an ethical basis.

The social purpose of industry may be loosely described rather than defined as the whole sum of the objectives in terms of human satisfactions, towards which industrial activities are directed. What, then, are these objectives? The part that industry is supposed to play in the modern community is a subject that has been variously discussed by sociologists, economists, politicians, philosophers, and other specialist groups, but the following have been the main lines of thought as to the primary purposes of industry:

1. The provision of the goods and services that the community needs or desires.
2. The provision of employment for the people of the community.
3. The provision of social satisfaction for those employed.
4. The earning of profit on the capital invested.

5. The basic value of the work itself; the old idea of craftsmanship for its own sake.

With the above list of purposes few would violently disagree. While the first—the provision of the goods and services which the community needs and desires—is an obvious purpose, it may be regarded from several points of view. In the past the "needs and desires of the community" have been regarded almost solely from the economic point of view. That the commodity or service would sell has usually been regarded as sufficient justification for its production or provision. This attitude has for some time, however, been gradually changing. As the consumer can often know little of the content of the product or the process of manufacture, he.has often been an easy prey. To exploit the consumer has almost ceased to be good business. Resnonsibility towards the consumer implies not only the production of the right goods, in the right quantities, at the right price, but also a recoinition that all needs and desires are not equally worthy. It is imperative not only to raise the standard of living but also to strive to improve the quality of life to raise the moral, social, intellectual and aesthetic standard. We may mention by ways of illustration the social costs which in any assessment of economic progress are to be debited against industry. They are costs to the community of the irresponsible exploitation of resources in private interests. To eliminate or minimize these costs to recognize that the power and liberty to exploit a country's resources are held in trust for the common good-this is part of the responsibility of managers. We are apt to forget that in these matters we have fallen far below the standard of some earlier civilizations. The ancient Greeks recognized that man is, in part, educated by or degraded by the environment in which he moves; they delighted in beautifying their public buildings, in providing public spectacles calculated to deepen the aesthetic sensibilities of the common man. The monuments of the Middle Ages still bear witness to the delight men took in beautifying their surroundings. It is an example an industrial age has neglected to its cost.

The third purpose of industry the earning of profit on the capital invested emphasizes the fact that without profits a business undertaking could not continue to exist, workers would lose their jobs, and capital would be unavailable. The managerial objective is often stated as being to "maximize profits." On this point, however, Professor Drucker has said: "Economists have for a long time tried to define the objective of business as 'Maximizing profits.' This is unfortunate-partly because their is no agreement on a definition of 'profit' which is one of the most elusive terms around-partly because 'profit' is a residual margin and not a result in itself."

In his opinion the manager must look for and find opportunity: his job is "to optimize opportunities." This involvea three activities. First there is the job of making the present business fully effective of making sure that the business is focussed on its opportunities and not on its problems. The second activity is to find and exploit the potential of the business. It is here that most innovation really comes into play. Any business offers tremendous opportunity for radical change through fairly minor imporvement in the rate at which it utilizes its potential. And increased productivity creates capital in that it makes the same resources capable of greater economic yield and thereby more valuable. Thirdly there is the task of making the future of the enterprise—now.

Finally, we come to the question of social purpose in industry. In so far as management has recognized that there is or should be any social purpose in industry it has usually been regarded as a departmental responsibility that of the personnel management department. Recent years have shown a remarkably increasing interest in personnel management. It is a belated recognition of the fact that industrial progress depends on both men and machines. Man is no longer regarded as simply an adjunct to the machine.

This development was largely the result of the experience of two world wars, when the nation's survival depended upon obtaining the maximum output from men and machines. The motive was perhaps as much utilitarian as humanitarian. Be that as it may, the result has been a deepend interest in the psychology of the worker. Without decrying in any way the value of the work done and the progress made, it may be remarked that the expression "personnel management" is in itself significant; significant of a tendency to regard people in the mass, and then as an abstraction, rather than as living human entities.

In the past, the personnel officer has been something betwixt and between a welfare officer and an industrial psychologist; the social aspect has been unduly neglected. Stress has been laid on those phenomena which were susceptible of measurement—heating and lighting, fatigue, accident proneness, incentive systems and the like. The criteria of successful managing, too, were conceived in measurable terms of increased productivity. There is no yardstick by which to measure social satisfactions, though they will ultimately determine the efficiency of the system.

The social problems entailed by the change from an established to an adaptive civilization are not peculiar to the workshop, factory or industry they are the problems of a civilization transformed and conditioned by industry. Before the industrial era men lieved mostly in villages; the small group was typical, and was almost self-sufficient; socially, it was self-sufficient. The village, or small town, was a community with a common way of life, common standards, recognized customs, established routines, accepted ways of thought, continuity in an acceptable way of life, the security and assurance that comes of belonging, the satisfaction of counting for something in a common purposeful round of activity this was the source and spring of those social satisfactions which an urban and industrial civilization has largely lost, and which must be recovered if healthy community social life is to be restored. It may be that, somewhat paradoxically, the factory, where men and women must perforce congregate, offers the best opportunity for effecting that restoration.

What are the chief needs? Security, stability, continuity some intrinsic satisfaction in work done as part of a common enterprise. The increasing realization of State responsibility for the welfare of the less forunate of its members, the sick, the needy, the unemployed, the aged, has removed some of the causes of unrest; it has helped to remove some of the fears that have hitherto beset the industrial worker. But state-organized social security schemes, admirable though they may be, can never provide that kind of security which we have in mind the feeling of having a niche of one's own in the social fabric of belonging to a social group which would be the poorer without us the security which a child feels when he thinks of home. The responsibility of the managers begins where state welfare schemes end; in a sense their effect is negative, the removal of fear; there still remains the positive task of creating an environment and an atmosphere in which man shall not only not fear sickness, unemployment, old age, but shall positively feel assured of such security, stability and continuity as can possibly be achieved in the particular work situation. Such assurance is often undermined by the everpersent fear of change. In this connection, the following comment by H. Whitehead deserves consideration:

Any executive from his own experience can cite instances where some needed change in routine has been patiently and clearly explained to a group, only to find in the end that the group has ruined its chances by resisting the change. At first, the group seems to acquiesce, impressed by the logic, but soon resentment or some similar sentiment indicates a reversal of attitude. Neither management nor the workers themselves can usually explain what has happened; but the fact is, nothing in the workers' daily experience has indicated the need for change; it presents itself not as a sensible adaptation to a visible situation, but as blow from management wrapped up in a tissue of unanswerable logic. The better the, logic the more irritating is the blow... No society or organization is averse to change, provided the initiative for that change takes place at the relevant level at that level where the daily activities have shown the need. Under those conditions, change will present itself not as an interruption. but as the natural flow of social living. . .change, to be acceptable to a group, must come from within and must appear as the visible need of its present activities.

It is common to regard the modern industrial worker as little more than a cog in a machine, in contrast with the medieval craftsman.

Tho difference is substantial, but can easily be exaggerated. Many medieval workers were not craftsmen, and of those who were many were probably more acutely conscious of the drudgery of the daily round the common task, than of the joy of creation. It is easy, too, for the more intellectual, introspective observer to over-stress the monotony of which the worker himself is often probably unconscious. Nevertheless, there is a real problem how to give the worker some pride in the work, and the feeling that the work is in itself worth while, and that it brings out such ability as he may possess.

The widespread application of automation will undoubtedly accentuate this problem. The technical possibilities of automation are clear, but as yet we know little of its social aspects. There is, therefore, great need for research, and for close consultation before industrial change, between managers and representatives of the workers, and to some extent also between them both and the Government.

That workers in any enterprise need some sense of common purpose in that enterprise is becoming increasingly recognized. When men are herded into large industrial establishments, the sense of common purpose must inevitably be diminished or lost. Yet industry has been organized in the past with an almost complete disregard of the human factors involved. Industrial organization, factory layout, technical processes, have been determined almost solely by economic and technological considerations.

Much, of course, has already been done to stimulate the interest of the worker and encourage his willing and active co-operation in the work of the enterprise. Incentive schemes for both individuals and groups; profit-sharing and copartnership; joint consultation; schemes for arbitration; selection and training schemes-all illustrate a general tendency to give the worker a deeper sense of responsibility, associate him more closely and identify his interests more intimately with those of the undertaking. The limited success of some of these policies and schemes suggests that they may be partly misconceived. It seems clear that too much emphasis has been placed upon the economic motive; as standards of living rise its importance will inevitably tend to diminish. It may be doubted, too, whether the desire of workers in general for a "say in the management" is quite so deep or so widespread as is some-times thought. A more fruitful field may well be found in the study of social relations within industry than in the cultivation of a subtle ingenuity in the elaboration of incentive schemes conceived in terms of money and what are often merely the symbols of power.

One comparatively recent, and hopeful, deveopment is the increasing attention that is being paid to the social psychology of the working group. In the paucity of social satisfactions outside the work environment, the worker will seek them increasingly within that environment. They will be sought in those groups, lacking definition in form and conscious organization, which simply grow when numbers are brought together. Man is a gregarious animal and will seek to satisfy that instinct by association with his fellows; he fulfils himself by participating in the common purposive social activity of the group. As H. Whitehead has pointed out, if members of the group do not find satisfaction in the performance of their daily tasks they will develop independent activities which do provide that satisfaction, and such activities may or may not further the general economic purposes of the undertaking. It is the task bf managers, by sympathetic study of such group activity to ensure that they do.

The expasion of repetitive jobs in, mass-production has laid emphasis on the so-called "social satisfaction" that may compensate for the lack of satisfaction from the job itself. Team-work is an important source of social satisfaction but the nature of team-work changes along with the technical basis of production. The more workers are involved in the planning and control of their work the greater is their job satisfaction likely to be.

Operatives on automatic processes are often spread thinly over a big area, and each of them covers an extensive part of the plant and so may become isolated though not where control is centralized. Yet they can obtain a new social satisfaction from technical co-operation with maintenance men and technical specialists. The three groups have a clear and important objective in common to keep the machine-line or the process running and this may prove more satisfying than membership of an operative team. Discipline on automatic processes is exercised more through the technical requirements of the plant than through differenees in status between employees. All told, the related functions of operatives, maintenance men and supervising technicians seem to provide a basis of team-work on automatic pocesses and may help to improve human relations.

F.J. Roethlisberger called attention to the significance of the social problem in industrial, national and international affairs. He pointed out that material provision is only one of the dutes of civilization, the other being the maintenance of co-opertive living. It is a mistake to think that if technical and material advancement is maintained human co-operation will somehow be inevitable. First class technical training is not sufficient in a modern and mechanical age: the study of social relations is equally important.

More recently, John Marsh, Director of the British Institute of Management, has said: "It is now realized that work is essentially a social process, a factory the place where people live and work together. Scientific and technological advances outstrip our knowledge of man's behaviour in reacting to these advances. One's awareness of this problem makes the progress of new developments in human relations and social welfare challenging and arduous, but essentially worth while."

❐

12

Strategy and Structure

THERE are six approaches to structure the organisation. They are: *(1)* Functional organisation structure, *(2)* Product organisation structure, *(3)* Geographical organisation structure, *(4)* Decentralised business divisions, *(5)* Strategic business units, and *(6)* Matrix organisational structure.

1. Functional Organisation Structure. Functional organisation structure is most widely used structure. Each functional departments consists of those jobs in which employees perform similar jobs at different levels. The commonly used functions are: marketing, finance and accounting, human resources, manufacturing, research and development and engineering:

> ***Strategic Advantages.*** *(i)* A functional structure would be effective in single business firms where key activities revolve around well defined skills and areas of specialisation. *(ii)* Indepth specialisation and focused concentration on performing functional tasks can enhance operating efficiency and the development of core competencies. *(iii)* This type of structure promotes maximum utilisation of up-to-date technical skills and enables the firm to capitalise on specialisation and efficiency. These are strategically important considerations for single business companies, dominant product companies and vertically integrated companies. *(iv)* The functional structure is most appropriate when firm compete on the basis of technical specialisation on efficiency in a relatively stable environment. *(v)* This structure promotes common values and goals among

employees of the department, facilitating coorperation and collaboration within the functional department.

Strategic Disadvantages. *(i)* The horizontal diversification of the business reduces the efficiency of the functional structure. *(ii)* The department members may see the activities from the narrow view point of the department rather than to total organisation. This aspect results in absence of inter-department coordination and cooperation. *(iii)* Interdepartmental policies further result in conflicts. This situation leads to indecision, delay in decision making or ineffective decision-making. *(iv)* Further, the narrow specialisations kill the initiative of entrepreneurs and the zeal of innovativeness and creativeness. Consequently, the firm may lose sensitiveness to the customer demands, technological changes and environmental demands. These limitations of functional structure may make the firm to reassess the suitability of the structure to the strategy and decide accordingly.

2. Product Organisation Structure. Activities are divided on the basis of individual products, product line, services and are grouped into department in product organisation structure. All important functions *viz.*, marketing, production, finance and human resource are contained within each department. This type of organisation structure overcomes many of the major limitations of functional organisational structure. Fig. given below presents the product organisation structure:

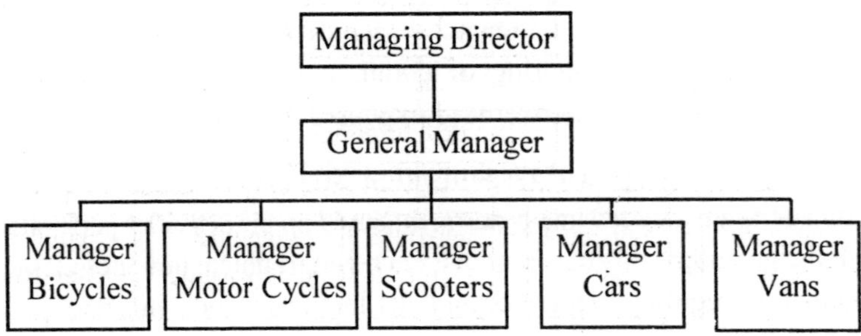

Fig. Product Organisation Structure

Strategic Advantages. *(i)* The product organisation structure is more appropriate than the functional from the organisation for firms producing multiple products. *(ii)* Coordination among functional areas like product design, producing, distributing, marketing is effective as all functions are performed in each department. *(iii)* Since, each department is independent, most of the decisions can be made at departmental level without involving the top managment in this process. It will result in fast decisions, enhancement of organisational competency to compete in rapidly changing environment. *(iv)* Responsibility and accountability for market share, sales, profit/loss is clearly fixed. Thus, either the credit for the success or blame for the failure of a product can be clearly attributed to a particular department. This advantage cannot present in case of functional organisation structure.

Strategic Disadvantages. Product organisational structure is also not free from limitations: *(i)* One of the major limitation is that unnecessary duplication of equipment and personnel among various departments. This results in loss of specialisation. *(ii)* Each department will have production, marketing, human resources, finance managers, secretarial and support staff, computers and testing equipment. As such specialised personnel and equipment cannot be produced. *(iii)* Some decisions like pay, promotion, product quality, design and pricing strategy may be inconsistent between departments. *(iv)* Interdepartmental conflicts arise regarding sharing of common resources, allocation of common and overhead expenses etc.

3. Greographical Organisation Structure. The activities or functions are grouped into department based on the activities performed in the geographical areas/regions. Each geographical unit includes all functions required to produce and market the products in a particular geographical area. Figure given below presents a geographical organisation structure. Multinational organisation, enterprise operating in diverse geographic markets or serving an expansive geographic area are organised based on the geographic structure. This strcuture is also used by chain stores, power companies, restaurant chains, dairy products, banking companies, insurance companies etc.

Strategic Advantages. The advantage of this type of organisational structure are : *(i)* Products and services are better designed to the climatic and cultural needs specific geographical regions. *(ii)* A geographical structure allows a firm to respond to the technical needs of different international area. *(iii)* Production and distributing products in different national or global locations may give the organisation to better serve the consumer needs of various nations. *(iv)* This organisation structure enables a company to adapt to varying legal systems. *(v)* It also allowed firms pinpoint the responsibility for profits or losses.

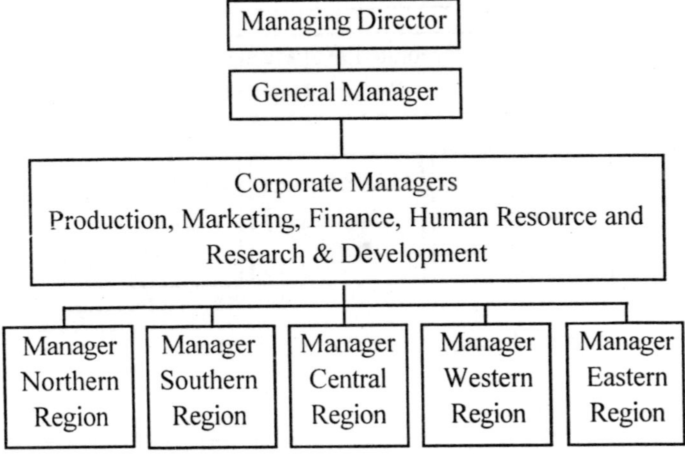

Fig. Geographical Organisation Structure

Strategic Disadvantages. This organisational structure is also not free from limitations. The limitations of the structure are similar to those of product structure. *(i)* Often more functional personnel are required. The firm cannot appoint specialist unlike in functional structure due to duplication of personnel. *(ii)* There would be duplication of equipment and facilities. *(iii)* Coordination of company-wide activities would be difficult. *(iv)* There would be a problem of imposing degree of uniformity and diversity. *(v)* It is difficult to maintain consistent company image or reputation. *(vi)* This structure adds another layer of management to run the geographic units.

4. Decentralised Business Unit Structure. Grouping activities based on product lines has been a trend among diversified companies since 1920. In a diversified firm, the basic organistional building blocks are its business units, each business is operated as a stand-alone profit centre. Fig. given below presents decentralised line of business type of organisational structure.

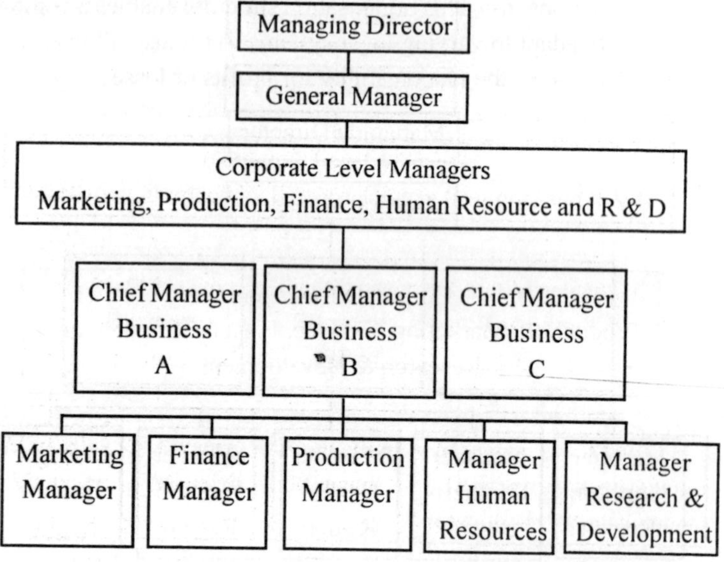

Fig. Decentralised Line of Business Type of Organisation Structure

Strategic Advantages. Functional structure and geographic structure are standard organisational building blocks in a single business firm. But, in multibusiness firms, the businensses are diversified. *(i)* Diversification is generally managed by decentralised decision-making and delegating authority and responsibility to a manager at each business unit. *(ii)* Each business unit would be managed by an entrepreneurially oriented general manager who is delegated with authority to formulate and execute business strategies. *(iii)* Each business unit operates as a stand-alone profit centre. Each business unit is structured on the bias of either functional structure or geographic structure depending upon strategy, key activities and operating requirements.

Strategic Disadvantages. The disadvantages are: *(i)* The major problem of this type of organisation structure is absence of mechanism for coordinating related activities across business units. *(ii)* General manager incharge of each business unit functions independently. It makes coordination a complicated task. Therefore corporate headquarters must devise some internal machanism for achieving strategic coordination and to capture strategic benefits. Coordination can be achieved by developing corporate R & D department, corporation sales force, sales force of closely related businesses, merging the order processing and shipping functions of business with common customers and consolidating the production of related parts.

The corporate managers can also build up strategic fit relationship involving skill transfer and technology transfer across business units. Corporate office can set up interbusiness task forces, standing committees, or project terms for the purpose of skills transfer and technology transfer.

5. Strategic Business Unit Structure. A single chief executive cannot control a number of decentralised units of a broadly diversified company. The business can be effectively controlled, if the related businesses are grouped into strategic units and the efficient and senior executive is delegated with the authority and responsibility for its management. The senior executive is delegated with the authority and responsibility for its management. The senior executive will in turn report the matter to the chief executive. This arrangement all improve strategic planning and implementation, though it adds one layer in the organisational hierarchy. Top management coordniates the interests of the diversified business units.

A strategic business unit is a grouping of business subsidiaries based on some important strategic elements common to each. The common or related elements could be an overlapping set of competitors, a closely related strategic mission, a common need to complete globally, an ability to accomplish integrated strategic planning, common key success factors and technologically related growth opportunities.

> ***Strategic Advantages.*** The advantages of this structure include: *(i)* reduction of the corporate headquarter's span of control. The chief executive at the corporate headquarters has to control the general managers of the strategic business units. *(ii)* This structure permits better coordination between division with similar mission, products, markets and technologies. *(iii)* It allows strategic management to be done at the most relevant level within the total enterprise. *(iv)* It helps to allocate corporate resources to areas with greatest growth opportunities *(v)* Business units are organised based on the strategically relevant method.

> ***Strategic Disadvantages.*** The strategic business unit structure also has certain disadvantages: *(i)* The first disadvantage is that corporate headquarters becomes more distant from the division. *(ii)* conflicts between/among the strategic business unit managers for greater share of corporate resources can become dysfunctional. *(iii)* Corporate portfolio analysis becomes complicated one in this structure.

6. Matrix Organisation Structure. Organisational structures discussed earlier have possessed a single chain of command. In other words, employees in the these structures reports to only one manager. But, the organisation structure possesses a dual chain of command.

Both functional and project managers exercise authority over organisational activities in matrix structure. Thus personnel in this structure have two superiors *viz.*, a project manager and the manager of the functional department.

A matrix organisational structure is appropriate when:

(i) Management attention must be focused on two or more key issues (technical issues, consumer needs, functional efficiency).

(ii) Large amounts of diverse information need to be processed.

(iii) Problem solving is complex (environmental uncertainty, inter-dependence among organisational units, complex products or technology).

(iv) Economies of scale require the sharing of human resource expertise to achieve high performance.

Strategic Advantages. The matrix structure is commonly used in the firms whose technological change is rapid. The advantages of matrix structure include: *(i)* the company can have the advantages of both project type of organisational structure and functional organisation structure. *(ii)* Functional personnel are paid for their services whenever, they are used by project managers. This practice enables the management to reduce the cost. *(iii)* This structure has considerable flexibility. The personnel can be transferred from one project to the other depending upon the need of the product. *(iv)* The lower level functional employees are highly motivated and satisfied with their job as they are involved in decision making. *(v)* Each project manager is incharge of a unit. Therefore, he can be developed as a general manager through performing general managerial functions.

Strategic Disadvantages. The significant strategic disadvantages of matrix organisational structure include: *(i)* greater administrative costs associated with its operation.

Personnel spend much of their time in meeting and exchanging of information to coordinate functional areas with projects. *(ii)* In view of the two forms associated in this structure, they are characterised by conflicts. The most critical conflict is between functional managers and project managers. *(iii)* Functional employees experience stress by working in matrix structure. Reporting to two bosses, creates role ambiguity and role conflict. Some companies reverted their organisational structures back to traditional structures from matrix structures due to these problems.

Strategies of business are not always static. They go on changing depending upon internal and external environmental factors. Hence, a single type of organisational structure is not suitable for all times and all situations. Blending the basic forms of organisation to match the structure to strategy in the units concerned is essential. Another option is to supplement special situation devices to the basic organisational structure. Three mostly used forms are:

(i) ***Project Team (or) Project Staff Approach.*** Project teams are created to handle special kinds of situations with a finite life expectancy. Project teams are self-sufficient work groups. These are created to supervise the completion of a special activity. The special activities includes: setting up a new technological process, starting up a new venture, producing a new product, initiating and completion of a joint venture and the like.

(ii) ***The Task Force Approach.*** Interdisciplinary assignments necessitate the formation of task force. A task force consists of top level executives and specialists in different areas from the organisation. The advantages of speical task force include; increased opportunity for creativity, open communication, cross-functional authority, effective integration of talents, quick conflict resolution, collaborative approach for problem solving.

(iii) The Venture Team Approach. Venture team is a group of individuals. The purpose of forming this team is to bring a specific product or a new business into being. The problems of venture team are: *(i)* Difficulty of deciding the manager to whom the report should be made, *(ii)* Source of founding to the venture *i.e.*, is the source from department or business or corporation? *(iii)* methods of keepíng the venture clear of bureaucratic and vested interests, and *(iv)* problem of coordinating large number of different ventures.

The suitability of structure to strategy is dependent on a number of situational factors. Absence of fit between strategy and structure leads to inefficient functioning of the company. The states of organisation development is an important factor that influence the match between strategy and structure.

MATCHING ORGANISATIONAL STRUCTURE TO STRATEGY

Every strategy is grounded in its own set of key success factors and critical tasks. Therefore, the internal organisation structure should be designed around the key success factors and critical tasks. The following five-sequence procedure is a useful guide for fitting organisational structure to strategy:

1. Pinpoint the key functions and tasks necessary for successful strategy execution.
2. Reflection on how strategy-critical functions and organisational units relate to those that are routine and to those that provide staff support.
3. Determine the degrees of authority needed to manage each organisational unit bearing in mind both the benefits and costs of decentralised decision-making.
4. Make strategy-critical business units and functions for the main organisational building blocks.

5. Provide the coordination among the various organisational units.

1. Strategy-critical Activities. Some activities and skills are generally critical in the execution of a strategy. In fact, much of the activities are performed in a routine manner even in the process of strategy implementation. The critical tasks to be performed only for strategy implementation include: tight cost control when the firm adopts the strategy of low-cost producer, special promotional appeal, tight quantity control to produce zero defect products, critical skills to produce distinctly qualitative products, and special design of the produce, when the company adopts the strategy of market leader. The critical activities in high-tech industries include: research and development, product innovation, developing new products, developing new uses of existing products, taking the laboratory results into the market quickly, testing the new products in the market etc. Thus, the strategy-critical activities vary according to the nature of the firm and competitive situation of the firm.

The firm in order to decide on the type of organisation structure should know the special tasks/functions to be performed and the right time for effective strategy execution. Further, the firm should also find out the vulnerable areas where malperformance of the tasks/functions seriously endanger strategic success. This effort will enable the management concentrate on the crucial areas in organisation building efforts.

2. The Structure-Follows-Strategy Thesis. The practice of matching organisation structure to the particular needs of strategy is a fairly recent and research based management development. Alfred Chandler, in his research study found that changes in a company's strategy bring about new administrative problems, which in turn, require a new or refashioned structure for the new strategy to be successfully implemented. A company's internal organisation should be reassessed whenever strategy changes. Otherwise, internal problems would crop-up and result in failure in strategy implementation. Structure follows strategy as organisational structure is only a means to an end rather than end itself. Organisational structure is a managerial tool in the process of achievement of organisational objectives. It is easy to coordinate strategic moves across functional areas, if functions, activities and responsibilities are efficiently organised to link strategy and structure.

ORGANISATIONAL CHANGE

Change is inevitable in a progressive culture. Change, infact, is accelerating in our society. Resolutions are taking place in political, scientific, technological and institutional areas. Sophisticated communication capabilities have increased 'telemarketing'; 'robotic' taking over some jobs currently performed by employees; man conquering the wonderland moon; are some examples that bear testimony of fastplaced, rapidly changing organisation. Organizations desire change in order to remain competitive, in order to remain in harmony with the ever-changing environment. Organizations also want to achieve internal stability because of the predictability and certainty it provides. Organisations handle the stability-change dilemma depending on the amount and type of innovation required. The organic organisation is, for example, suitable when frequent technological changes are required. Mechanistic organiszations, on the other hand, are oriented towards technological stability. Organizations, thus, resolve the stability-change dilemma by structuring in an organic way when the organization needs new ideas and frequent changes and by structuring in a mechanistic way whenever possible to obtain efficiency. The management must consider the human aspect of change before initiating any action. The man at the top responsible for the change, should take a decision of introducing change in the larger interest of the organisation and the workers but he must seek cooperation from those who are affected while managing the change.

Organisation is a social system. All parts of organisation affect all other parts. They are so interrelated that anything happening at one end is transmitting to the other end. This interrelationship develops also with the environment around it. When organisation functions for sometime, these relationship and interrelationship develops and gets established and gradually organisation obtains a systematised and orderly behaviour. An equilibrium is established in the whole system and any distrubance to such equilibrium excercises pressures on some elements which are accustomed to that way of life. In our dynamic industrial economy, several decisions are taken by the managers in performing their day to day obligation. Such decisions may involve changes in the investment pattern, organisational structure, work process, and methods of utilising the human resources of a firm or organisation to obtain the higher efficiency. But management does this only within prescribed limits established by public policies and sometimes by union agreements. People in organisation, always resist change, however well designed the change may be.

Organizations are, of course, learning to cope with the devastating rate of internal and external changes with the help of some fundamental changes in management philosophy and organizational technology. Modern organizations are highly dynamic, versatile and adaptive to the multiplicity of changes.

(i) Change basically results from *stimuli* from both outside and inside the enterprise. Organizational change refers to the alteration of structural relationships and roles of people in the organizations. It is largely structural in nature.

(ii) Change takes place in all organizations but at varying rates of speed and degrees of significance.

(iii) Finally, the enterprise can be changed in several ways. Its technology can be changed; its structure, its purpose, and other elements can be changed.

Change may affect an individual, a group, and the whole organisation. If the change is beneficial to parties affected, it may be immediately accepted. If, on the other hand, change affects no one the people will be quite indiffer‹ nt but if anyhow change is detrimental to their interest, they will resist the change to their full strength. The reaction is based upon not necessarily on facts but on their perception of the situation, *i.e.*, how they perceive the change.

Response to Change

Work change does not produce a direct adjustment but instead it operates through each employee's attitudes to produce a response conditioned by feelings towards the change.

Roethlisberger confirmed through various studies made in Howthorne plant that there was no direct relationship between the change and the response but it was attitude of the people that disturbed the set pattern. Each change is perceived and interpreted by individuals according to their own attitude and respond accordingly.

The attitude or feeling of people towards change is the result of several causes:

(i) One cause of such attitudes is the personal history of the individual which refers to biological processes of people, their backgrounds and their social experiences away from the work.

(ii) A second cause of a particular attitude is the work environment itself. It reflects the fact that workers as a members of the group are influenced by its norms, codes, and patterns of the group.

(iii) The attitude of workers are mostly governed by the group interests. This effect is named as Hawthorne Effect which refers that people individually interpret change, they often show their attachment to the group by joining hand with it in some uniform response to change. At times, there may be some illogical responses though unintended, but people respond just to show their affinity with the group, they are to follow other members of the group. For example, walkout by a few persons from a meeting to express their dissatisfaction over the situation may be psychology binding others to follow the path to affirm their cohesion to the group.

EFFECT OF CHANGE ON SOCIAL SYSTEM

The dynamic force of change affects the whole social system. All its elements, *i.e.*, its people, formal organisation, informal organisation, operating environment, communication pattern, decision making and patterns of cooperation, are bound to change. There is an equilibrium in all parts of a whole society. In trying to maintain the equilibrium, group develops responses to return to its perceived best way of life whenever any change occurs. Pressure produces counter pressure within the group which results in self-correcting mechanism by which balance is established. This self-correcting characteristic of organisation is called Homeostasis, *i.e.*, people act to establish a steady state of need fulfilment and to secure themselves from disturbance of that balance. Thus it is an idea of social equilibrium.

Following are some reasons of oganisational changes:

(a) Informal organisation is a must in every formal organisation and is a very important part of our existence, because many of our motivational forces find satisfaction in these relationships, when management likes to introduce any change that disturbs the informal relationship established among people.

(b) Changes in business conditions such as change in the quality of the product, change in the marketing system or practices, business cycles, change in industrial policy etc. all create disequilibrium in the work-environment and it needs adjustment accordingly.

(c) Man is a creature of habits. He feels irritated when change occurs in methods and procedures of work of which he is accustomed to. As it takes times to adjust to the new environment, it creates disequilibrium till the complete adjustment to the new environment.

(d) Change in the managerial personnel in the organisation may result in disequilibrium. A personnel may retire or change place, this will all affect the policies, practice, procedure and programmes of the organisation and the people are to adjust themselves accordingly.

(e) Technological or mechanical changes in machines, tools and equipments may bring change in the organisation. For example installation of an automatic machinary in place of old machinary, may result in displacement or replacement of people or loss of jobs to people and may create disequilibrium.

(f) The formal organisation structure establishes a formal line of command of authority and reponsibility in an organisation. Along with these lines, channels of communication and interpersonal relations are established. If there is a change in this formal organisational structure, there will be a change in the formal relationship which creates disequilibrium.

(g) Organisations once established can be said to be good for all times. Many defects may appear with the passage of time such as extention of the plant, change in managerial functions, evolution of complex organisation relationship etc. which cause imbalance and need correction. So, change is necessary to remove such deficiencies.

Thus, the above reasons emphasise change in the organisation which create imbalance in the relationship between employer and employee, and between employee and employee. So, people generally resist the change.

FACTORS OF CHANGE

Organisational change calls for a change in the individual behaviour of the employees. Organisations survive, grow, decline or die depending on the changing behaviour of the employees. Any organisational change whether introduced through a new structural design or new technology or new training programme basically attempts to make employees change their behaviour. It is because unless the behavioural patterns of the members change the change will have a little impact on the effectiveness of organizations. But behavioural changes are the most difficult and marathon exercises. They are not expected to be brought about overnight rather they devour more time. Lewin's model provides a useful vehicle for understanding change process in the organisation.

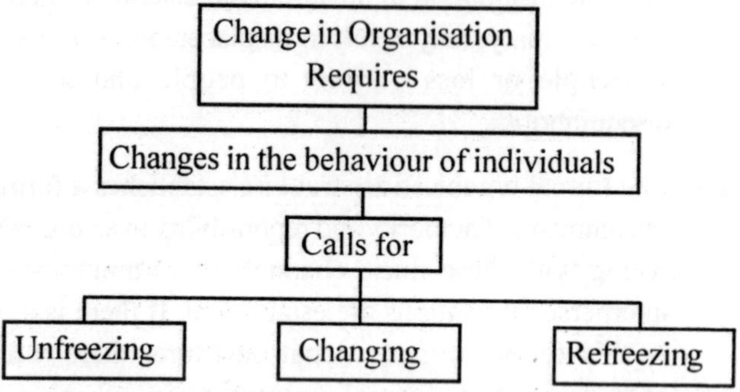

Unfreezing. It refers to making individual aware that the present behaviour is inappropriate, irrelevant, inadequate and hence unsuitables to the changing demands of the present situation. Edger Schien outlines the following elements which are vitally necessary during this unfreezing phase.

1. The physical removal of the individuals being changed from their accustomed routines, sources of information and social relationships.
2. The undermining and destruction of social support.
3. The consistent liking of reward with willingness to change and of punishment with unwilligness to change.
4. Demeaning and humiliating experience to help individuals being changed to see their old attitudes or behaviour as unworthy and think to be motivated to change.

Unfreezing is, thus, the breaking down of the existing mores, old taboos and traditions - the primitive way of doing things, so that the people are ready to accept new alternatives. It involves, discarding the orthodox and conventional methods and introducing a new dynamic behaviour that is most appropriate to the situation.

The essence of this unfreezing phase is that the individual is made to realize that his beliefs, feelings and behaviour are no longer appropriate or relevant to the current situation in the organization.

Changing. It is the phase where new learning occurs. When the individuals are convinced that their behaviour is inappropriate they happily come forward to accept the change. In order to change, it is not enough to sense that the current behaviour is inadequate. The necessary condition is that various alternatives of behaviour must also be made available in order to fill the vacuum created by unfreezing phase. During this phase of 'changing' individuals learn to behave in new ways; the individuals are provided with alternatives out of which to choose the best one. Kelman elaborately explains this 'moving' phase in terms of compliance, identification and internalizations:

(a) Compliance or force occurs when individuals are forced to change either by rewards or by punishment.

(b) Identification occurs when individuals recognize one among various models provided in the environment that is most suitable to their personality.

(c) Internalization occurs when individuals are forced to encounter a situation that calls for new behaviour.

Refreezing. During this phase individuals internalize the new beliefs, feelings and behaviour learned in the 'changing' phase. That is to say a person accepts the new behaviour as a permanent part of his behaviour repertoire. He has to practice and experiment with the new method of behaviour and see that it effectively blends with his other behavioural attitudes. It is very important for the manager concerned with the introducing change to visualize that the new behaviour is not extinguished soon. Ferster and Skinner have, in this connection, advanced the main reinforcement schedules, namely, continuous and intermittant reinforcements.

STEPS INVOLVED IN ORGANISATION WIDE CHANGE

Some changes are of such a nature that affects the whole organisation and has several consequential effects. For example, a promotion at higher level affects several hierarchical levels below. If the job of an individual is being changed, it will change his role set, also his self-concept which is in part a product of his culture, his reference groups and also his education and training. All these, he will bring in line with the formal task to display a cooperative behaviour. If the formal task role and the self-concept differ and cannot be in congruent there will be adaptive response either to leave the organisation or to make an attempt to change formal task role or to change the self-concept. In this way, any action has a chain reaction and causes a series of other changes, depending, naturally, upon the extent of its strength. Such changes that have a wide impact in the organisation, are organisation wide changes.

Any change in the organisation affects the people in terms of skills, status social relationship or otherwise but organisation wide change is just like a major surgical operation. If it remains unsuccessful, it may endanger the very existence of the organisation, and if successful, it may give a new life to the organisation. Therefore, there is a need of careful planning. Allen lists the following steps in this regard:

(i) development of clear objectives;

(ii) analysis of existing organisation;

(iii) preparation of an ideal plan;

(iv) trying out the plan;

(v) preparation of phase plan;

(vi) establihsment of uniform nomenclature.

To be on a safe side, it should be undertaken only when it is felt necessary and only with the proper planning for that we must try to understand what we have and what we would like to have. Such organisation wide changes should not be very frequent and we should have a time prospective and project into the future. This will facilitate identification of gap both in terms of men or materials and for this purpose an action plan should be prepared.

In implementing organisation wide change, it affects people throughout the organisation, so there may be many upsets and set backs. Status system titles and appellations may seriously be disturbed and designations should be immediately awarded as soon as the change is complete. Some people may be given training to re-equip them for handling new jobs. As change often evokes resistance, step should be taken to overcome them.

STRATETIC ADVANTAGES

Strategic advantage analysis is the process by which the strategists examine the firm's resources and capabilities in the key functional areas to determine where the firm has significant strength (and weaknesses) so that it can exploit the opportunities and meet the threats in the environment. The essential purpose of each analysis is to take advantage of the distinctive competencies of the firm by way of:

Following a course of action different from those of rival firms, developing a strategy which will provide different and better outcome than those of its competitors, and making it difficult for other firms to duplicate the strategy or enter the area of opportunity if the strategy works.

It is possible to list the factors and attributes which should be of common concern to the strategists in firms operating in a competitive environment. For the purpose Stevenson listed the following groups of factors.

1. Organisation

A. Top management interest and skill

B. Standard operating procedure

C. The planning system

D. The control system

E. Organisational form and structure

2. Marketing

A. Reputation

B. Product quality

C. Breadth of the product line

D. Knowledge of the customer's needs

E. Sales force

F. Customer force

3. Personnel

A. Number of employees

B. Experience

C. Technical skills

D. Employee attitude

4. Finance

A. Price-earning ratio

B. Financial size

C. Growth pattern

5. Technical

A. Basic research

B. Product development

C. Production techniques

D. Production facilities

Assessment of the strength & weakness of a firm for an analysis has following factors.

(1) Personnel

(2) Production

(3) Finance

(4) Research and Development

(5) Marketing

(6) Corporate Management

(1) Personnel. Human resource capabilities and organisational factors are closely interrelated. Together they constitute the corporate resources. The quality of managerial, technical and other employees, the organisational climate, union-management relations, personnel policies and practices and similar factors are crucial determinants of organisational effectiveness. Strengths and weaknesses relating to these resources should be analysed in terms of the following elements:

(a) ***Managerial (Leadership) Style.*** What are the characteristic features of managerial style with respect to delegation, participative decision-making, communication channels, and control?

(b) ***Union-management Relations.*** Is the degree of unionisation among employees of a high order? Does the management maintain harmonious relations with the unions?

(c) ***Corporate Image.*** Is the image of the company a source of loyalty and pride of the employees?

(d) ***Organisational Climate.*** How healthy is it?

(e) ***Employee Performance Record.*** How does it compare with similar firms? Has it been consistent?

(f) ***Personnel Policies and Practices.*** Are company policies effectively implemented with respect to staffying, promotion, training and development, compensation and benefits? How do the policies compare with competing firms?

(2) Production. Production management contribute a great deal to a firm's profitability through efficient use of capital and human resources. It needs to be mentioned that production, manufacturing and related functions are closely related with the marketing and distribution functions. The following aspects of production and operations management should be considered in the assessment of capabilities:

(a) ***Cost and Availability of Material and Components.*** What is the relative level of cost of raw materials and components? Are these adequately available?

(b) ***Plant Location.*** Is the location of plant facilities congenial from the strategic point of view?

(c) ***Purchasing and Inventory Control.*** Does the company have effective purchasing and inventory control systems?

(d) ***Capacity Utilisation.*** Is the production capacity adequate to meet existing and potential demand? Is the capacity fully utilised? If not, what is the extent of underutilisation?

(e) ***Cost of Operations.*** How do costs of operation compare with those of competing firms? How efficient is the system of cost control?

(f) ***Operations Procedures.*** How efficient are the procedures relating to design, scheduling, testing, tooling and quality control?

(g) ***Production Facilities.*** Are production facilities adequate, modern, and well maintained? How do the facilities compare with those of competitors?

(h) ***Production Control and Management Information.*** Are the management information and production control systems effective?

(3) Finance. The finance resources indicate to what extent the firm can make commitments to implement a strategy. Planned acquisition and utilisation of funds, expenditure control and the reporting of relevant financial and accounting information to the concerned managers as well as other parties are of crucial importance in every organisation. Assessment of the finance and accounting factors involves checking on the following aspects:

(a) ***Accounting System and Audit Procedure.*** Does the company have effective accounting systems for cost, budget and profit planning, and auditing procedures?

(b) ***Financial Planning and Budgeting.*** How efficient are financial planning and budgeting procedures?

(c) ***Relations with Owners (Shareholders).*** Are the company's devidend and profit retention policies consistent with shareholders.

(d) ***Financial Resources and Strength.*** Are long-term funds available or can be procured consistently with industry needs and relative to competitors?

(e) ***Capital Strcuture and Cost of Capital.*** Is capital gearing planned optimally? How does the cost of capital compare with that of industry and competing firms?

(f) ***Tax Planning and Tax Advantages.*** Does the company enjoy tax advantages and avail of tax concessions through tax planning?

(4) Research & Development. Development of new products and innovations in product design and production processes which constitute R & D functions are important parameters that often determine the success and future growth of industrial enterprises. R & D work may include exploratory (basic) research, new product or process research, improvement research, cost reduction research, and raw material adaptation research. The significance of these functions in a company lies in the competitive advantages which may accrue by way of new or improved products as also improvement in manufacturing processes leading to cost advantages. The capabilities of a company in this area can be analysed with reference to the following factors:

(i) What has been the result of R & D efforts during the last five years? How well are these efforts organised and managed.

(ii) How does the company's technical personnel compare with that of the competitor's?

(iii) What is the amount of R & D expenditure and what is the basis of investment outlay and recurring expenditure on R & D?

(iv) Is the work environment conducive to creativity and innovation? Are the managers well disposed towards innovation and change?

(v) Does the company have adequate R & D facilities, laboratories, equipment, tooling and testing arrangements? Are the facilities consistent with the latest scientific advancements? How efficiently are the facilities maintained and used?

(vi) What is the mix of basic, long term R & D projects and applied short term projects?

(5) Marketing. The marketing function is considered to be a key area not only because on its performance depends the success or failure of business activities, but also because it provides "a vital interface and communication link between the organisation and the external environment." The analysis of marketing capabilities should include the following elements:

(i) Has the advertising policy led to the establishment of a brand image?

(ii) Does the product line consists of a wide range and variety of designs and qualities?

(iii) Does the company have a separate market research unit, if so, how effective is it?

(iv) Does the firm have a sizable market share?

(v) How efficient and effective is the packaging and similar services?

(vi) In the policy consistent with competition, consumer preference, technological change and other environmental factors?

(vii) In what phase of the life-cycle are the main products : introductory, growth, saturation or declining phase?

(viii) How effective is it?

(viii) Do the sales depend on a few customers? If the products are for mass consumption, how effective is the sales force?

(x) How effective are the channels in terms of market coverage?

(6) Corporate Management. General management refers to the organisational function responsible for the overall performance of the firm. The capability of general management is thus defined as its propensity and its ability to engage in behaviour which will optimise attainment of the firm's objectives. This capability may be assessed by reference to the responsiveness of the firm to environment changes, and analysing the managers' willingness to respond and their competence, *i.e.*, ability to respond. While the managers themselves have a key role in determining their capability, the characteristics of the organisation through which they work are equally significant. Thus the managerial profit must be considered along with the organisational climate and organisational competence while diagnosing the general management capability. A profile of general management capability should therefore comprise the following aspects:

A. ORGANISATIONAL CLIMATE & COMPETENCE

(i) Culture

- Organisational attitude towards change (whether the organisation is hostile, passive or predisposed to change);

- Propensity towards risk (whether managers as a group are risk-averse, risk tolerant or risk-prone, whether they welcome novel risks or prefer only familiar risks);
- The time perspective in which the management perceives its problems (whether they rely only on past experience, prefer to deal with the present, or futuristic in outlook);
- The action perspective (whether organisational attention and energies are focussed on internal operations or external environment);
- The behavioural goals (whether thrust is on stability, efficiency, effectiveness, growth or innovation);
- What triggers change (is it crisis, unsatisfactory performance, or change is continuously sought after);
- Collective perception of the critical success factors (shared model of the world);

(ii) Power

- Distribution of power among groups with different cutlures;
- Stability of the power structure;
- Militancy of the power centres.

(iii) The organisational problem-solving skills and style (whether problem-solving is based on precedents, trial and error, optimisation of available alternatives, or generation of new alternatives);

(iv) The problem-solving process (whether compartmentalised, hierarchical, or decentralised and problem-centered); and

The management process-whether it is creative, anticipatory, or backward-looking;

(v) The information system (whether information used in managing are historical data, extrapolations, or wideranging with environmental scanning); and

The organisation structure—its flexibility and adaptability;

(vi) The technological aids to decision-making the models, computer programmes used; and Organisational capacity.

(vii) Managerial rewards system and incentives; and how are managerial jobs defined—is it narrowly circumscribed, or open, encouraging venture and initiative;

B. MANAGERS

(i) Capacity

- Personal work capacity and
- Work habits.

(ii) Mentality

- Their relative preoccupation with external v. internal problems; and
- The past v. future times orientation;
- Propensity to take risk;
- Perception of the critical success factors and behaviours; and
- Values, norms and personal goals of managers.

(iii) Power

- Power position of the manager in the firm and
- His ambitiousness and drive to use power.

(iv) Competence

- Talents and problem-solving skills;

- Leadership skills; and
- Knowledge about the firm and environment.

METHODS FOR ANALYSIS OF ORGANISATIONS ABILITIES

As in the case of environmental scanning, the relevant data for internal resources analysis may be available from different sources including verbal messages, phblished documents, study reports, etc. Some of the data gathered during environmental analysis may also be the basis of analysing and diagnosing internal capabilities. For instance, the technological environment may indicate the relative strength or otherwise of company's R & D efforts. Besides, data generated in the normal course of business operations is a veritable source as also the data provided by the management information system. Another source of data happens to be the annual reports of companies and other supplementary statements based on the accounting and financial records of the current and preceding periods.

Following are the methods of systematic assessment of the internal resource and identifying the areas of strategic advantages (Strength) & weaknesses (disadvantages) of an organisation:

1. Strategic Advantage Profile. A profile of strategic advantages (SAP) is a summary statement which provides an overview of the advantages and disadvantages in key areas likely to affect future operations of the firm. It is a tool for making a systematic evaluation of the strategic advantages factors which are significant for the compnay in its environment. The preparation of such a profile presupposes detailed analysis and diagnosis of the factors in each of the functional areas. The relevant data for the critical areas may go as a supplement of the profile. The following Strategic Advantage Profile relates to a food processing company in India.

The Strategic Advantage Profile is a summary statement of corporate capabilities, in summarising the functional competencies a comparative view needs to be taken in the light of external conditions and the time horizon of projections. For example, while comparing the level of inventory holding, one may find it do be relatively higher than that of competing firms; as such it should be regarded as a weakness. But if the market demand shows an upward trend, the apparent weakness should be considered a strength.

STRATEGIC ADVANTAGES PROFILE (SAP) OF ABC INDIA LTD.

Internal Area		*(+) Strength (–) Weakness*
(1) Corporate Resources	(+)	Management team comprises young, ambitious executives.
(2) Finance	(–)	No additional investment sicne 1980.
	(–)	Heavy reliance on fixed deposits and bank loans.
	(+)	Parent US company now interested in expansion.
(3) R & D	(–)	No R & D effort so far
	(+)	Backing in R & D expected from parent US company.
(4) Operations	(–)	Stagnating sales performance.
	(+)	Profits after tax picking up after 1993.
	(–)	Plant facilities are old.
(5) Marketing	(+)	Capable sales force; sales agents dispensed with.
	(–)	Shinking market for most products.

In the preparation of SAP one must also reckon the probability of the strength or advantage continuing in future and how long it can be relied upon. For, competitors are likely to be equally alert and may bridge the gap sooner or later. A company may identify its relative strength in the personnel area with highly skilled workmen and technical staff manning the production department; however, its production facilities may be old and outdated. It is obvious that the technical competence in the personnel area can hardly be regarded as a potential strength unless the company removes the weakness of obsolete production facilities.

The company should recognise the importance of its unique capabilities and capitalise the advantages rather than spreading its resources. At the same time, it must recognise the danger of relying on strengths in a particular area without simultaneously reckoning the capabilities in other interdependent units of activity. It is thus very well suggested that "a firm should develop a strategy over time which revolves around an area of distinctive advantages..., develop slack resources, and these can evolve into new areas of strength.

2. SWOT Analysis. The diagnosis of a firm's strengths and weaknesses can be fruitful only if the environmental factors and market conditions are considered along with the internal capabilities. This approach essentially involves matching of the internal capabilities with the environmental opportunities and threats, and is known as SWOT (Strengths and Weaknesses, Opportunities and Threats) analysis. In a way SWOT analysis may be said to consist of interlinking the ETOP and SAP. The extent of matching of internal capabilities and environmental conditions is reflected in the following schematic view of the position of ABC Industries Ltd.

The basic objective of this analysis is to provide a framework to reflect on the firm's ability to overcome threats and avail of the opportunities emerging in the environment. The dimensions of internal capabilities have relevance in so far as they relate to the environmental conditions. Hence, the analysis of comparative strengths and weaknesses requires linking internal capabilities with the characteristics of external environment.

ABC INDUSTRIES LTD.

MATCHING INTERNAL CAPABILITIES WITH ENVIRONMENTAL FACTORS

	- Internal Capabilities	*Environmental Factors*
(A)	Voluntary equity participation of dealers resluting in assured commitment.	Need for identifying design changes to cater to 'shifts' in fashion.
(B)	—cash generation on account of exports and yarn sales	Necessity of providing full range of of fabrics under one roof catering to 'family-purchase'.
(C)	—tax planning,	Restrictions in imports of fabrics.
(D)	Financial strength derived from: —ability to generate foreign exchange,	Willingness of consumers in various segments to pay high price to match the quality requirements.
(E)	Design capabilities to provide diversity of designs as also frequency of change.	Awareness of foreign fashions and wide range of designs of international standards.
(F)	Modern plant & machinery: production and technological capabilities of a high order.	Growth demand for high quality fabrics in different categories of blends.

Matching strengths and weaknesses with opportunities and threats requires that an organisation should direct its stengths towards exploiting opportunities and blocking threats while minimising exposure of its weaknesses at the same time. Thus, strategies, which are based on the matching of strengths and opportunities may be regarded as exploitative or developmental strategy. Those which direct strengths to threats may be called blocking strategies. If strengths are based on repair weaknesses, one may call it remedial strategy.

This analysis may provide the basis of a comprehensive approach to strategy. Capability in market research should enable an organisation to seek out market segments which are not so far identified by competitors. The same capability may be used to repair the present dependence on a narrow market segment. Cost efficiency of a firm may enable it to increase market share through an appropriate pricing strategy. With a strong financial position, the firm may imporve its production facilities or technological capability and thereby increase market share. If the weakness of a firm lies in its distribution network, or cost levels, the appropriate strategy should be to concerntrate on a market segment in which customers are less price conscious and prefer a service.

3. Functional-Area Profile and Resource-Deployment Matrix. Developed by Hofer and Schandel, this method requires the preparation of a matrix of functional areas with characteristics common to each, *e.g.*, focus of financial outlay, physical resources position, organisational system, and technological capability. It is required that the source outlay and focus of efforts over time in the respective functional areas be presented also in the form of a matrix. Such a profile is expected to indicate how the key functional areas stand in relation to each other and as compared with the competitors with respect to the deployment of resources and the focus of efforts in the respective areas.

The functional-area profile and the resource-deployment matrix obviously determine the interpretation and diagnosis of the data and constitute the basis on which strengths and weaknesses are to be identified. While appraising the capabilities in each functional area, the strategist should consider what the policies and approaches governing the operations in the area were, are and will be. In this process, one might discover that an element of strength could become a source of weakness in future. It is necessary that the analysis takes into account the position over a period of time. This would enable the strategist to see whether areas of advantage are being further strengthened or getting dissipated.

Piecemeal analysis of the capabilities in each functional area may be misleading. The relative strengths and weaknesses of the key functional areas should be considered together. If an organisation has developed competencies in one functional area, it needs to be examined whether the capabilities in other areas have compatible potentialities. Otherwise, the imbalance may lead to a position of weaknesses for the company as a whole. The element of strength in productive efficiency had to be viewed differently in the light of the firms marketing competence.

Another important aspect of capability analysis is the comparison of strengths vis-a-vis weaknesses. Emphasising strengths rather than weaknesses is often justified for it may be useful to take advantage of an opportunity on the basis of identified strengths rather than viewing weaknesses must be considered in the light of external conditions. This is usually done but only in relation to competing firms. That is internal resources are compared with those of competing firms whereas other dimensions of the environment might be equally important to warrant consideration.

❐

13

Foreign Collaboration Policy

COLLABORATION with foreign companies has been found to have special appeal as a growth strategy particularly in developing countries. Depending on the purpose in view, such collaborations may be classified as: Managerial, Technical and Financial. There are many advantages which a firm in the host country can derive from the collaboration deal:

1. Improving competitive abilities for domestic and export marketing;
2. Enlarging the scale of operations and reducing costs;
3. Developing indigenous production of components and spare parts;
4. Upgradation of existing technology or introduction of advanced technology, acquiring technical know-how, and facilitating transfer of technology;
5. Fostering cultural changes with respect to work ethos, attitude towards discipline, etc.;
6. Deriving the benefits of import substitution and increased foreign exchange earning;
7. Developing the brand image of products more quickly;
8. Securing foreign equity investment as a part of risk capital and enhancing the potential ability to raise necessary funds from the domestic capital market.

Benefits which may accrue to the foreign collaborators are:

1. Return on financial outlay;
2. Earnings by way of royalty and fees for technological collaboration, supply of drawings and documents technical and managerial know-how;
3. Market expansion in countries restricting hard currency imports.
4. Tax benefits derived in low-tax host countries. Royalties, technical fees, and service charges are taxed at a lower rate than profits;

Some Examples of Foreign Collaborations in India

The growth of many enterprises in India is attributable to the strategy of foreign collaboration. In recent years, a number of companies have decided to join hands with foreign companies providing for technical financial and managerial collaboration. Some of these are mentioned below:

Maruti Udyog tie up with Suzuki of Japan for the manufacture of passenger cars and vans;

Hindustan Teleprinters Ltd., tie up with Olivetti of Italy to make electro-mechanical teleprinters and electric typewriters. Financial and technical collaboration of TISCO. UK promoting Tata Robins-Fraser Ltd., a company manufacturing material handling equipments of various kinds and undertaking 'system contracts' for such equipments.

Technical collaboration of Nirup Synchrome Ltd., with Acna Chimica Organica S.P A., a division of Montedison, Italy, for the manufacture of synthetic dyes;

Financial and technical collaboration of Bajaj Tempo Ltd., with West German Daimler-Benz AG:

Technical collaboration of Noduran Founders Maharashtra Ltd., with SKF-GISAG of East Germany (GDR).

Joint ventures promoted during the last four years by DCM, Hyderabad Allwyn, Punjab Tractors, and Eicher Motors in collaboration with Japanese companies—Toyota, Nissan, Mazda, and Missubishi respectively, to manufacture light commercial vehicles;

In addition to this 'orientation' of foreign collaborations, they also suffered from a number of other disadvantages.

1. The practice of multiple collaborations led to the introduction of standards of various countries (in raw materials, spare parts, designs, specifications, and even terms of measurement) into the Indian industry even for very similar products or within the same firm. This multiplicity led to large inventory accumulation and uneconomic locking up of working capital. It also hindered standardisation and variety reduction which are so essential for raising industrial productivity;

2. The government permitted multiple collaborations, *i.e.* repetitive import of the same or similar technology. This resulted in repetitive payments without additing to the stock of technical knowledge in the country;

3. Foreign collaborations have helped the growth of monopolies and concentration. They joined hands with the big business houses and the latter were only too eager to enter into understanding with them since the presence of foreign links often conferred certain strategic advantages (patent, resources, foreign exchange, etc.) enabling the big business houses to diversify and expand;

4. The most important part related to the presence of various restrictive clauses in the agreements. Some restrictions imposed were: *(i)* the technology cannot be passed on to anyone else, in some cases even after the expiry of the

agreement; *(ii)* manufacturing is to be carried out according to the specifications laid down by the collaborator and no local adaptations can be made; *(iii)* control over overseas purchase was exercised through the provision that it had to be made directly or indirectly through the collaborator; *(iv)* production was tightly controlled at times through the posting of foreign technicians; *(v)* controls over the pricing and marketing of the products were exercised by requiring that a part of the production was to be sold to the collaborator's subsidiary in India at a fixed commission or that specified firms were to be made the sole selling agents; and *(vi)* right to export was also restricted by provision that exports could be done only to specific countries or on certain preconditions.

5. The terms of payment were also drawn up so as to squeeze out the maximum payment under one head or other. Generally 5 per cent of the annual turnover for 10 years as royalty plus 5 per cent of the imported plant cost as technical fees in the case of royality-cum-technical fees, or 10 per cent of the issued capital as lumpsum payment for technical fees alone, were the limits of official policy. However, these tended to become routine;

6. The terms of agreements were mostly weighted in favour of the foreign collaborators and were against Indian interests. This arose on account of the lack of bargaining power in the Indian side and the government's eagerness to acquire foreign participation in the face of foreign exchange shortage;

7. Since the responsibility of specification and supply of equipment was entrusted to the foreign collaborators, there was close tie-up between the designers and suppliers resulting not only in price mark-up but also in over-import of equipment. Sometimes equipments were imported even when they were available locally, sometimes they remained idle for want of spares.

REGULATORY CONDITIONS GOVERNING THE SETTING UP OR INDIAN JOINT VENTURE ABROAD

(1) Formation of a limited company is a must for participation in a joint venture abroad; only corporate bodies are allowed such participation as per the Guidelines of the Government of India.

Under Sec. 27 of the Foreign Exchange Regulation Act, 1973 (FERA) approval is required to be obtained for the proposed venture *(a)* from the Ministry of Commerce, GOI, in Case of industrial joint ventures, *(b)* from the Ministry of Finance (Deptt. of Economic Affairs) in the case of non-industrial joint ventures.

After approval of the Ministry concerned a formal approval for the project is to be obtained from the Reserve Bank of India (Exchange Control Deptt.) Application for this purpose should be accompanied by: *(i)* Copies of the application with annexures submitted to the Ministry and approval received; *(ii)* Copy of the project/feasibility study report of the project: and *(iii)* Copies of the Memorandum and Articles of Association as well as of the Certificate of Registration of the overseas joint venture company.

Also under Sec. 27 of FERA, permission must be obtained by Indian residents to accept appointment as Directors on the Board of the joint venture company, for which application has to be made to the Ministry of Finance (Deptt. of Economic Affairs). Approval is generally given for a period of two years, which may be renewed on application. The permission so granted is to be submitted for approval of the Reserve Bank of India.

(2) The joint venture agreement finalised and executed on consultation with the solicitors should be submitted to the Ministry of Commerce for approval: and a copy of the agreement, as approved by the Ministry, submitted to the concerned office of the Reserve Bank.

(3) Prior approval has to be obtained front the Ministry of Industry (Deptt. of Company Affairs) for investment in the shares of the overseas joint venture company under Sec. 372 (4) of the

Companies Act. The time specified in the approval for such investment must be adhered to, and if it is likely to be delayed suitable extension of times should be applied.

(4) For entitlement of deduction of certain payments received from the overseas joint venture company u/s 80-O of the Income Tax Act, 1961, an application in the prescribed form along with the copy of joint venture agreement has to be submitted to the Central Broad of Direct Taxes, New Delhi, on or before the last day of October of the relevant assessment year.

(5) Registration with the related Export Promotion Council to avail of export incentive, excise duty concession, etc., and enrolment with the Regional JCCI & E for cash compensatory support and REP licence the also necessary.

(6) Permission for export of machinery to the joint venture company against equity participation has to be obtained from the Commerce Ministry. On application .giving details of each item of such machinery including FOB value in Indian Rupees price in foreign currency break up of FOB value against a lakh shares will be issued by the joint venture company and the balance value if any, to be received by the Indian company.

(7) Half yearly progress reports have to be submitted to the Ministry of Commerce till the project is fully implemented and a copy of the same submitted to the RBI.

(8) After the project is fully implemented, annual performance report in the prescribed format is to be submitted every year to the Ministry of Commerce together with the copy of audited Balance Sheet and Profit and Loss Account of the joint-venture company, and a copy of the report with annexures is to be sent to RBI.

Indian Govt. Policy on Foreign Collaboration

The inflow of foreign private investment and the import of foreign technology have been subject to Government regulation in most developing countries. This has been so essentially for two reasons.

(i) To ensure industrial growth in conformity with national priorities. The contribution of foreign capital and foreign technical collaboration in different respects having been found to be of significance also prompted governments in third world countries to be less enthusiastic about foreign participation. Indian Government policy in this respect has changed over time.

(ii) To prevent the continuation and emergence of foreign vested interests.

The regulatory framework and Government policy with respect to foreign investment and collaboration were spelt out in July 1980 along with the industrial policy statement presented in Parliament. The policy was modified in May 1990, and a new policy initiative announced in July 1980.

Policy Statement, July 1980

Advanced Technology for Economics of Scale: In a number of cases Indian industry has not been able to compete in markets abroad because the scale of output which is related to the level of domestic demand is too small to give them the advantage of modem technology and economies of scale. In cases where a larger production base would increase the competitiveness of Indian industry abroad, Government will consider favourably the induction of advanced technology, and will permit creation of capcity large enough to make it competitive in world fiarkets.Provided substantial exports are likely. The purpose of introducing such a policy would be not only to encourage exports but also to enable industry to produce better quality products at lower cost which will ultimately benefit the consumer in terms of price and quality.

The Indian industry must earmark substantial resources for R & D to constantly update technologies with a view to optional utilisation of scarce resources, better service to the consumer achieving greater exports. We also have to lay greater emphasis on bringing the benefit of the latest R & D to the medium and small Units.

There has already been considerable simplification and streamlining of licensing procedures. Nevertheless, there is scope for further improvement in reducing the period of time taken for disposal of applications for the creation of new capacities, proposals for substantial expansion and the production of new items. It is proposed to speed up the processes of examination and decision-making and also to examine the possibilities of further rationalisation and simplification of the system of industrial licensing.

The industries where no foreign collaboration, is considered necessary are specified. The import of technology may be considered by Government even in these fields if they conform to the guidelines referred to in the statement on Industrial Policy.

Government will take active measures to facilitate the transfer of technology from efficiently operating units to new units. Companies which have well established R & D organisations, and have demonstrated their ability to absorb, adapt and disseminate Modern technology will be permitted to import such technology, as will increase their efficiency and cost effectiveness. This will not only lead to saving of foreign exchange but would also ensure self-sufficiency and higher exchange earnings.

Guidelines for Approval. The following are some of the important guidelines for approval of proposals for foreign collaboration (financial and or technical):

1. ***Equity Participation.*** Government's policy towards permitting foreign equity participation will continue to be selective. Such participation has to be justified having regard to factors such as the priority of the industry, the nature of the technology involved, whether it will enable or promote exports which may not otherwise take place, and the alternative terms available for securing the same or similar technological transfer. The ceiling for foreign equity participation is 40 per cent although exceptions can be considered on merit.

The foreign share capital should be by way of cash without being linked to tied imports of machinery and equipment or to payment for know-blow, trade marks, brand names, etc.

Keeping in view the need to provide additional facilities to promote investment in the country from Oil Exporting, Developing countries, which have large financial resources but not the type of technology that the country needs, it base been decided that foreign proposals from these countries need not be associated with transfer of technology from the equity holders, and that such investment may be of a portfolio nature. Within the framework of the investment policy of the Government, it has been decided to provide the following facilities:

(a) Investment of the aforesaid pattern may be allowed in hotels.

(b) Loans should also be allowed to be raised abroad for such joint ventures provided the terms are reasonable.

(c) Investment may also be allowed in new hospital projects and such hospitals should have adequate provision for outdoor and emergency medical service to the general public, and also for a minimum percentage of occupancy by Indian public.

(d) Investment from oil-exporting developing countries may be permitted in new companies even if it is in the nature of portfolio investment.

(e) The new companies should be export-oriented or should undertake manufacturing activities covered under Appendix-I of the press Note of 2nd February, 1973.

(f) Such investments should not exceed 40 per cent in the equity.

2. ***Renewal of Collaboration Agreement.*** Applications for extension of collaboration agreements are scrutinised

carefully and extensions are agreed to only in those cases where Government is satisfied that there is need for them. Application for extension may be considered in the following circumstances:

(a) If the collaboration agreement involves the manufacture of a large number of items and the Indian party could start manufacturing some of the items only at a later stage. In such cases, extension is granted only in respect of these few items the manufacture of which started later;

(b) If it is felt that such extension would be in the interest of exports of the manufactured products. Even where extensions are considered and granted, every effort is made to reduce the rate of royalty payable, with regard to the nature of the product and the period of extension;

(c) If the item of manufacture is sophisticated and it is necessary that the period of collaboration should be extended for a short period to enable the Indian party to fully absorb the know-how.

3. ***Technical Collaboration.*** Technical collaborations are considered on the basis of annual royalty payments, which are linked with the value of actual production. The percentage of royalty will depend on the nature of technology but should not ordinarily exceed 5 per cent. Royalty is calculated on the basis of ex-factory selling price of the product net of excise duties minus the cost of standard bought out components and landed cost of imported components. Royalty payments are subject to Indian taxes. Wherever appropriate, payment of a fixed amount of royalty per unit of production will be preferred.

Lumpsum payments may also be considered in appropriate cases for the import of drawings, documentation and other forms of know-how. In deciding on the reasonableness of such payments, account will be taken of the value of production so that the lumpsum and the recurring royalty, if any, is an acceptable proportion of the value of production. Such payments will be subject to applicable Indian taxes. The lumpsum payments should be phased out as follows:

1/3rd after agreement has been taken Oil record,

1/3rd to be paid on the transfer of documentation, etc., and 1/3rd to be paid at the commencement of production or after completion of 48 months of the signing of the foreign collaboration agreement whichever is earlier.

Policy, May 1990

While making certain changes in the industrial licensing policy in May 1990, the government also announced certain decision with respect to foreign investment and collaborations with the object of attracting inflow of technology more effectively. Foreign investment up to 40 p.c. equity was decided to be allowed on an automatic basis. The landed value of imported capital goods in such cases was to be allowed up to 30 p.c. of the value of plant and machinery. As regards transfer of technology, if import of technology was considered essential they would be free to conclude an agreement with the foreign collaborator without obtaining any clearnance from the Government. Two conditions were laid down in that connection; *(i)* Royalty payment should not exceed 5 p.c. on domestic sales and 8 p.c. on exports; *(ii)* If lumpsum payment was involved in technology import, the proposal must be submitted for clearance lay Government, but decisions would be communicated to the entrepreneur within 30 days.

Acquisition of Technology Through Foreign Collaboration

Foreign technical collaboration may involve agreement for supply of technical know-how, engineering services in respect of specific projects, patent or trade mark agreement, and agreement for supply of plant, machinery and other equipment. The technology policy of the Government of India announced on 3rd January 1983 envisaged import of technology in selected areas for its efficient absorption and adaptation appropriate to national priorities and research. In accordance with this policy, acquisition of technical know-how or services is governed by the following principles:

(i) There shall be a firm commitment for absorption, adaptation and subsequent development of imported know-how through adequate investment in R and D by importers of technology.

(ii) The collaboration agreement should necessarily provide for horizontal transfer of technology.

(iii) The company importing technology trust built up its engineering and R and D centre to assimilate, update and indigenise the technology in defect improvements as required within the shortest possible time.

To give effect to the objectives underlying its technology policy, the Government passed the Research and Development Cess Act, 1986, and notified the Rules framed thereunder in October 1987 to be effective from 1st December 1987. The Act and. Rules provide for the levy and collection of a cess at the rate of 5% on all payments made for the import of technology with a view to encouraging the commercial application of indigenously developed technology and adapting imported technology wider domestic application. The cess is payable on payments for import of technology, including:

(i) Payments made towards the cost of drawings and designs, publications and services of technical personnel.

(ii) Payments made to foreign collaborators or to any other person for or in connection with deportation of technical personnel to India in accordance with the approval granted by the Central Government or the Reserve Bank of India. If the technology package includes supply of plant and machinery, and acquisition of patent and trade marks, payment for the same will also be regarded as payment towards or in connection with import of technology and hence will be liable to the levy of cess.

(iii) Payments made towards import of technical know-how approved by Central Government in terms of any foreign collaboration agreement.

Harmful Effect's of the Operations of MNCs on Indian Economy

The operations of MNCs open up the possibilities of interference in the industrial (and other) activities of the recipient country and are thus resented by the 'nationalist' thinkers. Their arguments against the operations of. MNCs can be summed up as follow:

1. ***Payment of Dividends and Royalty.*** A large sum of money flow out of the country in terms of payment of dividends, profits, royalties, technical fees and interest to the foreign investors. For instance, remittance made abroad by private sector companies stood at Rs. 72.26 crores in 1969-70. This rose to Rs. 398.9 crores in 1981-82 and further to Rs. 8135 crores.

   It would be revealing to point out that Caltex which had a total investment of Rs. 16.92 crores in India, remitted profits, amounting to Rs. 43 crores in the period 1968-70. ESSO with a total investment of Rs. 29.58 crores remitted profits totaling Rs. 83 crores during the same period.

2. ***Political Interference.*** Because of their immense financial technical power, the MNCs have gained the necessary strength to influence the decision making processes in underdeveloped countries. Though they do help in transferring technology to underdeveloped countries, it has been often found that models and patterns of industrial development and technologies transferred are not in harmony with the interests of the host countries. The governments of underdeveloped countries have also felt threatened by the direct and indirect interference of MNCs in their internal affairs. The autonomy and sovereignty of the host countries

is in danger. Because of these reasons, the governments of various countries have sought to restrict the activities of MNCs in their economies through a battery of administrative controls and legal provisions.

3. ***Technology Transfer not Necessarily Conducive to Development.*** As far as transfer of technology to underdeveloped countries is concerned, the behaviour pattern of MNCs reveals that they do not engage in R and D activities within the underdeveloped countries. Their R and D efforts are concentrated in laboratories in the home country or in other industrialised countries. Though R and D activities continue to be centralized in the parent country, the host countries have to bear the bulk of their costs since the affiliates of the MNCs in these countries remit payments on this account generally in relation to their sales volume. Such payments by the affiliates are generally over and above those remitted in the form of royalties and technical fees to the parent firm. The satisfaction expressed on technology transfer is partly misconceived also on account of the fact that MNCs which generally command a semi-monopolistic position in their product lines do not transfer their first-line or most advanced technology until foreign firms compel them to do so. In many cases, the technology transferred is of a capital-intensive nature which is not useful from the point of view of a labour surplus economy. In fact, continued insistence on the import of such technology can have serious consequences for the economy of the host country since unemployment will increase. Also, market will fail to grow and this constraint alone would suffice to restrain the rate of growth from increasing.

4. ***Distortion of Economic Structure.*** MNCs can inflict heavy damage on the host country in various forms such as suppression of domestic entrepreneurship, extension of oligopolistic practices (such as unnecessary product differentiation, heavy advertising, or excessive profit taking),

supplying the economy with unsuitable technology and unsuitable products, worsening of income distribution by distorting the production structure to meet the requirements of high-income elites, etc. Modern Marxist economists (Paul Baran, for example) argue that foreign investment (especially through multinational corporations) opens up the doors of 'neoimperialism' and 'exploitation'.

CONCESSIONS GRANTED BY GOVT. TO FOREIGN COLLBORATION

Policy Initiative, July 1991

As a part of the changes in industrial policy announced on 24 July 1991, the Government also initiated changes in its policy relating to foreign investment and foreign collaboration agreements. In sum the decisions are as follows:

1. In respect of industries other than the high priority industries, automatic permission would be given subject to the same guidelines as above if no free foreign exchange is required for any payments.

2. All other proposals will need specific approval under the general procedures in force.

3. No permission would be necessary for hiring of foreign technicians, foreign testing of indigeneously developed technologies. Payment may be made from blanket permits or free foreign exchange according to RBI guidelines.

4. Automatic permission would be given for foreign technology agreements in high priority industries up to a lumpsum payment of Rs. 1 crore, 5 p.c. royalty for domestic sales and 8 p.c. for exports, to total payment of 8 p.c. of sales over a 10 year period from date of agreement or 7 years from commencement of production. The prescribed royalty rates are net of taxes and would be calculated according to standard procedures.

5. To provide access to international markets, majority of foreign equity holding up to 51 p.c. equity would be allowed for trading companies primarily engaged in export activities. While the thrust would be on export activities, such trading houses shall be at par with domestic trading and export houses in accordance with the Import-Export policy.

6. Approval would be given for direct foreign investment upto 51 p.c. foreign equity in high priority industries There shall be no bottlenecks of any kind in this process. Such clearance would be available if foreign equity covers the foreign exchange requirement for imported capital goods.

7. While the import of components, raw materials and intermediate goods, and payment of know how fees and royalties would be governed by the general policy applicable to other domestic units, the payment of dividends would be monitored through the Reserve Bank of India so as to ensure that outflows on account of dividend payments are balanced by export earnings over a period of time.

8. Other foreign equity proposals, including proposals involving 51 p.c. foreign equity which do not meet the criteria under *(i)* above, will continue to need prior clearance. Foreign equity proposals need not necessarily be accompanied by foreign technology agreements.

Foreign Collaboration and MNCs

A common form of MNC participation in Indian industry is through entering into collaboration with Indian industrialists. Foreign collaboration agreements are made between Indian companies and foreign parties, involving sale of technology, as well as use of foreign brand names for the final products. The enormity of Foreign collaborations entered into by the Indian companies would be clear from the fact that in nearly all of the new industries in the large or medium size group, privately or publicly owned, set up after independence, some collaboration agreement was present. Trends of liberalisation in the 1980s' gave substantial spurt to foreign collaborations. This would be clear from the fact that the annual average number of foreign collaboration approvals by the Government witnessed a big jump from 319 during the period 1975 to 1980 to over 771 between !981 and 1988. In fact, of the total 12,760 foreign collaboration agreements approved in 40 years between 1948 and 1988. As many as 6,165 (*i.e.* 48.3 per cent) have been approved during the eight years between 1981 and 1988. This is a direct result of the liberal policy on technology imports being pursued by the government in recent years.

While there have been collaboration agreements with a number of countries, the largest number of collaborations has been with the U.S.A. followed by the West Germany and the U.K. In recent years there has been a spurt in collaboration agreements with Japan. Of the total of 6,165 collaborations approved between 1981 and 1988, the USA accounted for 1,245 followed by West Germany 997, the UK 963 and Japan 600. The other important countries are France (315), Switzerland (265), Italy (232), Sweden (155) and Neatherlands (130).

Study of these foreign collaborations reveals certain interesting results. Thus, a large number of agreements were concluded for the manufacture of products which were non-essential or which could be produced with help of local technology. These items included vaccum flasks, lipstick, toothpaste, cosmetics, brassiers, ice-cream, gin, beer, biscuits, dry batteries and readymade garments. Not only were collaborations granted for these products, they were often in multiple numbers and were renewed on expiry. Clearly such collaborations were often directed to serve the needs of high income groups and to take advantage of a foreign brand name.

Characteristics of Multinational Corporations

The MNCs have certain characteristics, among which the more important are as follows:

1. ***Giant Size.*** The assets and sales of MNCs run into billions of dollars and they also make supernormal profits. For example, the General Motors' yearly operating revenues exceed gross national product of all but a dozen or so countries. It has more than 40 subsidiaries in 26 countries, with its centralised decision-making apparatus being located in the United States. The IBM's physical assets are worth round 7 billion dollars. ITT has 708 subsidiaries in 67 countries on 6 continents. It is the biggest multinational, accounting for USA's one-third balance of payments. Such is the enormous size of MNCs.

2. ***International Operations.*** In such a corporation control resides in the hands of a single institution. But its interests and operations sprawl across national boundaries. An MNC operates through a parent corporation in the home country. It may assume the form of a branch or a subsidiary in the home country. If it is a branch, it acts for the parent corporation without any local capital or management assistance. If it is a subsiiliary, the majority control is still exercised by the foreign parent company, although it is incorporated in the home country. The foreign control may range anywhere between the minimum of 51 per cent to the full 100 per cent. An MNC thus combines ownership with control The branches and subsidiaries of an MNC operate under the united control of the parent company.

3. ***Oligopolistic Structure.*** Through the process of merger- and takeover, etc., in course of time an MNC acquires awesome power. This coupled with its giant size make it oligopolistic in character.

4. ***Spontaneous Evolution.*** MNCs usually grow in a spontaneous and unconscious manner. Very often they develop through creeping incrementalism. Many films have become international by accident. At times, firms have also established subsidiaries abroad due to wage differentials and better opportunities prevailing in the home country.

5. ***Collective Transfer of Resources.*** An MNC facilitates a multilateral transfer of resources. Usually this transfer takes place in the form of a "package" which includes technical know-how, equipments and machinery, raw materials, finished product, managerial services, and so on. MNCs are composed of a complex of wodely varied modern technology ranging from protraction and marketing to management and finance.

Regulation or Multinational Corporations

In view of that fact the MNCs do possess a potential that can be gainfully exploited, most of the underdeveloped economics have chosen to regulate their activities rather than to dispense with them altogether.

1. The government may allow collaboration in certain selected industries or certain selected regions where the operations of MNC is felt highly suitable.
2. The threat of nationalisation is an effective tool of regulation. Although nationalisation should be resorted to only its the extreme situations, the very fact that it on be exercised makes the corporations act in a disciplined manner.
3. The host country may lay down certain export criteria.
4. MNCs may be allowed to invest for specific periods. Thus, after a certain period of time restrictions may be imposed on foreign holdings, or there may be provision for gradual disinvestment.
5. A multi-tax system may be followed by the government. The MNCs be taxed at a higher rate.

Finally, MNCs may be asked to carry out a minimum fixed share of their total research and development activities within the host countries.

Reasons for the growth of multinationals are manifold, the important ones being as follows:

1. ***Technological Superiorities.*** The main reason why MNCs have been encouraged by the underdeveloped countries to participate in their industrial development is on account of the technological superiorities which these firms possess as compared to national companies. The underdeveloped countries regard transfer of technology from MNCs useful on account of the following reasons: *(a)* Industrialization represents the most important way out of underdevelopment and the resources of these countries are insufficient to sustain the industrial progress on their own; *(b)* Local manpower rematerials, local capital equipment etc. have to be optimally exploited and these countries are unable to accomplish this; *(c)* Depending totally on local companies would require heavy imports of raw materials capital equipment machinery and technical knowledge whereas MNCs bring these on their own; and *(d)* The underdeveloped countries have to face stiff competition for selling their products in international markets. Unless their goods meet international standards and quality specifications, they cannot sell. MNCs help them in producing such goods.

2. ***Product Innovations.*** MNCs have Research Development Departments engaged in the task of developing new products and superior designs of existing products. Therefore their production opportunities are far greater as compared to national companies.

3. ***Marketing Superiorities.*** A multinational firm enjoys a number of marketing superiorities over the national firms: *(a)* It possesses a more reliable and uptodate market information system; *(b)* It enjoys market reputation and faces less difficulty in selling its products; *(c)* It adopts more effective advertising and sales promotion techniques; and *(d)* It has efficient warehousing facilities due to lower inventory requirements.

4. ***Financial Superiorties.*** A multinational firm enjoys the following financial superiorities over the national firm:

(a) It has change financial resources with which it can easily turn all circumstances in its favour; *(b)* It maintains a high level of funds utilization by generating funds in one country and using them in another; *(c)* It has easier access to external capital markets; and *(d)* Because of its international reputation it is able to raise more international resources. Even investors and banks of the host country are eager to invest in it.

5. ***Expansion of Market Territory.*** As the operations of a large-sized firm expand and as its international image builds up it seeks more and more extension of its activities beyond the physical boundaries of the country in which it is incorporated.

Foreign Collaboration in Foreign Trade

Foreign trade or international trade refers to the exchange of goods and services between two nations. The whole volume of foreign trade of a country consists of its purchases from, and sales to, other countries during a particular period. Purchase of goods from a foreign country is known as 'import trade' and sale of goods to another country is known as 'export trade'. But when goods are imported from a country with the objective of exporting them to some other country, it is known as '*entrepot trade*'.

Foreign trade can be bilateral or multilateral. Where trade is between any two nations, it is bilateral. Foreign trade is multilateral when a country buys from and sells to more than one country. Foreign trade is more complicated as compared to the internal trade of a country. An important reason for this is that each country has it's own currency system and the currency of one country is not acceptable in another country. Therefore, foreign trade involves the exchange of currency first and the exchange of goods afterwards. There are many difficulties in the foreign trade because of geographical distance, physical barriers and lack of personal contacts between exporters and importers. Moreover, foreign trade is also subject to certain restrictions by the Government of the country concerned. No trader is free to export or import goods without the prior permission of the Government.

Advantages of Foreign Trade

Foreign Trade offers the following advantages:

(a) Better Use of Resources. Foreign trade facilitates international division of labour and specialisation. It permits different countries of the world to manufacture or produce those products which they can manufacture or produce economically. It reduces waste of resources in the production of uneconomical goods.

(b) Equalisation of Prices Between Countries. Foreign trade leads to enqualise the prices of various commodities throughout the world. Whenever the prices of commodity are rising in a country, it can increase the level of its import to check the rise in prices. Similarly, a commodity in abundance can be exported to avoid situation of glut in which the commodity will fetch an unreasonably low price.

(c) Economic Growth. Foreign trade helps in the growth of under-developed or developing economies. Such countries can import machines and equipments, technical know-how, etc., from the developed countries and utilise them to exploit their natural resources.

(d) Economies of Large Scale. Because of specialisation brought about by foreign trade, economies of large scale can be achieved. Foreign trade helps in carrying production or manufacture not only for home consumption but also for external consumption. This generates several economies of large scale production.

(e) Employment. Foreign trade facilitates the growth of industries engaged in manufacturing goods for export purposes. This generates greater employment.

(f) Higher Standard of Living. Most of the countries do not have resources to produce everything they require. In the absence of foreign trade, the citizens of a country would not be able to consume those products which are not produced there. Foreign trade provides such products and increases their standard of living.

(g) International Brotherhood. Because of foreign trade, different countries are dependent upon one another. Each country can have access to the goods that it does not produce itself. Similarly, a country with surplus of certain goods can make them available to the countries facing their shortage. This promotes goodwill and cordial relation among various nations.

Problems of Foreign Trade

Foreign trade gives birth to a large number of problems in the exchange of commodities between different nations. Some of the important problems are as under:

(a) Currency. Every country has its own currency system and the currency of one country is not in circulation in the other country. This creates a problem in the foreign trade. The traders have to fix the rate of exchange between two currencies before they enter into any foreign trade transaction.

(b) Credit Worthiness of Dealers. The value of goods involved in foreign trade in fairly high. Every exporter is interested to know the credit worthiness of the importer and every importer wants to know reliability of the exporter. It takes a long time to verify from references given by the parties to the foreign trade transactions.

(c) Rules and Regulations. Every country has imposed restrictions in the import and export of goods to protect its economic and political interests. These restrictions are created by various laws, regulations and customs formalities enforced by the governments of different countries.

(d) Language. Each country has its own language and also often its own script this creates a problem of communication between dealers of different countries knowing different languages.

(e) Time Lag. Since there is a wide gap between the time the goods are despatched by the exporter and the time when they are received and paid for by the importer the capital of the exporter is blocked for along period.

(f) Transport and Risk. Because of distance between the countries and the physical barrier, there is a problem of transportation of the good. The risk to the goods during transit is also higher.

EXPORT TRADE PROCEDURE

In India exports are regulated by the Central Government under the provisions of the Imports and Exports Control Act, 1947. The Central Government announces rules and regulations and procedures to be valid for export of goods from time to time. The general procedure for exporting the goods involves the following steps:

1. Receipt of Enquiry. The first step in the export trade is the receipt of an enquiry from an importer or his agent by the exporter. An enquiry is a request by a prospective purchaser regarding price, quantity and quality of goods which he intends to purchase: The reply of such an enquiry is in the form of quotation. Both enquiry and quotation should contain the full details of the goods required, their description, catalogue number, Sizes, rates or other distinguishing features, the number or quantity, time and method of delivery, method of packing, and in case of a quotation the price and terms of sale.

2. Enquiry about Credit. After accepting the order of the importer the exporter will proceed to find out the credit-worthiness of the importer. The exporter will like to satisfy himself about the credit other buyer from various sources before despatching him the goods. Generally, the exporter asks the importer to send a letter of credit to him. The importer will open an account with his banker and get a letter of credit in favour of the exporter of the banker of the exporter.

3. Receipt of Order. When the importer accept a quotation he will place an order with the exporter either directly or through some specialised agency known as indent house. The order or indent contains the importers instructions concerning the goods to be exported. It gives full particulars of goods with regard to size, quality, shipment required, etc., and also states the price, the importer is willing to pay. An indent may be open or close. An open indent leaves the selection of goods to the agent while a close indent gives full particulars of the goods required.

4. Obtaining the Licence. As said earlier exports are subjects to the provisions of Imports and Export Control Act, 1947. In exercise of the power granted by the Act, the Central Government issues from time to time, an export control order bringing various items under control. The goods covered by such order cannot be exported unless an export licence is secured, The goods liable to export control are listed in the schedule attached to the Export Control Order, 1962 issued by the Central Government.

In order to obtain export licence, the exporter has to apply to the controller of export in a prescribed form. He has also to submit a challan to be obtained from a Government Treasury on payment of the prescribed free under the head export licence fee and an income tax verification declaring that the exporter is paying income tax regularly. After the controller of exports is satisfied, the exporter will be issued an export certificate on licence which is normally valid for a period of three months from the date of issue.

5. Securing the Shipping Order. The exporter has to enter into an agreement with a shipping company or its agent for hiring space in a ship for transporting the goods to the importer. The shipping company will give a shipping order which contains instructions to the. Captain of the ship to receive the specified quantity of goods from the exporter mentioned therein. Sometimes the consignment is very big the exporter may charter a whole ship or a major part of ship. Such all agreement is known as a Charter Party. The Charter Party may be of two types—Voyage Charter Party and Time Charter Party.

6. Compliance with the Exchange Regulations. The exporter has to make a declaration that he, will surrender the foreign exchange to the extent of full value of the export of goods to the Reserve Bank of India within a prescribed period. This declarations necessary under the Foreign Exchange Regulations Act, 1947. A prescribed form of declaration is used for this purpose. The exporter should specify the full particulars of the value of the goods, method by which payment is expected and name of the dealer in the foreign exchange through whom the documents are to be negotiated.

7. Fixation of Exchange Rate. The rate at which the currency of one country is exchanged for the currency of another country is called the exchange rate. The exchange rate keeps on fluctuating. Since there is a good time gap between the despatch of goods by exporter and the receipt of payment, it is necessary that the exchange rate at which the payment would be made by the importer should be fixed before hand so that variations in the exchange rate do not affect adversely the interest of either the importer or the exporter.

8. Packing ana Marking. Packing may be under taken by the exporter or by a firm of packing agents. It is an extremely part of the export procedure and should receive careful attention of the exporter. While packing the goods, it should be ensured that all the instructions given by the importer in this regard are strictly followed. Packages should not be too bulky to be handled. A package must be compact so that the cargo occupies the minimum space and facilitates convenient handling. It should be noted that the shipping company charges freight not only for the weight of the cargo but also the space occupied. So care should be taken to pack the maximum of cargo in the minimum of space. Packing should also ensure safety of the goods during the process of handling and transportation.

9. Bill of Lading. A Bill of lading is a document by which the shipping company acknowledges the receipt of goods expected to be carried in its ship to the port of destination specified therein in return for the payment of freight. It serves three purposes. Firstly, it is a quasi negotiable documents of title to the goods. It can be transferred to another person by endorsement and delivery. Secondly, it acknowledges receipt of goods on board. Thirdly, it is an evidence of the terms of contract of affreightment between the shipper and the ship owner. The bill of lading is issued by the shipping company on presentation of the mate's receipt at the shipping company's office.

If the Mate's Receipt contains any remark regarding any defect in the packing of the goods, the same is noted in the bill of lading.

10. Mate's Receipt. Goods may be delivered to the dock or the ship. When delivery is made to the dock, a dock receipt or wharfinger receipt is issued to the exporter. But when the goods are directly handed over to the Captain of the ship or his assistant, called the 'Mate' the exporter will get a Mate's Receipt. The exporter has to hand over a copy of the shipping bill and the shipping order to the Captain of the ship who will inspect the goods and will issue a clean receipt if he is satisfied with the packing of the goods. If the packing is defective, the Captain of the ship issues a receipt to the exporter which will specify the defect in packing.

11. Customs Formalities. The exporter has to observe certain customs formalities before the goods can leave the country. He has to prepare the shipping bill in triplicate and an application to export in duplicate. The shipping bill is a printed form in which the exporter is required to mention his name, description of goods, name of the ship which is to carry goods, the port of destination and the name of the importer it is available from the customs office. There are different forms for different classes of goods, namely, free goods, dutiable goods and bonded goods. There is also a specified form of application to export which is available with the Landing and Shipping Dues Office of the Port Trust. The exporter presents both the forms to the Landing and Shipping Dues Office. He also pays the shipping charges that he is called upon to pay. The shipping bill and a copy of the application to export duly endorsed for payment for shipping charges are returned to the exporter who will present them to the customs office. The customs authorities scrutinise the documents and ask the exporter to pay the duty, if any. Two copies of the shipping bill are returned to the exporter.

12. Insurance. Before the goods are despatched, they are insured against sea peril. The insurance policy is also to be sent to the importer along with the bill of lading. Generally, the shipping companies refuse to carry the goods unless they are insured and the commercial banks also refuse to discount the documentary bills of exchange unless they are accompanied by the insurance policies.

The marine policy is a document setting out the contract for insuring the goods against the perils of sea. It can be made out in favour of one person and may be assigned to another by simple endorsement and delivery.

13. Certificate of Origin. As the name implies the certificate indicates the origin of the exports and is issued by a Trade Consul or some other authorised persons or by the Secretary of a Chamber of Commerce. This certificate is required for purpose of calculation of import duties. Some countries give preferential treatment of certain friendly nations in the matter of payment of customs duties under trade agreements.

❐

14

Foreign Trade Policy

ECONOMIC development is characterised by the growth of the foreign trade sector and the structural changes in the economy are usually reflected in the changes in the direction and composition of foreign trade. Government of India earlier imposed many types of restrictions has relaxed its export and import policy recently. The objective of commercial policy of India is to transform the business sector according to the Objectives of national development.

In India, the trade is required because of following reasons:

1. To have favourable balance of payments and increase in foreign exchange reserves.
2. To protect domestic industries from the competition from rest of the world.
3. To encourage import substitution.
4. The encourage exports and for export promotion.
5. To keep foreign exchange reserves upto a reasonable extent.
6. To develop economy of India.

The role of foreign trade has become very important in India. The value of foreign trade has been increased many folds since the introduction of first five year plan. The value of foreign trade Rs. 1972 crores in 1950-51 increased to Rs. 75,698 crores in 1990-91. If we look at data of foreign trade, then we find that the gap between export and import value is continuously increasing like Import and

Export control Act. 1947 etc. steps to reduce the gap between export value took many steps like import and export control Act, 1947 etc. to reduce the gap between export value and import value. Now we shall discuss import and Export act, 1947 in detail.

IMPORTS AND EXPORTS (CONTROL) ACT

The Imports and Exports (control) Act 1947, amended from time to time empowers the central government to prohibit or control certain imports and exports in the public interest.

The act enables the Central Government to make provisions for prohibiting, restricting or otherwise controlling:

(a) The import, export, carriage, stores of goods of any specified desription; and

(b) The bringing into any part or place in India of goods of specified description intended to be taken out of India without being removed from ship or conveyance in which they are being carried.

The Government can also prohibit, restrict or impose conditions on the clearance, whether for homes consumption or for shipment abroad, of any goods or class of goods imported into India.

There are provision in the Act according to which imported goods or materials can be confiscated in certain cases. An authorised person, as specified in the Act, may enter, at any reasonable time, any premises in which any imported goods or materials which are liable to confiscation under this Act are suspected to have been kept or concealed, and inspect such imported goods or materials as he may think fit. Such kinds of inspections may be made by the authorised person of any books of account or other documents of things which, in his opinion, will be useful for, or relevant to, any proceeding under this Act. If the authorised person has any reason to believe that any such imported goods or materials or documents are secreted in any place, he may enter into the search such place or premises for them. If the authorised person has any reason to believe that any imported goods or materials are liable to confiscation under this Act, he may seize them. Where it is not practicable to seize andy such goods or materials, the authorised person any serve on the owner of the goods or materials an order that he shall not remove, part with or otherwise deal with, the goods or materials, except with the previous permission of such authorised person.

Any imported goods or materials in respect of which:

(a) any condition of the licence of letter of authority, under which they were imported, relating to the utilisation or distribution of such goods or materials, or

(b) any condition relating to the utilisation or distribution of such goods or materials subject to which they were received from, or through, a recognised agency, or

(c) any direction given under the control order with regard to the sale of such goods or materials, has been, is being or is attempted to be, contravened shall, together with any package, covering or receptacle in which such goods are found, be liable to confiscation and, where such goods or materials are so mixed with any other goods or materials that they cannot be readily separated, such other goods or materials shall also be liable to confiscation.

It has been laid down in the act that any authorised person may stop, or compel to land, as the case may be, any conveyance or animal which is suspected to be used or is about to be used for the transport of any imported goods of materials liable to confiscation under this Act, and search/examine the conveyance and the goods or materials in the conveyance or on the animal.

Any means of transport which has been is being or is attempted to be, used for the transport of any imported goods or materials which are liable to confiscation under this act, shall be liable to confiscation unless the owner of the means of transport proves that it was, is being or.is about to be, so used without the knowledge or connivance of the owner himself, his agent, if any, and the person in change of the conveyance or animal, and that each of them has taken all reasonable precautions against such use.

IMPORTS (CONTROL) ORDER

In exercise of the powers conferred by the impors and exports control Act 1947, the central government made on 7th December, 1955, an order namely, the Imports (Control) Order, 1955. This Order has been amended from time to time.

This Imports (Control) order prohibits the import of any goods of the description specified on schedule I of the order except under, and in accordance with, a licence or a customs permit granted by the central government or by any officer specified in schedule II of the order.

The order lays down that it, in any case, it is found that the goods imported under licence do not conform in every respect *(i)* to the description or value of the goods as contained in the licence, or *(ii)* to the other conditions relating to such goods, contained in, or applicable to the licence, the Import of Such Goods shall be deemed to be Prohibited.

The order states that the licensing authority issuing a Licence under this order may issue the same subject to one or more of the conditions stated below:

(i) That the goods converted by the licence shall not be disposed of except in the manner prescribed the licensing authority or otherwise dealt with without the written permission of the licensing authority or any peron duly authorised by it;

(ii) That the goods coverd by the licence on importation shall not be sold or distributed at a price exceeding that which may be specified in any direction attached to the licence;

(iii) That the applicant for a licence shall excute a bond for complying with the terms subject to which a licence may be granted.

A licence granted under the order shall also be subject to the conditions contained in schedule *V*, which deals with certain payment conditions, "Actual user" conditions applicable to import licences issued to "Actual User", and conditions applicable to licences issued for the import of capital goods.

It has also been laid down that it shall be deemed to be a condition of every such licence that:

(i) No person shall transfer and so person shall acquire by transfer any licence issued by the licensing authority except under, and in accordance with, the written permission of the authority which ranted the licence or any person empowered in this behalf by such authority;

(ii) The goods for the import of which a licence is granted shall be the property of the licences at the time of import and thereafter up to the time of clearance through the customs. (There two conditions, however, shall not apply to licences issued to the State Trading Corporation of India, the Minerals and Metals Trading Corporation of India and other similar institutions or agencies owned or controlled by the central overnment and which are entrusted with the canalisation of imports. The above two conditions shall also not apply to the licences issued to eligible Export Houses for the import of goods meant for disposal to actual users under the import policy for registered exporters);

(iii) The goods for the import of which a licence has been granted shall be new goods, other than disposal goods, unless otherwise stated in the licence.

A licence granted under this order may contain such other conditions, not inconsistent with the Act or this order, as the licensing authority may deem fit.

A licence shall comply with all the conditions imposed or deemed to be imposed under the order.

The Order also deals with the details of matters like refusal of licence; amendement of licence; power to debar from importing goods or from receiving licences or allotment of imported goods; power to suspend importation of goods; grant of licences or allotments of imported goods power to keep in abeyance applications for licences or allotments or imported goods. Cancellation of licences; declaration as to the value, sort, quality etc. of imported goods; uilistion of imported goods; power to make directions for the sale of imported goods in certain cases; exceptions from this order, etc.

EXPORT CONTROL ORDER

In exercise of the powers conferred by the imports and exports (control) Act, 1947, the central government on 24th March, 1977, made an order called the Exports (control) order, 1977.

The exports control order restricts the export of certain goods. Accordingly, no person shall accordingly, no person shall export any goods of the description specified granted by the central government or by an officer specified in schedule II of the order {clause 3(1)}. The same rule is applicable to exports to Pakistan {Clause 3(2)}.

Notwithstanding anything contained in sub-clauses (1) and (2) mentioned above, goods specified in schedule III of the order may be exported on fulfilment of the terms and conditions specified therein.

The order states that if, in any case, it is found that the value, sort, specification, quality and description of the goods to the exported are not in conformity with the declaration of exporter in those respects, or if the quality and specification of such goods are not in accordance with terms of the export contract, the export of such goods shall be deemed to be prohibited.

It has been laid down in the exports (control) order that a licence granted under this order may contain such condition, not inconsistent with the Imports and Exports (Control) Act, 1947, or this order, as the licensing authority may deem fit.

It shall be deemed to be a condition of every licence that:

(i) No person shall transfer and no person shall acquire by transfer any licence issued by the licensing authority except under, and in accordance with, the written permission of the authority which granted the licence or of any other person empowered in this helf by such authority,

(ii) The goods for the export of which the licences has been granted shall be the property of the licence at the time of the export.

The licence shall comply with all the conditions imposed or deemed to be imposed under the relevant clause of the order.

The order also deals with the details of matters like refusal of licences amendment of licences, power to debar from receiving licences of exporting goods, power to suspend grant of licences or permission to export goods, cancellation of licences, declaration as to value, sort, quality, etc., of exported goods, prohibition regarding making, signing, etc., of any documentation, statement of document, exemptions from the order, etc.

FOREIGN TRADE ACT, 1992

Foreign Trade (Development and Regulation) Act, 1992 replaced the Imports and Exports (Control) Act, 1947. The objective of the Act is to provide for the development and regulation of foreign trade by facilitating imports into and augmenting exports from, India and for matters connected therewith or incidental thereto.

The main provision of the Act are as follows:

1. Power to Make Provisions Relating to Imports and Exports. Section 3 of the Act deals with the powers to make provisions relating to imports and exports. According to this Section, the Central Government may by order published in the official gazette, make provision for *(i)* the development and regulation of foreign trade by facilitating imports and increasing exports, and *(ii)* prohibiting, restricting or otherwise regulating the import or export of goods. Section 5 authorises the Central Government to formulate and announce, by notification in the Official Gazette, the export and import policy and also, in like maner, to amend that policy.

2. Importer-Exporter Code Number. According to Section 7, no person shall make any import or export except under an Importer-Exporter Code Number granted by the Director General or the officer authorised by the Director General in this behalf , in accordance with the procedure specified in this behalf by the Director General. Section 8 states that if any person has contravened by law relating the Central Excise or Customs of Foreign Exchange or has committed any economic offence under any other law in force at that time, or the Director General has reason to believe that person has made any export or import in a manner gravely prejudicial to the trade relations with other countries, the Importer-Exporter Code Number given to him can be cancelled. In such circumstances, the person whose code number has been cancelled or suspended will not be entitled to import or export goods except under a special licence granted.

3. Issue, Suspension and Cancellation of Licence. According to Section 9, the Director General or an officer authorised by him may, after making an enquiry, grant or renew or refuse to grant or renew a licence to import or export goods. In the event of suspension or cancellation of the licence of any person to import or export goods. he shall be provided a reasonable opportunity of being heard.

4. Director General of Foreign Trade. Section 6 provides for the appointment of Director General of Foreign Trade by the Central Government for the purposes of this Act. The Director General replaces the Chief Controller of Imports and Exports under the Imports and Exports (Control) Act, 1947. His job is to advise the Central Government in the formulation of the export and import policy and he shall be responsible for carrying out that policy.

5. Power Relating to Search and Seizure. According to Section 10, the Central Government may authorise any person for the purpose of exercising such powers with respect to entering such premises and searching. inspecting and seizing of such goods, documents, things and conveyance, subject to such requirements and conditions, as may be prescribed.

6. Penalty for Contravention. According to Section 11, no export or import shall be made by any person except in accordance with the provisions of this Act, the rules that orders made thereunder and the export and import policy for the time being in force. Any contravention to this provision will invite a penalty not exceeding one thousand rupees or five time the value of the goods in respect of which any contravention is made or attempted to be made, whichever is more. Failure to pay the penalty could lead to the suspension of the Importer-Exporter Code Number of the person. Section 11 further state that where any contravention of any provision of this Act or any rules or orders made thereunder or the export and import policy has been is being, or is attempted to be made, the goods shall be liable to confiscation by the Adjudicating Authority. Section 14 provides that before imposing any penalty or confiscating goods. the person concerned would be given a proper notice in writing and would also be given an opportunity of being heard.

7. Appeal and Revision. Section 15 lays down that any person aggrieved by any decision or order made by the Adjudicating Authority may appeal against any such decision or order within a period of fortyfive days from the date on which the decision or order was served on him. The Appellate Authority can, if it so wishes, futher extend the period by thirty days, and can, at its discretion, dispense with the penalty to be deposited by the appellant either unconditionally or subject to such conditions as it may impose. The Appellant Authority may, after giving to the appellant a reasonable opportunity of being heard, confirm, modify or reverse the decision or order appealed against. The order made in appeal by the Appellant Authority shall be final. Section 16 confers the power on the Central Government to examine the records of any proceeding in which a decision or an order imposing a penalty or redemption charge or adjudicating confiscation has been made and against which no appeal has been preferred, for the purpose of satisfying itself as to the correctness, legality or propriety of such decision or order and make such orders thereon as may be deemed fit.

COMPOSITION OF FOREIGN TRADE

In order to study the composition or structure of India's foreign trade, it is necessary to analyse the changing pattern of imports and exports.

Pattern of Imports. Inputs have been classified into Bulk imports and non-bulk imports. Bulk imports are further subdivided into petroleum, oil and lubricants (PoL) and non-PoL items such as consumptions goods, fertilizers and iron and steel. Non-bulk items such as consumption goods (which include electrical and non-electrical machinery), pearls, precious and semi precious strong and other items.

The structural changes in imports since 1951 show:

(a) rapid growth of industrialisation necessitating imports of capital goods and raw materials.

(b) growing imports of ıaw materials on the basis of liberalisation of imports for export promotion; and

(c) declining imports of foodgrains and consumer goods due to the country becoming selfsufficient in food gains and other consumer goods through agricultural and Industrial growth.

TREND OF PRINCIPAL IMPORTS

Foodgrains. The imports of food grains were necessitated by the partition of the country and the growing demand for food for the rising population. The average annual imports of food grains which were about Rs. 200 crores during the first plan rose to Rs. 161 crores during the second plan, further increased to an average rate of Rs. 241crores during the third plan. The drought of 1965-66 further worsened the situation and consequently, foodgrains imports worth

Rs. 1,201 crores were made during the three years *i.e.* 1966-67 to 1968-69. During the 5-years period (1980-81-1984-85) food grains worth Rs. 66 crores were imported a negligible figure indeed. But during 1991-1992, they again rose to Rs. 395 crores. In later years the share of foodgrains fill almost to zero. The import of foodgrains during the year 1999-2000 was of Rs. 222 crore and it declaimed sharply to Rs. 20 crore in 2000-2001. This has happened mainly because of continuance rise in the production of food grains in the country.

Mineral Oils. Imports of mineral oils are also on the increase. India is short in the supply of mineral oils, especially petroleum. Annual import of mineral oil during 1969-70 to 1973-74 averaged Rs. 226 crores. On account of the sharp increase in the prices of crude announced by the organisation of petroleum exporting countries, during 1973-74 alone, petroleum imports were of the order of Rs. 569 crores. Their annual average during 1974-75 to 1979-80 was of the order of Rs. 2,063 crores. Though the share of mineral oils in imports has declimed from 45.1 per cent in 1990-91 to 39.6 per cent in 1999-2000 but it has increased from Rs. 10,816 crore to Rs. 54,649 crore during the period in abosolute terms.

Machinery. This item includes electrical and non-electrical equipment. In a country which is rapidly industrialising her economy imports of machinery are bound to increase. Compared to the average annual import of machinery which was about Rs. 1991 crores during the 1951-61, the annual average during the third plan rose to Rs. 472 crore. During the fourth plan, they were of order to Rs. 484 crore. Machinery imports during Seventh Plan jumped to Rs. 6,415 crore annually and further to Rs. 11,895 crore during the year 1999-2000.

Metals. India imports iron and steel and also some non-ferrous metals. The annual average imports of ferrous and non-ferrous metals which were about Rs. 54 crores during the first plan have gone up steadily with every plan and are about Rs. 2,450 croes during 1985-86 and 1989-90 Import of metals on such a large scale is necessitated by the vast programmes of industrial expansion, development of railways and hydro-electric projects. With improvement in capacity utilisation of our steel plants, imports of iron and steel should be cut down. During 1990-91 metals worth Rs. 1,528 crore were imported which futher increased to Rs. 3,789 crore in 1999-2000.

Chemicals Drugs and Medicines. There has been an increase in the imports of chemicals, drugs and medicines. The anual average of these items was about Rs. 55 crores during the third plan. Imports of chemicals, drugs and medicines rose to Rs. 113 crores per annum on the average during the Fourth plan. During 1980-81 and 1984-85 annual average imports of this item rose to Rs. 660 crores. They further rose to Rs. Rs. 2,289 crore in 1990-91 and to Rs. 12,420 crore in 1999-2000.

Pearls and Precious Stones. The imports of pearls and precious stones averaged Rs. 223 crores during 1974-79 and they have further increased to Rs. 2,405 crores per annum for the period 1985-86 to 1989-90. Part of these imports is meant to satisfy the demand of the afluent sections and part of these imports serve as raw material for the handicrafts export industry. It may be noted that the India imported pearls and precious stones worth of Rs. 3,738 crore in 1990-91 and it further increased to 23,556 crore in 1999-2000.

Fertilisers. Following the adoption of the new strategy in Indian agriculture, the imports of fertilizers were stepped up. The average annual imports of fertilizers which stood at Rs. 28 crores during 1966-67 to 1968-69. During 1980-81 to 1984-85 the annual imports of fertilizers were of the order of Rs. 698 crores. As a consequence of liberalisation, fertilizer imports jumped to Rs. 1,436 crores in 1985-86 and were of the Rs. 1,114 crores per annum on an average during 1985-86 to 1989-90. Imports of fertilizers touched a level of Rs. 1,765 crore in 1990-91 and Rs. 6,063 crore in 1999-2000.

The data related to average annual principal imports is shown in the following table.

AVERAGE ANNUAL IMPORTS OF PRINCIPAL COMMODITIES

Items	1951-52 to 1960-61	1980-81 to 1984-85	1985-86 to 1989-90	1990-91 to 1999-2000
1. Foodgrains	141	374	516	624
2. Machinery	191	2,515	6,415	14,976
3. Mineral Oils	77	5,264	4,498	27,469
4. Metals	93	1,448	2,450	7,003
5. Chemicals	44	660	1,868	1,921
6. Fertilisers	–	698	1,114	4,707
7. Pearls and Precious Stones	–	730	2,405	9,993

PATTERN OF EXPORT

Exports of India are broadly classified into four categories:

(i) Agriculture and allied products which include coffee, tea, oil cakes, tobacco, cashew kernels, spices, sugar, raw cotton, rise fish and fish preparations, meat and meat preparations, vegetable oils, fruits, vegatables and pulses;

(ii) ores and minerals include manganese ore, mica and iron ore;

(iii) Manufactured goods include textiles and ready-made garments, jute manufactures, leather and footwear handicrafts including pearls and precious stones, chemicals, engineering goods and iron steel; and

(iv) mineral fuels and lubricants.

Table : Classification Indian Exports

(Rs. crore)

	1970-71	*1980-81*	*1991-92*	*1999-2000*
1. Agriculture and Allied Products	487 (31.7)	2,057 (30.6)	7,638 (17.3)	24,301 (15.2)
2. Ores and Mineral 164	413 (10.7)	2,281 (6.2)	2,643 (5.2)	3,970 (2.5)
3. Manufactured Goods	772 (50.3)	3,747 (55.8)	32,384 (73.5)	1,28,761 (80.6)
4. Petoleum Products	13.28 (0.8)	102.2 (0.4)	905.2 (.23)	168 (0.1)
5. Others	99.0 (6.5)	465 (6.9)	717 (1.6)	2,361 (1.5)
Total	1,535 (100.0)	6,710 (100.0)	44,042 (100.0)	1,59,561 (100.0)

Data given in table reveal that traditional exports dependent upon agriculture and mineral wealth accounted for 42 per cent of total exports in 1970-71, their share has, however, declined to about 18 per cent in 1999-2000 in 1970-71 to about 80.6 per cent in 1999-2000. An interesting feature of the changing pattern of exports is the sharp increase in the share of manufactured products. Obviously, the structure of Indian exports is changing in favour of manfactured goods and petroleum products whose combined share has gone up from about 51 per cent in 1970-71 to about 81 per cent in 1999-2000.

Exports of Principal Commodities

Tea. Tea is one of the most important items of Indian exports. It had the first position in our exports in certain years. The average annual exports of tea were Rs. 106 crores during the first plan period. Tea exports further picked up to touch Rs. 195 crores in

1960-61. But later they declined. Tea exports earned Rs. 1,985 crores during 1999-2000.

Cotton Yarn and Manufactures. During the first plan period, the average annual exports of cotton yarn and manufactures touched Rs. 81 crores, but they declained to a small figure of Rs. 55 crores during the Third plan. On account of relatively high cost in Indian textile industry, Indian found it diffcult to capture the international market. In fact high costs were due to rising labour cost and use of old and worn-out machiner. In the post-devaluation period exports of cotton textiles have increased on account of their competitiveness in the international market. During 1970-71 and 1991-2000 exports of cotton (yarn and manufactures) improved from Rs. 75 crores to Rs. 18,151 crores.

Engineering Goods. In 1970-71 exports of engineering goods were of the order of Rs. 130 crores, During the 1970's engineering exports surged forward. In 1976-77, they exceded Rs. 500 crores and in 1999-2000 they were of the order of Rs. 22,325 crores, this is really creditworthy.

Readymade Garments. In recent years, the exports of cotton apparel or ready-made garments have shown significant improvement. These exports were just Rs. 9 crores in 1970-71. They jumped to Rs. 196 crores in 1974-75. During 1999-2000 cotton apparel exports touched a record of Rs. 20,649 crores. This indicates the increasing importance of this item in our exports.

Leather and Leather Manufacturers. One of the traditional items of Indian exports is raw hides and skins. But recently, in the exports of this item, the proportion for leather and leather manufactures to raw hides and skins is on the increase. This is really a healthy development. India earned about Rs. 39 crores in 1960-61 from this item. It touched Rs. 486 crores in 1979-80 and rose further to Rs. 6,891 crores during 1999-2000.

Handicrafts. The exports of Indian handicrafts assumed great importance in the 1970s. From a low level of Rs. 70 crores in 1970-71 they increased to Rs. 120 crores in 1972-73 and stood at Rs.

6,285 crores in 1989-90. The most important item among the handicrafts was pearls and precious stones which averaged Rs. 3,177 crores during 1985-86 to 1989-90. At present, the single largest item of export in handicrafts. During 1999-2000 handicrafts exported were of the order or Rs. 37,568 crores.

Iron ore. Indian exports iron ore. India earned about Rs. 30 crores per year from iron ore during the first first plan. During 1970-71 exports of iron ore rose to Rs. 117 crores and touched Rs. 1,175 crores during 1999-2000. This is an unhealthy development. India should increase the share of steel in exports by utilising iron ore in her own steel plants.

Changing Structure of Exports

The structure of Indian exports is typical of a developing economy. India has traditionally been an exporter of agricultural raw materials and manufactures based on agricultural raw materials. There has been a continuous decline in the share of agricultural raw materials and allied products. One reason for the relative decline of food, beverages and tabacco in the total exports is the increase in population and consequent increase in domestic consumption of these goods, Accordingly, the export surplus in many traditional commodities like tea has not been increasing as much as the Government would have wished. In this connection, the growing importance of certain products in this category should be noted, *i.e.*, fish and fish products, cashew kernels and coffee.

We should not, however, conclude that only non-traditional items are to the fore and the traditional items have suffered are treat. Exports of traditional items are also expanding, though probably not to the extent desired. Examples are the respectable growth in cotton fabrics, tea, leather and leather manufactures etc.

Thus the pattern of India's exports indicates that:

(a) The Indian economy is being diversified and both traditional and non-traditional items of exports are growing in importance.

(b) India is now in a position to take advantage of both favourable demand situation and attractive price assituation in international markets and this explains the expansion in the exports of many traditional and non-traditional items.

(c) The large expansion of engineering goods is partly the result of pick-up in demand in industrial countries and also from the Middle east countries which have undertaken infra-structural projects like roads, ports and rail construction, tele-communication and civil construction.

(d) While some commodities have tremendous exports poetential (*e.g.* handicrafts, engineering goods and readymades), others (like sugar, jute, yarn and manufactures, iron and steel) have fluctuated hopelessy.

DIRECTION OF INDIA'S FOREIGN TRADE

Our trade with East European socialist countries *viz.*, U.S.S.R. Poland, Romania, Bulgaria, Hungary, East Germany, Czechosolovakia and Yugoslavia has developed in recent years. The main items of imports from these countries are iron and steel, non-ferrous metals, chemicals, capital equipment, railway stores, paper, medicines and pharmaceuticals and petrolium products. The imports of most of these commodities are of crucial help for our core projects and several industries of strategic kernels, tobacco, oil seeds, leather, metallic ores, jute manufactures etc.—the traditional items of Indian exports. The composition of imports from these countries suggests the significance of the trade from the viewpoint of economic development. In 1960-61 India imported 4 per cent of her total imports from this region and exported about 8 per cent of her total exports to this region. But soon after the Indo Chinese conflict in 1962 and Indo-Pak war in 1965 our trade relations with the East European Socialist countries improved remarakably. In 1969-79 this group cf countries accounted for 18 per cent of total imports and about 22 per cent of our exports. U.S.S.R. the chief contributor and accounted for nearly 84 per cent of trade with this region. By 2000-

2001 India's imports from East European countries declined to about 1 per cent and our exports to these countries which declined to 14 per cent in 1979-80 further fell to about 2 per cent in 2000-2001 with the disintegration of the soviet Union into common wealth of independent states (CIS) Trade relations with these countries are undergoing a change.

Our trade with the countries in Asia and oceania has been of great significance. Our exports of these countries which were about 28 per cent of total import in 1951-52 increased to 32 per cent in 1969-70. As against it, imports from these countries declined from about 23 per cent in 1951-52 to 19 per cent in 1969-70 (Refer table 13) the ECAFE* region was of great significance and four countries, viz, Japan, Austalia, Iran and iraq were very important.

Table—Direction of India's Foreign Trade

Region/Country	*1980-81*		*2000-2001*	
	Exports	*Imports*	*Exports*	*Imports*
(1)	*(2)*		*(3)*	
1. OECD of which	3,126 (46.6)	5,747 (45.8)	1,07,238 (52.6)	92,090 (39.9)
(a) European Union	1,447 (21.6)	2,639 (21.0)	47,561 (23.4)	48,015 (20.8)
(i) Belgium	144 (2.2)	296 (2.4)	6,718 (3.3)	13,112 (5.7)
(ii) U.K.	395 (5.9)	731 (5.8)	10,512 (5.2)	14,472 (6.3)
(b) North America	806 (12.0)	1,851 (14.8)	45,509 (22.4)	15,588 (6.7)
(i) Canada	62 (0.9)	332 (2.6)	2,999 (1.5)	1,814 (0.8)
(ii) U.S.A.	744 (11.1)	1,519 (12.1)	42,570 (20.9)	13,774 (6.0)
(c) Other OECD	708 (10.5)	932 (7.4)	14,168 (6.9)	28,487 (12.3)
(i) Japan	598 (8.9)	749 (6.0)	8,198 (4.0)	8,416 (3.6)
2. OPEC	745 (11.1)	3,490 (27.8)	22,223 (10.9)	12,358 (5.4)

Contd.

(1)	*(2)*		*(3)*	
3. Eastern Europe	1,486 (22.2)	1,296 (10.3)	6,020 (2.9)	3,884 (1.7)
USSR/CIS	1,226 (18.3)	1,014 (8.1)	4,061 (2.0)	2,365 (1.0)
4. Developing Countries	1,266 (18.9)	1,971 (15.7)	59,381 (29.2)	50,865 (22.0)
(i) Asia	880 (13.1)	1,428 (11.4)	45,858 (22.5)	38,647 (16.7)
5. Others	65 (0.9)	45 (0.4)	350 (0.2)	8 –
Total 1 to 5	6,711 (100.0)	12,549 (100.0)	2,03,571 (100.0)	2,30,873 (100.0)

However, due to increasing importance acquired by the import of Crude oil, OPEC countries have assumed very great significance in our import. These countries acounted for barely 8 per cent in our total imports in 1970-71 but as against it their share in 1980-81 has jamped upto about 27.8 per cent. Much of the increase is due to the sharp hike in the price of oil and does not indicate a corresponding increase in the quanitity index, of imports. On the export front also our exports to OPEC countries have also increased from 6.4 per cent in 1971-72 to about 11 per cent in 2000-2001 with a fall in the international price of oil, the share of OPEC countries in our imports declined to 5.4 per cent in 2000-2001.

The share of Japan in our export which was about 8.9 per cent in 1980-81 has come down to 4.0 per cent in 2000-2001. As against it, the share in our imports from these two countries has also declined from 6.0 per cent to about 3.6 per cent during the same period.

India has a great potential for increasing her foreign trade with Asian countries, because the Indian manufactures can be readily acceptable in these countries. Similarly, India can import raw materials for her growing industries from these relatively more under-developed regions. This is evidenced by the fact that during 2000-2001, imports from this region accounted for 16.7 per cent of our total imports whereas they were in the range of 11.4 per cent in 1970-71 to. On the export side, there has been a gradual and steady improvement and exports to this region increased from 13.1 per cent during 1980-81 to a level of nearly 22.5 per cent in 2000-2001.

It would be of interest to examine the direction of trade with reference to some important countries. U.S.A. U.K. west Germany U.S.S.R. Japan, Saudi Arabia, Australia and Canada were the 8 countries of significance in our trade. The share of these 8 countries in our exports has ranged between 54.7 and 41.6 per cent during 1980-81 to 2000-2001. As against it, their share in our imports has ranged between 46 and 24.5 per cent during this period.

Although U.K. was of prime importance in our foreign trade before independence, U.S.A. was growing in importance up to 1970. During the Seventies, especially after the Indo-Pak war of 1971, U.S.S.R. has grown in significance in our foreign trade. On the import side, the share of U.K. was the highest in 2000-2001 followed by USA, Belgium, Germany, Japan, Saudi Arabia and Switzerland. On the export side, Indian exports to U.K. were always higher than the exports to U.K. and subsequently exports to U.S.A. but during the Third Plan, the exports of U.S.A. levelled off with exports of U.K. and subsequently exports to U.K. fell futher to an abnormally low level of about 5 per cent. Our imports from West Germany were on the increase till 1965-66, but have declined since then. As against it, our exports to this country have been of the order of 2-3 per cent of total exports in the past but have risen to about 2 per cent in 2000-2001. Japan and U.S.S.R. are both growing in importance in our foreign trade. We had trade relations with Japan in the pre-war period, but trade was cut off during the war. It has been revived again. With U.S.S.R. Although our foreign trade is of recent origin, the share of imports was 1.0 per cent in 2000-2001 as against 8.1 per cent in 1980-81. Similarly the share of exports of USSR has risen from 1.0 per cent in 1951-52 to 18 per cent in 1980-81 but declined to 2.0 per cent in 2000-2001. Iraq and Iran also became important especially for oil imports, but due to continued Iran-Iraq was imports from these two countries became negligible but imports from Saudi Arabia rose to 1.3 per cent and from Indonesia to 1.8 per cent in

2000-2001. With the distintegration of Soviet Union our trade with this retio has suffered a serious setback.

Some salient features of the changes in the direction of trade in the post-independence period may be noted here.

(i) **New Trading Partners.** Before Independence, U.K. was the principal trading partner for India, accounting for 34 per cent of India's exports and 30 per cent India's imports. After Independence, even though India has continued to be a member of the British commonwealth, she has succeeded in getting new trading partners. Besides U.K. other countries of importance are U.S.A. U.S.S.R. West Germany, Japan and members of OPEC. Thus an important future of the new direction of trade since 1951 is the increasing in the number of trading partners for India. This spatial or geographical diversification has helped India to go for diversification of industries along with specialisation in certain goods, and secure new markets for her products.

(ii) **Larger and More Attractive Outlets for Exports.** India has been diversifying her exports to match her imports. Naturally, she has to search for new countries to sell her goods. Even though U.K. continues to buy a larger volume of goods from India, it has been relegated to second and even third place. U.S.A. has become the biggest buyer of Indian goods. Likewise, UAR, Honkong and Japan along with U.S.A. and UK constitute the first five leading countries absorbing 42 per cent of India's exports. These are rich countries with high national and per capita income and they manufactures, specially carpet backing, leather manufacturers and non-traditional items such as marine products, pearls and precius stones, etc. Middle East countries offer a good market for Indian exports.

(iii) **Larger Sources of Imports.** The increase in the number of countries from whom we by has been necessitated by many factors peculiar to the post-World War II. For one thing, the planned economic development and the tremendous increase in the requirements for machinery, equipment, industrial raw material, etc. could not be met by U.K. alone, or even by USA. For another reason, grant of aid and other assistance by international institutions like the World Bank allowed India to by from the cheapest sources (through global tenders). Thirdly, tied aid and grants from some countries willing to help India in per planning effort necessitated India to import from particular countries. Fourthly, foreign exchange shortage with reference to some capitalist countries induced India to make bilateral rupee arrangements with U.S.S.R. and other socialist countries. Finally, since the hike in the price of oil in 1973 India's imports from Iran, Iraq, Kuwait, Saudi Arbia and other members of the OPEC have gone up.

Scope for Direction. The share of Africa and South America is only marginal. These are rich continents with very bright future. India should cultivate trade relations with these countries-they could offer huge markets for India's exports. Likewise, the scope of India's exports to the development countries of the Middle East Asia is vast and in recent years, India is increasingly cultivating these markets. The Composition of imports by source reveals that OECD countries as a group accounted for the largest share in India's imports accounting for 40 per cent in 2000-2001. This was followed by the developing countries (excluding members of the OPEC) whose share was about 22 per cent. OPEC and East European countries accounted for 5.4 per cent and 1.7 per cent respectively in India's imports in 1991-92.

The destination-wise share of India's exports shows sufficient diversification. In 2000-2001, the share of exports going to industrial market economies as represented by OECD group was 52.6 per cent, while developing countries accounted for 29.2 per cent. The countries of OPEC accounted for 10.9 per cent of our total exports. During recent years, the share of countries of Asia and Pacific region in particular has been increasing in our exports. The economic survey reviewing the position mentions: "There has been a high growth in exports/imports to/from India to developing countries of Asia (excluding members of the OPEC). Some of these economic (Korea, Singapore, Malaysia, Hong Kong and Taiwan) have withnessed continued economic growth along with significant trade liberalisation and economic deregulation. Therefore, these economies provide excellent opportunities for export thrust. On the other hand, India's exports may have to contend with uncertainty in East European market arising out of proposed economic reforms underway. Exports from India will now have to face increasing competition in view of switch over by these economies to trading based on world prices and convertible currencies."

INDIA'S TRADE POLICY

The trade policy played an important role in the development of advanced countries like U.S.A., U.K., Germany, France, Japan etc. It restricted their imports and provided a sheltered market for their own industries so that could develop rapidly and promoted their exports so that expanding industries could secure foreign markets. India, however, did not have a clear trade policy before independence, though some type of import restrictions-known as discriminating protection was adopted since 1923 to protect a few domestic industries against foreign competition. It was only after independence that a trade policy as a part of the general economic policy of development was formulated by India. The time period of India's Trade Policy can be divided into five different phases:

1. First Phase (1947-48 to 1951-52)
2. Second Phase (1952-53 to 1956-57)
3. Third Phase (1956-57 to June 1966)
4. Fourth Phase (1966-67 to 1977-78)

5. Fifth Phase (1978-79 to 1990-91)

6. Sixth Phase (1991-92 and onwords)

First Phase. During the first phase up to 1951-52. India could have liberalised imports but on account of the restrictions placed by the U.K. on the utilisation of the sterling balances, she had to continue wartime controls. Since our balance of payments with the dollar area was heavily adverse, an effort was made to screen imports from hard currency areas and boost up exports to this area so as to bridge the gap. This also necessitated India to devalue her currency in 1949. By and large, the Import policy continued to be restrictive during this period. Besides this, restrictions were also placed on exports in view of the domestic shortages.

Second Phase. During the second phase (1952-53 to 1956-57) liberalisation of foreign trade policy. Import licences were granted in a liberal manner. An effort was also made to encourage export by relaxing export controls, reducing export duties, abolishing export-quotas and providing incentives to exports. Liberalisation led to a tremendous increase in our imports but exports did not rise appreciably. Consequently, here was fast deterioration in our foreign exchange reserves.

Third Phase. During the third phase which began in 1956-57; the trade policy was re-oriented to meet the requirements of planned economic development. A very restrictive import policy was adopted and the import controls further screened the list of imported goods. On the other hand, a vigorous export promotion drive was launched. The trade policy assumed that a lasting solution to be balance of payments problem lies in the promotion and diversification of our export trade. Not only should the export of traditional items be expanded, but export of newer items should also be encouraged. Similarly, import substitution industries should also be encouraged so that dependence of foreign countries should also be encouraged so that dependence on foreign countries be lessened. It was in this period that India's trade policy was thoroughly reviewed by the Mudaliar Committee (1962).

Fourth Phase. The fourth phase stated after the devaluation of the rupee in June, 1966. During this period trade policy attempted to expand exports and strangely liberalised imports too. Actually, export promotion was given a big boost through the acceptance and implementation of the recommendations of the Mudaliar committee (1962). The major recommendations included increased allocation of raw materials to export-oriented industries, income tax relief on export earnings, export promotion through import entitlement, removal of disincentives, and setting up of Export Promotion Advisory Council, a ministry of International trade, etc. When these export promotion measures did not succeed and adverse balance of payments persisted, the government of India undertook devaluation on the rupees in 1966 as a major step to check imports and boost exports. Initially devaluation was not successful and the adverse balance of payments worsened during the annual plans. But during the Fourth plan, the trade policy was quite successful in restricting imports and promoting exports. This period continued till 1977-78.

Fifth Phase. During the last phase (1978-79 onwards), the Government adopted a policy of import liberalisation, with a view to encourage export promotion. During Janata rule import liberalisation was also adopted to augment domestic supply of essential goods and to check rise in price level. Import-export policy of the Indian government attempted to achieve such objectives as: *(i)* to provide further impetus to exports; *(ii)* to provide support to the growth of indigenous industry; *(iii)* to provide for optimum utilisation of the country's resource endowments, especially in man power and agriculture; *(iv)* to facilitate technology up-gradation with special emphasis on export promotion and energy conservation; *(v)* to provide a stimulus to those engaged in exports and in particular, to manufacturing units contributing substantially to the export efforts; and *(vi)* to effect all possible savings in imports. Thus it is clear that the present trade policy has been to stimulate economic growth and export promotion via import liberalisation.

Import liberalisation along with export promotion at a time when *(a)* prices of imported goods were rising such faster, and *(b)* foreign markets for Indian goods were depressed, resulting in huge adverse balance of trade and payments from 1979-80 onwards. Instead of curtailing imports, the Tandon Committee (1981) recommended a policy of vigorous export promotion and further import liberalisation as a means of export promotion. The IMF loan (1981) had also stipulated that India should use export promotion and not import restriction as the strategy for controlling adverse balance of payments. Such a trade policy has forced India almost into a debt trap and the Indian bureaucrats are knocking at the doors of Aid India consortium and other advanced countries to bail India out.

While framing the export-import policy (1985) the Government was guided by the recommendations of Abid Hussain Committee. Whereas the committee emphasized the need for striking a balance between export promotion and import substitution, the Government in its wave of import liberalisation permitted a much greater quantum of imports in the name of export promotion and capital goods imports for technological upgradation. Thus, grave distortions have appeared in the process of implementation of the recommendations of the committee's report which need to be rectified.

Sixth Phase (New Trade Policy and Trade Liberalisation). The massive trade liberalisation measure adopted since 1991-92 to mark a major departure from the relatively protectionistic trade policies pursed in earlier years. The main features of the new trade policy since 1991 are as follows:

1. ***Free Imports and Exports.*** In the pre-reform period, India's trade policy regime was complex and combersome. There were different categories of importers, different types of import licences, alternate ways of importing etc. Substantial simplication and liberalisation in all these respects has been carried out in the reform period. Under its commitment to the World Trade Organisation (WTO) India, in November 1997, agreed to phase out all curbs on 2,714 tariff lines over a six year phase out period starting April 1, 1997. However, USA did not agree to this schedule and appealed

to the WTO which ruled against India. As a result, India has to remove all quantitative restrictions by April 1, 2001. After the announcement of Exim Policy, 2000-2001 the number of items on which quantitative restrictions remain in 715 and exim policy 2001-02 removed quantitative restrictions on the balance 715 items. Thus in line with India's commitment to the WTO quantitative restrictions on all import items have been withdrawn.

2. ***More Facilities to EOUs and EPZs.*** The 1992-97 policy conferred higher benefit to 100 per cent export oriented units (EOUs) and units in export processing zones (EPZs) over those exporting from the domestic tariff area (DTA). The EOU and the EPZ schemes have now been extended to newer activities and services. By a separate notification, such units dealing with broad agro-based products can sell 50 per cent (twice the normal) output in the DTA. This can prove to be a powerful initiative for boosting exports.

3. ***Decanalisation.*** A large number of export and imports used to be canalised through the public sector agencies in India. The supplementary trade policy announced on August 13, 1991 reviewed these canalised items and decanalised 16 export items and 20 import items. The 1992-97 policy decanalised imports of a number of items including newsprint, non-ferrous metals, natural rubber, intermediates and raw materials for fertilisers. However, 8 items (petroleum products, fertilisers, edible oils, cereals, etc.) were to remain canalised. Large scale decanalisation is an important step towards opening up more areas of the economy to the private sector. The Exim policy 2001-02 put 6 items under special list. These itmes would be allowed though state trading agencies.

4. ***Trading Houses.*** The 1991 policy allowed export houses and trading houses to import a wide range of items. The government also permitted the setting up of trading houses

with 51 per cent foreign equity for the purposes of promoting exports. Under the 1992-97 trade policy, export houses and trading houses were provided the benefit of self certification under the advance licence system, which permits duty free imports for exports.

The 1994-95 policy introduced a new category of trading houses to be called Super Star Trading Houses. To attain the status of a Super Star Trading House, an exporter must have registered an average FOB value of exports of Rs. 925 crore during the preceding three years or Rs. 1,387.50 crore during the preceeding year. On the basis of NFE criterion, an exporter must have registered an average net foreign exchange (NFE) value of exports of Rs. 740 crore during the preceding three years or Rs. 1,100 crore during the preceding year. These houses will be entitled to membership of apex consultative bodies concerned with trade policy and promotion, representation in important business delegations, special permission for overseas trading and special import licences at enhanced rate.

5. ***Export Scheme for the Services Sector.*** Since trade in services is becoming increasingly important for our country a new scheme called the "Export Scheme for the Services Sector" has been introduced. Under the scheme, person who render professional services have been allowed to import capital equipment at a concessional rate of duty of 15 per cent. The export obligation to be achieved by them will be in the form of the foreign exchange earned by them, regardless of whether the services are rendered in India or abroad.

6. ***Export Promotion Capital Goods Scheme.*** The Export Promotion Capital Goods (EPCG) scheme has been revamped by having only one window with a concessional customs duty rate of 15 per cent with export obligation (earlier there were two windows—15 per cent and 25 per

cent). The 1994-95 policy simplified the EPCG scheme and third party exports were permitted for purposes of fulfilment of export obligations. The 1995-96 policy placed the services sector at par with the supply of goods under the Export Promotion Capital Goods (EPCG) scheme. This ensures rich dividends for several companies in wide ranging sectors like financial services, banking, hotels and airlines, advertising, software and legal firms. In March 1996, the EPCG scheme was enhanced by inclusion of 'mining' in the definition of manufacture for the purpose of export-import policy.

7. ***Export Promotion Industrial Parks.*** A centrally sponsored Export Promotion Industrial Parks scheme was introduced in Aug. 1994 with a view to involving the State governments in the creation of infrastructural facilities for export-oriented production. It provides for 75 per cent of capital expenditure towards creation of infrastructural facilities limited to Rs. 10 crore of grant to the State government. So far 11 parks have been completed.

8. ***Duty Exemption Scheme Enlarged.*** The duty exemption scheme has been strengthened under which imports are provided at two concessional rates of 15 per cent and 25 per cent subject to appropriate export obligations. The exporters have been given a choice to opt for advance import licences under the duty exemption scheme either under quantity based or (for the first time introduced) value based norms. This will given greater flexibility to the exporter to import and export goods within the overall value limits and without any quantitative restrictions except in the case of sensitive goods.

9. ***Rationalisation of Tariff Structure.*** In its Final Report published in January 1993, Chelliah Committee had advocated drastic reductions in import duties. The committee expressed the opinion that the rupee had depreciated

considerably in the eighties and the early nineties, pushing up the level of protection to Indian industries considerably. For instance, the committee pointed out that in the seven year period 1985-86 to 1992-93, the real exchange rate of the rupee has depreciated by 57.45 per cent. This had pushed up the cost of the imports considerably leading to very high levels of protection to the Indian industry. The Committee, therefore, recommended that the prevailing import duties be rationalised and drastically lowered by 1997-98 so that parity in prices of goods produced domestically and internationally can be established. Action on the recommendations of the Committee, the Finance Minister announced substantial cuts in import duties in the 1993-94, the 1994-95 and the 1995-96 Budgets. The 1993-94 Budget reduced the maximum rate of duty on all goods from 110 per cent to 85 per cent except for a few items including passenger luggage and alcoholic beverages. The 1994-95 Budget further brought down the maximum rate of duty from 85 per cent to 65 per cent. This was brought down to 50 per cent in the 1995-96 Budget, to 40 per cent in the 1997-98 Budget and further to 35 per cent in the 2000-2001 Budget. In the budget 2002-03, the Finance Minister announced that by the year 2004-05, there would be only two basic rates of custom duties, namely 10 per cent and 20 per cent. For the year 2002-03, the peak custom duty rate has been reduced from 35 per cent to 30 per cent.

Rupee Depreciation and Convertibility. Prior to the devaluation of 1966, one US dollar was equal to Rs. 4.76. After the devaluation in 1966, one U.S. dollar became equal to Rs. 7.50. The system of fixed exchange rates was abandoned by most countries in 1973. The Government of India also abandoned it and pegged Indian rupee to a basket of currencies of the countries which are her major trading partners. This floating exchange rate system has been in operation since September 1975. Under the new system, the rupee started to slide against the dollar and other major currencies of the OECD countries. By the end of 1990, one US dollar had become equal to Rs. 18.07. The rate, Rs. per SDR, was 7.58 in 1970 and reached Rs. 25.71 by the end of 1990. The Government devalued the rupee in early July 1991 which led to a depreciation in the value of the rupee against the five major international currencies by roughly 22 per cent.

(i) ***Partial Convertibility of Rupee.*** The Finance Minister announced the liberalised exchange rate mechanism system (LERMS) in the Budget for 1992-93. Under this system a dual exchange rate was fixed under which 40 per cent of foreign exchange earnings were to be surrendered at the official exchange rate while the remaining 60 per cent were to be converted at a market determined rate. The foreign exchange surrendered at official rate was to be used for the import of essential items (like crude oil, petroleum products, fertilisers, life saving drugs, etc.) and the foreign exchange converted at the market rate was to be used to finance all other imports. Since the official exchange rate was lower than the market rate, this system meant taxing the exporters to subsidize the government's bulk imports. The implicit export tax was between 8-12 per cent and was highly resented by exporters.

(ii) ***Full Convertibility on Trade Account.*** The 1993-94 Budget introduced full convertibility of the rupee on trade account. Side by side, the official RBI rate also stayed on for the conversion of items not permitted under the unified markets rate, *i.e.*, more than half a dozen of invisible items of current account as well as capital account. In addition, various exchange control norms of the Reserve Bank remained in operation all along, albeit with some relaxation of provisions.

(iii) ***Full Convertibility on Current Account.*** In February 1994, the Reserve Bank undertook several steps towards achieving current account convertibility when it announced relaxation in payment restrictions for a number of invisible transactions and liberalisation of exchange control regulations upto a specified limit relating to *(a)* Exchange Earners' Foreign Currency (EEFC) Account; *(b)* basic travel quota; *(c)* studies abroad; *(d)* gift remittances; *(e)* donations; and *(f)* payments of certain services rendered by foreign parties. India achieved full convertibility on current account on August 19, 1994 when the Reserve Bank further liberalised invisible payments and accepted obligations under Article VIII of the IMF, under which India is committed to foresake the use of exchange restrictions on current international transactions as an instrument in managing the balance of payments. Many other relaxations of restrictions on current transactions were announced in later years.

After the country moved to a single market-determined exchange rate system in March 1993, the rupee exhibited goods stability and for over two years after March 1993, the rupee-dollar exchange rate remained steady at about Rs. 31.6. After reasonable stability the Indian rupee, in August 1997, experienced a mild attack on contagion emanating from currency turmoil in East Asia. Beginning in the second week of November, 1997, the exchange rate of the rupee against the dollar came under renewed downward pressure. The rupee depreciated to a low of Rs. 40.36 per dollar by January 16, 1998. and fell further to Rs. 48.58 per dollar at the end of January 2002.

The Government of India has introduced convatibility on capital account in stages. For this the Union Budget, 2002-03, announced following measures:

1. There will be full convertibility of deposit scheme for Non-Resident Indians.

2. The schemes which do not offer full convertibility to NRIs will be discontinued from April 1, 2002.

3. NRIs will be free to repatriate in foreign currency their current earnings in India such as rent dividend, pension, interest and the like based on appropriate certification.

4. With a view to liberalising the capital account transactions it is proposed to put foreign currency Convertible Bond (FCCB) scheme under the automatic route upto $ 50 million.

5. Indian mutual funds will now be allwed to invest in rated securities in countries with fully convertible currencies, within the existing limits.

6. Corporates with proven records can set up educational chairs in educational institutions abroad from their foreign exchange earnings.

7. Indian companies wishing to invest abroad may now invest upto US $ 100 million on an annual basis through the automatic route, up from the existing limit of US $ 50 million.

The Government of India announced the new Exim policy for the 5 year period (2002-07) on March 31, 2002. The highlights of this new policy are the following:

1. Indian banks have been allowed to set up offshore banking units in special Economic Zones to attract foreign direct investment.

2. The promote the export Hardware and Software industry, the government modified Electronic Hardware Technology Park (EHTP) scheme. Now this sector will face zero duty regime under information Technology Agreement. The government has allowed free import of equipment and other goods used aborad for more than one year.

3. Exim policy has initiated a member of measures in the field of agriculture, cottage sector and handicrafts, small scale sector etc. Exim policy has removed all quantitative restrictions on all agricultural products excepts jute and onion. The Govt. has earmarked Rs. 5 crores for the promotion of exports of cottage sector and handicrafts. Three towns namely Tirpur, Panipat and Ludhiana have been granted special status for their export excellence. The Government has allowed the import of rough diamonds on zero custom duty basis.

4. Like focus LAC (Latin Amercican Countries) launched in 1977, the government had been launching focus Africa since April 2002. In the first phase 7 countries will be focus. Links with CIS (Commonwealth of Independent States) to be revived. To encourage relocation of industries in India plant and machineries would be permitted to be imported without a licence, where the depreciated value of such relocated plants exceeds Rs. 50 crore.

5. To make the system, trust based, the following measures have been taken:

   (i) Penal interest rate for bonafide defaults to be brought down from 24 per cent to 15 per cent.

   (ii) No seizure of stocks in trade so as to disrupt the manufactuing process affecting delivery schedule of exports.

6. With a view to reducing transaction cost, govt. has introduced various procedural simplifications. For example a new 8 digit commodity classification for inputs has been introduced. It will help to eliminate the classification disputs and hence transaction costs and time.

7. The Government has decided to abolish Duty Exmption Entitlement Certificate (DEEC) book. The govt has withdrawn annual advance licence requriement. Now the

exporters can avail of advance licence for any value. The government granted to continue value cap exemption on 429 items.

The Government hopes that as result of the Exim Policy (2002-07) India will be able to capture 1 per cent of global share of trade by 2007, up from the present level of 0.67.

Critical Evaluation of the New Trade Policy. The trade policy reforms initiated in 1991 have shifted its eruphasis from inward-oriented to an outward-oriented policy. Due to liberalisation, the level of protection of Indian industry has declined significantly. Many people view the foreign trade sectors as the leading sector of the economy—a sector will change the face of the economy. But economists have raised serious doubts against it because of the relative importance of home market, the nature or the degree of State intervention, and the acquisition or development of the technology. Hence it will be very difficult to capture 1 per cent of global share of trade by 2007.

DEVALUATION OF RUPEE

Devaluation of a currency means lowering of the value of a currency in terms of gold or in terms of other currencies. The difference between devaluation and depreciation is that while develuation is the reduction of the value of a currency by the government, depreciation stands for automatic in the value of a currency by market forces. But in substance, both mean the same thing-lower value for a currency in terms of foreign currencies and both have similar effects. When the local currency depreciates in value and the foreign currency appreciates in value, the foreign commodities are made costly and hence imports are checked while the local commodities are made cheap and hence exports are promoted. Thus, a tendency towards a favourable balance of payments is created.

Conditions for the Success of Devaluation. The immediate effect of devaluation of a currency will be reflected in the increase in exports and decrease in imports. This is to be expected since, by devaluation the domestic currency will become cheap and, therefore, the domestic goods will also become cheap to foreigners, while the foreign currency will become costly and, therefore, foreign goods will become costly to consumers of the devalued currency. But curtailing imports and by expanding exports, devaluation creates favourable balance of payments and removes the chronic adverse balance of payments which had existed earlier. It will, however, the successful only under the following favourable circumstances:

(a) ***Cost-price Structure.*** There should be no change in the cost price structure in the devaluaing country. Only the external value of the currency unit has been reduced through devaluation. But it is possible for costs and prices within a country to change for two reasons : First, the merchants and speculators may raise the prices of those goods whose imports have been cut off or reduced owing to devaluation. Seconldy, imports which have now become costly because of devaluation may form a significant part of the consumption of the working and middle classes, in which case, the cost of living will rise, necessitating higher wages and higher prices. As a result of these reasons, the cost-price structure in the devaluing country may change and thus may prevent the favourable effects of devaluation to come into existence.

(b) ***Elasticity of Demand.*** The demand for imports and exports should be elastic. If Indian demand for foreign goods is inelastic, that is, whatever be the price of the foreign commodities, India will buy more or less the same amount; the total value of imports will increase as a result of devaluation. At the same time, if foreign demand for Indian goods is inelastic, India will not gain anything by lowering its price level through devaluation, for the same amount will be sold whatever be the price and, therefore, as a result of devaluation the total value of exports will fall. Thus, if the demand for imports and exports is inelastic,

devaluation will worsen the balance of payments situation by increasing the total value of exports. It can be successful only if demand is elastic on both sides—that is, demand for imports is elastic, and as a result when the prices of foreign goods are high due to devaluation, imports will be curtailed; likewise, demand for exports by the foreigners is also elastic and as a result, when the local goods are cheap, exports will be stimulated.

(c) ***Co-operation of Other Countries.*** The efficacy of devalution of a currency by a country will depend upon the co-operation of foreign country or countries whose currencies have appreciated as a result of devaluation. Foreign countries will experience contraction of demand for their exports from the devaluing country, while their own demand for the goods of the devaluing country will expand due to lower exchange rate of the latter's currency. The natural tendency under the circumstances is to retaliate. This may take the form of high tariffs to prevent imports from the devaluing country or grant of subsidies to push up exports of devaluation of their currencies too.

India devalued its currency for the first time in 1966. Prior to the devaluation of 1966, one US dollar was equal to Rs. 4.76. After the devaluation in 1966, one U.S. dollar became equal to Rs. 7.50. The system of fixed exchange rates was abandoned by most countries including India and government pegged Indian rupee to a basket of currencies of major trading partner countries. Now government adopted floating exchange rate system, which resulted into the depreciation of the rupee against dollar and major currencies of the OECD countries. The government again devalued rupee in July 1991 which led to a depreciation in the value of the rupee against the five major international currencies by roughly 22 per cent. The purpose of this devaluatin was to boost the exports of goods and contain imports by making them cheaper and costlier respectively.

After the devaluation of currency the exports and imports both have gone in absolute terms. The value for exports gone up from U.S. $ 17,865 million in 1991-92 to U.S. $ 44,560 million in 2000-2001. Similar by the imports have also gone up from $ 19,411 million to $ 5,05,036 million during the same period. Hence the trade balance has increased from $ 1,546 million to $ 5,976 million during 1991-92 to 2000-2001. This shows that devaluation did not help in narrowing the trade deficit.

If we compare the growth rate of foreign trade pre-devaluation period with post-devaluation period, we find that devaluation has not made any significant impact on foreign trade.

During 1980-81 to 1989-90 the Growth Rate of Exports was 8.1 and Imports was 7.2. During 1990-91 to 1999-2000 it was 8.6 (Exports) and 9.6 (Imports).

This trade reveals that growth rates of exports has increased marginally and growth rates of imports has increased significantly. The main cause for high increase in imports is their inelastic demand trade liberalisation policies the Govt. Near stable export growth rate and higher import growth rate has widen the deficit in trade balance. Thus devaluation has not affected foreign trade sector significantly and India is still facing deficit it its trade balance.

❒

Index